Innovation, Growth and Social Cohesion

NEW HORIZONS IN THE ECONOMICS OF INNOVATION

Series Editor: Christopher Freeman, *Emeritus Professor of Science Policy, SPRU – Science and Technology Policy Research, University of Sussex, UK*

Technical innovation is vital to the competitive performance of firms and of nations and for the sustained growth of the world economy. The economics of innovation is an area that has expanded dramatically in recent years and this major series, edited by one of the most distinguished scholars in the field, contributes to the debate and advances in research in this most important area.

The main emphasis is on the development and application of new ideas. The series provides a forum for original research in technology, innovation systems and management, industrial organization, technological collaboration, knowledge and innovation, research and development, evolutionary theory and industrial strategy. International in its approach, the series includes some of the best theoretical and empirical work from both well-established researchers and the new generation of scholars.

Titles in the series include:

Technological Learning and Competitive Performance
Paulo N. Figueiredo

Research and Innovation Policies in the New Global Economy
An International Comparative Analysis
Philippe Laredo and Philippe Mustar

The Strategic Management of Innovation
A Sociological and Economic Theory
Jon Sundbo

Innovation and Small Enterprises in the Third World
Edited by Miene Peter van Dijk and Henry Sandee

Innovation, Growth and Social Cohesion
The Danish Model
Bengt-Åke Lundvall

The Economics of Power, Knowledge and Time
Michèle Javary

Innovation in Multinational Corporations in the Information Age
The Experience of the European ICT Industry
Grazia D. Santangelo

Environmental Policy and Technological Innovation
Why Firms Accept or Reject New Technologies
Carlos Montalvo Corral

Government, Innovation and Technology Policy
An International Comparative Analysis
Sunil Mani

Innovation Networks
Theory and Practice
Edited by Andreas Pyka and Günter Küppers

Innovation, Growth and Social Cohesion

The Danish Model

Bengt-Åke Lundvall

Professor of Economics, Department of Business Studies, Aalborg University Denmark

NEW HORIZONS IN THE ECONOMICS OF INNOVATION

Edward Elgar

Cheltenham, UK • Northampton, MA, USA

Published by
Edward Elgar Publishing Limited
Glensanda House
Montpellier Parade
Cheltenham
Glos GL50 1UA
UK

Edward Elgar Publishing, Inc.
136 West Street
Suite 202
Northampton
Massachusetts 01060
USA

Paperback edition 2004

A catalogue record for this book
is available from the British Library

Library of Congress Cataloging in Publication Data

Lundvall, Bengt-Åke, 1941–
   [Danske innovationssystem. English]
   Innovation, growth and social cohesion: the Danish model/Bengt-Åke Lundvall.
      p.cm. – (New horizons in the economics of innovation)
   Rev. and updated version of Det danske innovationssystem.
   Includes bibliographical references and index.
      1. Technological innovations–Economic aspects–Denmark. 2. Technology
   and state–Denmark. I. Title. II. Series.

HC360.T4 L867 2002
338'.064'09489-dc21

ISBN 1 84064 743 4 (cased)   2002020233
      1 84542 216 3 (paperback)

Typeset by Cambrian Typesetters, Frimley, Surrey
Printed and bound in Great Britain by MPG Books Ltd, Bodmin, Cornwall

To Birte

Contents

Figures

Tables

Boxes

Preface

This book is a revised and updated version of a report published in Danish in the autumn of 1999 (the DISKO report). That report was addressed to policy-makers and to other students of innovation policy in Denmark and it brought together the results of a big interdisciplinary project on the 'Danish innovation and competence-building system in comparative perspective'. The project started in January 1996 and was financed by the Danish Agency for Trade and Industry. When the report was published in the autumn of 1999 it was presented at a seminar where leading representatives of eight national agencies (covering respectively industrial policy, economic policy, competition policy, labour market policy, vocational training, education policy, science policy and technology policy) were given an opportunity to comment on the analysis in the report and its policy recommendations.

On the basis of the report and the discussion at the seminar, the Danish Agency for Trade and Industry worked out a policy memorandum for the government where many of the recommendations from the report were included. Less than a year later the Danish government presented its new plan for industrial development – dk 21 – to mark the new millennium. The most striking feature of dk 21 was that no less than eight ministries were involved in its preparation and responsible for its realization. Some of the recommendations in the DISKO report appear in the plan while others do not. And, of course, there are elements in dk 21 which have nothing to do with the DISKO project and also elements that go against the logic in the DISKO report. These typically reflected the IT, high-tech and NASDAQ euphorias that reigned everywhere at that time.

Even so, it is obvious that this was a process of close interaction between academic research and policy learning from which certain lessons may be drawn. The first lesson is that in the new context of the learning economy there is a need for research that combines approaches from different disciplines and for research that goes across traditional sector boundaries. One of the major problems of policy-making in the new context of globalization and rapid change is that the sharp division of responsibilities among ministries and authorities makes it impossible to develop coherent strategies to cope with the new challenges. And the organization of policy research tends to follow the dividing lines of the policy world: often it is the case that each ministry has its own community of researchers connected to it. Labour market expertise does not reflect much on innovation and innovation policy experts know little about labour market dynamics

Of course, analytical work cannot operate completely without delimitations – theories about everything are not useful. What follows is also specialized but it is so in a different dimension. The specialization consists in the application of a systemic perspective on processes of socio-economic change that relate to competence-building and innovation. The objective of the exercise – to create a more satisfactory knowledge foundation for policy-making and to stimulate policy learning in the new context – also gives the analysis a certain direction.

When presenting the results of the DISKO project for an international audience we have two objectives. One is to inspire similar analytical efforts in other countries. The quite recent concept of the innovation system is now becoming widely used among academic scholars in all parts of the world. This study might be helpful in inspiring the design of empirical studies broadening the concept and making it more relevant for economic development in less-developed as well as more-developed economies.

The second major objective is to present the analysis of the Danish case as one input in a process of international policy learning especially at the European level. My involvement in the preparation of the Portuguese Presidency of the European Council made it clear to me that policy coordination in Europe could benefit from a study of the DISKO type and also that there are specific characteristics in the Danish model that might help to bridge the gap between Anglo-Saxon pro market ideas and a Continental emphasis on social security.

The fact that the Danish economy is, at the same time, one of the most rapidly growing economies over the 1990s and one of the most equal societies in the world in terms of income distribution makes it an interesting alternative to the US model where growth has been established through growing inequality. In the introduction and in the final chapter I will present the research results of DISKO in this light. In the first chapter I will give some general observations relating innovation and growth to social cohesion in the learning economy. In the final chapter I will discuss what lessons, if any, can be drawn from the Danish case.

This book is the result of a joint effort by researchers connected with the IKE (International Competitiveness and Industrial Development) group at the Department of Business Studies, Aalborg University. The project has been a central part of the research programme of the IKE group and the national research network DRUID (Danish Research Unit on Industrial Dynamics).

The DISKO project has involved 15 researchers over a three-year period, including five PhD students. Twelve reports have been published and five PhD theses using data from the project have been successfully defended. In this book, I have drawn heavily on these reports and on specific contributions from

Jesper Lindgaard Christensen, Ina Drejer, Allan Næs Gjerding, Birgitte Gregersen, Björn Johnson, Kenneth Jørgensen, Preben Sander Kristensen, Frank Skov Kristensen, Reinhard Lund, Poul Thøis Madsen, Peter Nielsen, Søren Nymark, Anna Rogasczewska, Anker Lund Vinding and Søren Voxted. I would like to extend to them here my warmest thanks for an exciting and fruitful collaboration and also for the contributions they have made directly to the content of this book.

A special thanks to Poul Thøis Madsen and Jesper Lindgaard Christensen who played key roles in coordinating this complex project. Thanks also to student assistants that included Michael Dahl, Lars Dyhrberg, Durita Eliasen, Stig Andreas Garde, Pia Gertsen, Birgitta Jacobsen, Jens Erik Majgaard Jensen, Peter Livoni, Jesper Koch Olsen, Toke Reichstein, Jens Rygaard and Lars Schmidt. I want to thank our secretary Dorte Køster for yet once again offering her kind and efficient support all through the project.

Without the support from the Danish Agency for Trade and Industry and from the Ministry of Business and Industry that financed the empirical studies and two of the PhD grants, the project could not have taken place. I would also like to take this opportunity to thank everyone who contributed to the collection of knowledge that took place in this project in connection with surveys and case studies. A special thanks to the participants in our advisory committee who generously took time out of their busy schedules to discuss the contents of this project. The translation of the original Danish text has been done by Beth Stauter and in the final editing I was helped by Gro Stengaard Villumsen. Aalborg University has been generous in supporting the project through all its phases.

Aalborg, August 2001
Bengt-Åke Lundvall

Introduction: innovation and social cohesion in a learning economy

The radical change in the wider context in which national economies evolve, collaborate and compete has been alluded to along different dimensions and in different types of discourses. Some emphasize globalization and that nation states tend to loose some of their autonomy. Others point to the growing importance of knowledge for economic development and refer to the 'knowledge-based economy'. Yet others give information technology a key role in the process of change and some go as far as referring to a 'new economy' where old trade-offs between high rates of growth and stability have been relinquished.

The hypothesis put forward here and underlying the analysis all the way through is that we are moving into a 'learning economy' where the success of individuals, firms, regions and countries will, more than anything else, reflect their capability to learn. The speed-up of change reflects the rapid diffusion of information technology, the widening of the global market-place, with the inclusion of new strong competitors, deregulation and less stability in market demand. The acceleration in the rate of change implies that knowledge and skills are exposed to a depreciation that is more rapid than before. Therefore, the increase in the stock of knowledge might be less dramatic than it looks at first sight (OECD 2000b).

Different national economies exposed to the same transformation pressure have different capabilities to innovate and to cope with change and they have also established different principles and institutions for distributing the costs and benefits of change. The actual transformation they go through will reflect systemic differences in the way they innovate and build competence. They will be specialized differently, characterized by different institutional set-ups and the political culture will promote different types of state intervention to cope with the challenges raised by the transformation. We summarize such differences by referring to different national systems of innovation and competence-building. This signals that in the learning economy we need a wider perspective than the one associated with normal use of the term 'national system of innovation'.

To understand the process of transformation, it is useful to analyse and understand how specific national systems respond to global trends and challenges. Some national systems may, for historical reasons, be better prepared to cope with the new context than others. Some systems may be more innovative than others when it comes to developing policy strategies and institutional reforms that respond to the new challenges. The Danish system of innovation and competence-building is small in global terms but it has certain characteristics that makes it interesting as a 'model' for international institutional learning. Denmark has one of the most egalitarian societies in the world in terms of income distribution and at the same time it has an income level that is among the highest in the world. It has a high degree of gender equality, and well-developed local democracy.

The Danish system has some interesting features also when it comes to understanding transformation in the learning economy. As we will see, the system is obviously based on learning and on the use of competence in production and innovation. But it is not a high-technology economy and it is not an economy where formal science plays the most important role in processes of innovation. Our analysis of the Danish case thus illustrates that knowledge management and innovation policy involves a much broader set of institutions than those included in a traditional conceptualization of a national innovation system. In this sense, it may inspire broader strategies of policy-making and institutional reform. This may be especially important for other small countries and for developing countries where the focus on an isolated small science sector as the basis for knowledge-based development may actually be harmful to economic development.

Another specific reason for presenting the analysis of the Danish innovation and competence-building system to a wider audience has to do with the current stage of European integration where international benchmarking in different areas has become a major activity aiming at strengthening policy coordination at the European level. To strengthen the insight into the differences and similarities between European national systems of innovation and competence-building is important in order to avoid 'naive benchmarking' (Lundvall and Tomlinson 2001). Finally, the focus on Danish institutional characteristics may be helpful in overcoming some of the European contradictions between Anglo-Saxon pro-market strategies and Continental emphasis on state regulation and social security.

FROM THE NEW ECONOMY TO A NEW ECONOMIC POLICY?

The 'new economy' is a concept with many different meanings and connotations. In the financial journals it signalled, at least until the NASDAQ crisis in late 2000 and early 2001, that there is a new type of company connected to information technology and especially the Internet that grows very rapidly and constitutes attractive investment objects. In the realm of macro-economic debate the focus was on the new possibility of long-term, if not eternal, stable and strong economic growth (OECD 2000a; 2001b).

There has been certain envy in Europe of the new magic formula that apparently could guarantee permanent growth and low unemployment in the US. The downside – extreme and growing economic inequality – has been recognized and the general idea has been to integrate the positive aspects of the US model and combine it with 'social cohesion'. The European governments have thus given strong priority to increasing the role of venture capital and to stimulate the use of computers and the Internet. E-commerce and E-learning are among the areas given highest priority in Brussels.

The idea of using the US experience as a benchmark for economic policy and institutional reform has been undermined by the fact that in the US, the new economy, with the recession, has started to behave very much like the old economy. And the slowdown in economic growth has at its centre the very same financial institutional set-up – household investment in the stock market and a vibrant market-dominated financial system – that was regarded as a model for Europe just a year ago. The extreme focus on Internet and ICT sectors in the stock exchange created the financial bubble that is now bursting, and the heavy involvement of households contributes to the recession.

There is little doubt that technologies related to computers, telecommunications and the Internet have a great potential to increase productivity in the long run. But they will typically do so over a long period since they need to be supported by institutional and organizational change as well as by skill formation. The surprisingly strong and stable economic US growth can only to a minor degree be explained by the real effects of information technology and the Internet.

The most important factor has probably been the US economy and the US dollar remaining highly attractive for foreign capital, and the room for expansionary economic policy obtained hereby. The other two factors that may be of special importance are to do with access to labour reserves. At the bottom of the skill pyramid, the presence of a big hidden illegal labour reserve has had an anti-inflationary impact. At the top of the skill pyramid, the inflow of young ambitious scholars, not least from Asia, into the US university system has helped to avoid lack of academically trained labour.

The connection between the pattern of economic growth and information technology is certainly there. The extreme optimism created by 'new economy' hype has probably postponed the recession but also made it more painful to get out of. The Japanese financial bubble experience and the vain efforts to get out of stagnation illustrates how difficult it may be to overcome a bubble-based recession when both inflation and nominal rates of interest are low. What might come out of the US 'new economy' experience might at the end, actually, be 'a new economic policy' much more willing to accept high inflation in order to bring real rates of interest down. If this should happen Europe might take it as a 'benchmark' for reforming its EMU rules and its passive role in both monetary and financial policy.

FROM THE KNOWLEDGE-BASED ECONOMY TO THE LEARNING ECONOMY

Structural analysis of industrial developments shows that the sectors most intensive in their use of knowledge inputs such as R&D and skilled labour are the ones that grow most rapidly. Also, the skill profile is upgraded in almost all sectors in the economy. The most rapidly growing sectors in terms of employment and value-added are, in most OECD countries, knowledge-intensive business services. These observations have led more and more analysts to characterize the new economy as 'knowledge-intensive' or 'knowledge-based', and there is little doubt that there has been a relative shift in the demand for labour toward more skilled workers. Even so, this term may be misleading because it does not fully capture the dynamics of what is going on.

The acceleration in the rate of change implies that knowledge and skills are exposed to a depreciation that is more rapid than before. The alternative hypothesis put forward here is that we are moving into a 'learning economy' where the success of individuals, firms, regions and countries will, more than anything else, reflect their capability to learn. So far the studies of national systems of innovation have given too little emphasis to the sub-system related to human resource development. This includes formal education and training, labour market dynamics and the organization of knowledge creation and learning within firms and in networks. This sub-system is now confronted with very strong needs for social invention in all national systems and quite a lot of the peculiarities of national systems are rooted in it. This is reflected in the use of the concept of national innovation system in this book. It has been widened to include all organizations and processes that contribute to competence-building.

The new context of accelerating change also calls for rethinking knowledge management at the level of the firm and innovation policy at the regional, national and European level. Industrial relations and the role of trade unions also need to be reassessed. While knowledge production and policy-making through decades have been characterized by growing specialization, the learning economy calls for lateral thinking and for an integration of separate perspectives and strategies.

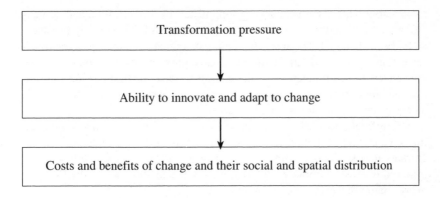

Source: Archibugi and Lundvall 2001, p. 6.

Figure 1   The basic model relating transformation pressure to the ability to innovate and to costs and benefits of change

INNOVATION POLICY AS ONE ELEMENT OF A COORDINATED STRATEGY

As indicated by the title of the book the focus is on innovation and social cohesion. This is reflected in our broad definition of 'innovation policy' and in the fact that we take into account how other policy areas influence or are influenced by innovation. Above, in Figure 1, some of the crucial aspects of the learning economy are illustrated with a simple model, where transformation pressure is linked to innovation and organizational change and to the costs and benefits of change. Through this model we can also see how different policy fields interrelate to each other and require coordination.

Transformation Pressure

One of the most fundamental factors affecting the transformation pressure is technical change. A second major factor is the competition regime. Governance regimes – the role of ownership and finance in managing the firms – affect the intensity but also the direction of the transformation pressure. Finally, the macroeconomic stance affects transformation pressure.

The development and widespread use of new technologies and especially of information and communication technologies has transformed fundamental aspects of the economy such as time and space. The wider set of competitors in world trade also reflects deregulation of trade and international financial flows as well as transport technologies that make it less and less expensive to move commodities and people over long distances. Privatization and deregulation increase the transformation pressure on parts of the economy that have so far been sheltered. These are the main factors that have increased the transformation pressure. To this should be added certain mechanisms that reinforce this tendency by introducing circular causality. Selection mechanisms in product and labour markets favour change-oriented organizations and individuals and thus increase the transformation pressure.

It is difficult to see what mechanisms within the economic sphere could halt this tendency. The full impact of information technology has yet to be felt; new entrants into world trade are on their way and further deregulation may be imposed in most countries by international organizations such as the IMF, the World Bank, the WTO, OECD and the EU.

The main limits to the process might be 'exogenous' and have to do with increasing costs in terms of potential social and environmental crises that might trigger popular resistance and political intervention. Popular resistance has become a real issue; after Seattle it has become increasingly obvious that globalization and international rule-setting are of broader concern in society in the developed as well as in the less developed countries.

Ability to Innovate and Adapt to Change

A key to successful innovation is to have a strong knowledge base including an R&D capacity and a well-trained labour force. But as indicated by the concept of an 'innovation and competence-building system', many different agents, organizations, institutions and policies combine to determine the ability to innovate. Adaptation to change can take many forms and this is the subject of some of the most heated ongoing debates on economic policy. Flexible labour markets may be at the core of adaptation in some systems while others adapt more through functional flexibility within organizations. The creation of new firms may be a key to adaptability and innovation in some systems while others rely more on innovation and reorienting the activities of existing firms. In this book the focus will be on technical innovation, the introduction of learning organizations, the establishment of networking and on hiring and firing as different possible responses to the growing transformation pressure.

The new demands on the ability to innovate reflect a new mode of knowledge production. The new context puts a premium on interactivity within and between firms, and between firms and the knowledge infrastructure. These changes are reflected in new and more stringent demands regarding the qualifications of employees and management. Services, and especially knowledge-intensive services, tend to become much more important, both in their own right and for overall industrial dynamics.

Costs and Benefits of Change and their Social and Spatial Distribution

The different forms of adaptability characterizing an innovation system will distribute costs and benefits of change differently. In the US system most of the costs are left to the individual. In Japan the firm has covered the costs of their employees. In most European countries the state takes on the cost collectively through insurance systems or needs-oriented systems. In Southern Europe the traditional family still plays an important role in caring for young and old people while the public welfare state has taken over most of this responsibility in Scandinavia. The UK system is the one closest to the US model and here neither the family nor the public sector takes a strong responsibility for those who lose in the game of change.

Data seem to indicate that, on balance, the distribution of benefits and costs has become more uneven during the last decade, at least within the OECD area. Profit shares have grown at the cost of wage shares in all parts of the OECD since the middle of the 1970s (OECD 1994a, p. 22). Earning differentials between skilled and unskilled workers have grown in the Anglo-Saxon countries and differences in employment opportunities between more- and less-skilled labour categories have increased in those, as well as in the other European countries (op. cit., pp. 22–3). The EU program for targeted socio-economic research (TSER) demonstrates that the convergence of differences in income between rich and poor regions in Europe came to a halt in the 1980s (Fagerberg, Verspagen and Caniolis 1997).

Another set of costs arising from rapid change and which now needs to be tackled are those relating to global and local environmental problems: old and new industrialization and the intensification of transport locally and globally increasingly threaten the basic conditions for human life.

ON THE NEED FOR POLICY COORDINATION AND ESPECIALLY FOR A NEW NEW DEAL

This simple model demonstrates a need for coordination of a wide set of policies. Competition policy and macroeconomic policies need to take into account the capability to innovate and adapt in the national economy. The policies and institutions affecting the distribution of costs and benefits of change need to be designed in such a way that they do not undermine social capital and so that they contribute to the capability to innovate and adapt. Finally, all the policy areas relating directly to innovation and competence-building are crucial for economic growth and competitiveness.

A problem is that some of these policies are determined at the European level while others are respectively national or regional. There has been a tendency to move policies affecting the transformation pressure to the European level (common competition policy and the EMU) while leaving the other policies to the lower levels.

Another problem is that different national political cultures in Europe may give rise to different types of responses to the growing transformation pressure. Somewhat simplified, we can identify at least four different policy strategies (in real life these strategies tend to appear in different mixes in different nation states):

- Neo-liberalism: accept the increase in transformation pressure and leave it to the individual to cope with the costs of change.
- Neo-protectionism: reduce the pressure in order to reduce the costs for the individual.
- Old new deal: accept the increase in transformation pressure and compensate the losers *ex post*.
- 'New New Deal': invest *ex ante* in people and regions especially exposed to the transformation pressure – 'life-long learning with a social dimension'.

It is a serious problem for the European Union that the big member states tend to adhere to different strategies in these respects. The UK tends toward neoliberalism, France toward neoprotectionism and Germany toward the old new deal. In this book we use the Danish model as our basis for strongly recommending a common European movement in the direction of what we call the 'New New Deal'. Such a movement does not rule out a need to introduce mechanisms that reduce the transformation pressure, for instance through global agreements on regulation of financial markets. Neither would such a move make it unnecessary to use the old new deal instruments to help those who cannot be integrated into the learning economy.

ON THE NEED FOR NEW RULES OF THE GAME AT THE GLOBAL LEVEL

In the present era of the globalizing learning economy there are contradictions in the economic process that threaten learning and competence-building. Financial speculation seems to become more and more unhampered because it is now finance capital that judges what is 'best practice' among firms as well as among governments. This power of financial capital is one of the major factors that speed up the rate of change and thereby the need for accelerating learning. At the same time, the uninhibited rule of finance capital gets into serious conflict with some of the fundamental prerequisites for the sustainability of the learning economy.

On the one hand, short-term economic calculations and speedy processes of decision-making (especially in financial flows) are becoming more and more important. On the other hand, competition depends more and more on dynamic efficiency rooted in knowledge or knowledge-related resources with long-term characteristics. These resources often take a long time and sustained efforts to build, but they may be quickly destroyed. The speed-up of change puts a pressure on social relationships in traditional communities. It contributes to the weakening of traditional family relationships, local communities and stable workplaces. This is important since the production of intellectual capital (learning) is strongly dependent on social capital. To find ways of re-establishing the social capital destroyed by the globalization process is a major challenge. Learning and innovation are interactive processes, which depend on trust and other elements of social cohesion.

It is a fundamental paradox that financial capital has been so successful in establishing itself in a dominant position in a 'learning economy'. Financial capital takes on a 'smart appearance' but basically it is 'silly'. This can be illustrated by different examples. In 1997 the Nobel Prize in economics was given to two US economists. Less than a year later those same two economists were responsible for hedge fund operations that brought the US and the global financial system to the brink of collapse. In Denmark the nationwide competition in investing in financial assets was won by a schoolboy without any earlier experience. The daily discourse in financial newspapers is characterized by a complete lack of consistency. It is quite legitimate for a commentator to propose one explanation for rising market values one day and exactly the same explanation for falling values the next day. No other area is so influenced by herding behaviour, and to define what it is that constitutes 'competence' is in this area obviously not simple. In economics the complete lack of 'wisdom' is compensated by the exaggerated technical complexity of mathematical models and econometric techniques.

These contradictions in the learning economy increase the need for policy coordination at the international level. A much stronger role for international agreements and rule-setting that rein in some of the wildest aspects of financial capital is needed. The Tobin tax is a modest proposal in this direction. As a first step to create a more long-term and stable context for learning processes it should be welcomed. Given the current US unwillingness to join any kind of multilateral agreements, a realistic first step toward global rules might be that Europe and other global regions establish some regulation of inflows and outflows of finance. This might at the same time help to build a more balanced and stable global economic system where there is not one single dominating economic power.

LEARNING BY COMPARING AND BENCHMARKING

In this book we assume that political actors, policy-makers and scholars in other countries can learn something important from the study of the Danish system of innovation and competence-building. This kind of international institutional learning is radically different from the now so popular idea of 'international benchmarking'. Actually, showing the broad picture of a national innovation and competence-building system and thinking about it as a 'model' from which lessons can be learnt helps to understand the limits of 'naive benchmarking' and the impossibility of simply transplanting a single 'best practice' unchanged from one national system to another.

It is true that some of the underlying ideas behind benchmarking may be useful in relation to policy learning. To focus the attention on alternative ways used elsewhere of doing things and to reflect on what possibly could be learnt from these observations is useful and it gives rise to a process of 'learning by comparing'. But benchmarking might also be highly problematic and give rise to biased processes of institutional reform.

The very idea implicit in what we have named 'naive benchmarking' (Lundvall and Tomlinson 2001) – that there, in any narrowly defined domain, always exists one unique 'best practice' way of doing things and that this way, always, could and should be transferred from one context to another – is methodologically unsound. It is contradicted by almost everything we know from research on innovation and institutional learning. This research tells us, for instance, that the normal situation is one of coexistence of different good ways to do things, that this coexistence, and the diversity it gives rise to, is what makes systems adaptive and innovative, that what seems to be best practice in one period will quite obviously not be so in a later period and, finally, that the systemic context determines what is a good practice and what is a bad practice.

Benchmarking may also undermine democracy if taken too literally and too far. The very term 'benchmarking' indicates that what is at stake is a technocratic fine-tuning of procedures where political values and fundamentally different interests may be safely neglected. This might be less problematic in private sector benchmarking where there is a search for more effective ways to organize certain economic activities (but even here such procedures will often become elements in power games between different interest groups).

When it comes to agreement on how to design national labour market institutions or research and education institutions it is, of course, much more problematic to pretend that what is at stake is just a search for a 'pure efficiency' solution. One reason is that these institutions have become even more fundamental for income distribution issues and for issues related to citizenship. If we leave it to the expert to decide what is best practice and forget to consult the citizens, we will contribute to a kind of withdrawal from politics that seems to be one of the problems following in the wake of globalization processes.

BENCHMARKING ACROSS SYSTEMIC CONTEXTS

The idea of one unique 'best practice' way of doing things is not compatible with a system's approach. The system's approach assumes that normally the context – defined in its economic, technical, geographic, historical and cultural dimensions – has a great influence when it comes to determining what is best practice.

The concept 'innovation system' was introduced in the middle of the 1980s (Lundvall 1985, p. 55) to capture the relationships and interactions between R&D laboratories and technological institutes on the one hand, and the production system on the other hand. The first widely diffused publication that used the concept of a 'national system of innovation' was the analysis of Japan by Christopher Freeman (1987). The concept was definitely established in the innovation literature as a result of the collaboration between Freeman (1988), Nelson (1988) and Lundvall (1988) in the collective work on *Technology and Economic Theory* (Dosi et al. 1988).

A system's approach to innovation makes it more complex to interpret the results of benchmarking and to define action on the basis of benchmarking. For example, it does not support strategies that have as their exclusive aim to increase the R&D budget. Different types of competence matter more or less depending upon the prevailing industrial structure and institutional set-up of the national economy. Other factors have to be taken into account such as the demand side and user competence. Crucially, what matters most are relationships between the different elements of the system, and it is often extremely difficult to get good indicators for 'connectivity' and social capital. Having excellent universities does not help if the interaction with competent users of academic research is weak.

Most of these factors are localized and cannot easily be changed. To neglect the local, regional and national context when selecting and introducing new ways of doing things would be highly problematic, and to benchmark only those policies and institutions that share all of these conditions would, on the other hand, reduce the number of comparable units to a handful or even to zero.

THE PORTUGUESE PRESIDENCY AND THE OPEN METHOD OF COORDINATION

The Portuguese Presidency in the spring of 2000 introduced to the European Council an institutional innovation referred to as the 'Open Method of

Coordination' and one way this idea has been made operational by national administrations, and especially by the different parts of the Commission, has been through the introduction of international benchmarking at the level of specific sector policies.

The implementation of benchmarking is expected to take place differently in different policy areas. At regular meetings representatives of national government will meet to consider progress made in specific areas of policy and it is assumed that this will also give inspiration for learning from each other's experiences. It is assumed that 'benchmarking' your own economy and using good practices from other countries as benchmarks is a way to stimulate progress toward shared objectives and instruments.

At the Lisbon Summit there were few reflections on the limitations of benchmarking. Since then some of the critical points made above have been considered, not least the reference to the importance of taking the systemic context into account. In an important document from the Portuguese Presidency distributed at the end of the Presidency period (Council of the European Union, 9088/00, 14 June 2000) the use of benchmarking and its relationship to the open method of coordination was further discussed and clarified. In this document it is pointed out that the open method of coordination aims to organize a learning process about how to cope with common challenges of the global economy in a coordinated way while also respecting national diversity. Further it is specified that benchmarking is only one element in the open method of coordination.

It is specified that the open method is 'open' because best practices should be assessed and adapted in their national context and because monitoring and evaluation should take the national context into account in a systemic approach. The open method is also open in the sense that the method should invite the participation of the various actors of civil society.

INNOVATION POLICY, SYSTEMIC CONTEXTS AND THE US AS A 'BEST-PRACTICE' NEW ECONOMY

In the recent documents covering innovation policy (Communication from the Commission to the Council and the European Parliament, COM (2000) 567 final) there is also a tension between the recognition of the coexistence of specific national innovation systems (op. cit., 8) and the frequent references to the need to diffuse 'best practice' among member countries.

Some of the small national systems (Finland, the Netherlands, Denmark and Ireland) seem to be most successful in terms of innovation according to these preliminary attempts to establish an Innovation Scoreboard. It is interesting to note that this result coincides with the preliminary OECD analysis of economic growth in the new economy where some of the same small countries appear together with the US and Australia as the most successful ones in terms coping with the new context (OECD 2000a; 2001b).

Even so, there is a strong tendency in the Innovation Scoreboard report to emphasize the US as the leader and Europe as the laggard in terms of innovation. *Ad hoc* arguments are used to diminish the weight to be put on the good performance of small European countries. The report also seems to neglect the fact that in the central documents from the period of the Portuguese Presidency the objective is to combine competitiveness with social cohesion. The possibility that the small welfare economies illustrate a type of new economy, completely different from, and actually more sustainable than, the US type is not seriously considered.

At the same time this example demonstrates the limitations of using benchmarking in narrowly defined and separate policy areas. In order to understand what lies behind the relative success of the small countries it is necessary to understand how social and cultural dimensions are co-evolving with organizational and techno-economic developments.

At the Lisbon Summit in the summer of 2000, the Portuguese Presidency attempted to overcome the classical tension between the Anglo-Saxon emphasis on 'flexibility' in labour markets and the Continental emphasis on social security by combining the dynamic perspective of innovation with an emphasis on social cohesion. As will be seen, the Danish system represents a peculiar combination of successful incremental innovation, high rates of mobility in labour markets and a shared positive perception among most workers and citizens of social security paid by taxes. This is one reason why we believe that useful lessons may be learnt from the Danish case.

Another reason to pay attention to the Danish case when it comes to design institutions and policies is that the Danish system seems to cope quite well with the new context of the learning economy. The Danish economy is not strongly specialized in the production of high technology (with the exception of pharmaceuticals), but it is quite successful in using the new technologies including information and network technologies and the outcome in terms of employment and growth has been quite satisfactory especially over the decade of the 1990s.

EMPLOYMENT, PARTICIPATION RATES AND PRODUCTIVITY GROWTH

In Chapter 1 we discuss the relevance of the book in the specific Danish situation. We show that labour market participation rates are already high and that at best only limited increases can be obtained by further efforts to mobilize those outside the labour market. Therefore policies aiming at stimulating

productivity growth become especially important. Understanding the work-
ings of the national innovation system helps to coordinate these policies.

We also argue that it makes a difference if the mobilized workers join the
labour market of their own free will or if they are forced into it by workfare
programmes. A special weakness of the Danish system raised in Chapter 6 is
the weak integration of workers with a different ethnical background. In this
area there is need for innovative and more far-reaching solutions that open up
entry into the regular labour market for workers who have been excluded from
normal working life for a longer period.

In the context of European policy coordination increasing participation
rates has been defined as a common objective. Denmark illustrates better than
most countries some of the major benefits and costs that high participation
rates bring along. There is little doubt that the high participation rates have
been one element in the emancipation of Danish women. It has also in many
other respects contributed to wealth creation and equality. The high degree of
individualization and leaving it to public sector institutions to care for children
and older people may be seen as a positive or a negative aspect depending on
the value norms you start from.

Under all circumstances this is one area where 'benchmarking' needs to be
combined with wide democratic debates on what kind of society people want.
Just using the Nordic countries as benchmarks for countries such as Spain and
Italy without popular debate is not acceptable.

CHARACTERIZING THE DANISH INNOVATION SYSTEM

In Chapters 2–4 the basic concepts of 'innovation', 'innovation system' and
'national innovation system' are introduced. Data on the relative performance
of the Danish economy in terms of innovation are presented in Chapter 2. In
Chapter 3 the fact that innovation is an interactive and systemic process is
illustrated by Danish data on patterns of cooperation among firms, and among
firms and knowledge institutions in connection with product innovation. In
Chapter 4 it is demonstrated that the patterns of cooperation indicate that the
Danish system remains national while becoming increasingly open to knowledge flows from abroad.

Chapter 5 characterizes the Danish innovation system in terms of specialization both when it comes to high-versus low-technology products and in
terms of specific industries and technologies. It is shown that Denmark shares
with other small highly developed countries a relatively weak specialization in
high-technology products. Chapter 6 broadens the innovation system perspective by introducing specific characteristics of the labour market, the education
system and the financial markets. It is demonstrated that these elements of the
broader system of innovation and competence-building tend to support a Danish

mode of innovation that is incremental and experience-based. Chapter 7 studies how the Danish system copes with the growing transformation pressure of the learning economy. It is shown that, at the level of the single firm, efforts to innovate and to introduce new forms of organization has to some degree overcome the job losses triggered by the increased transformation pressure.

KNOWLEDGE MANAGEMENT AT THE LEVEL OF THE FIRM

Chapters 8–13 put the focus on how firms adopt learning organizations, invest in human resources, enter into network relationships and hire and fire personnel. In Chapter 8 the focus is on the introduction of organizational traits characteristic of learning organizations. Chapter 9 analyses the knowledge production and knowledge flows between sectors and firms. Chapter 10 and Chapter 11 analyse network formation between firms and between firms and knowledge institutions respectively. Chapter 12 studies how firms make use of different types of continuous education and vocational training. Finally, Chapter 13 links organizational change at the level of the firm to the conduct of the firm in the labour market. Hereby, we establish a feedback effect from the micro-dynamics at the firm level to the dynamics in the labour market as a whole.

The analysis of the Danish case demonstrates, firstly, that the movement toward a learning economy is real. More firms tend to introduce learning organizations and give strong priority to the development of skills. It also shows that for most sectors the increasing transformation pressure tends to stimulate the movement in this direction. The performance of firms that have introduced traits characteristic of learning organizations is stronger in terms of productivity and employment growth.

Secondly, it is shown that there are quite important differences in how the increasing transformation pressure affects conduct among sectors. This is reflected in substantial differences between sectors regarding how far they have developed their models of knowledge management. While big manufacturing firms and business service firms are more advanced in terms of establishing learning organizations, the laggards are found in transport and especially in construction industries.

A third important result is that the predominance of small and medium-sized firms and the incremental mode of innovation in Denmark are reflected in the mode of knowledge management. Inter-firm networking is especially important in Denmark while the interaction with universities is less developed than abroad. Publicly organized and financed training and continuous education programmes are important in Denmark while firms' in-house investment in training courses is more limited. High rates of inter-firm mobility and less-developed geographical mobility promote learning in regions with a specialized industrial profile (industrial districts).

One of the most innovative features of the DISKO project is that it links on the one hand, firms' innovation activities and the wider diffusion of new organizational practices and, on the other hand, the overall labour market dynamics. This makes it possible to illustrate the model presented in Figure 1. The result is interesting. It shows that firms that introduce new organizational practises and engage in innovation, on average, create more jobs and also more stable jobs than firms that do not engage in change.

What is perhaps more surprising is that they create more jobs and more stable jobs also for unskilled workers. This gives a more optimistic scenario for the future of the learning economy than we expected when we started the project. Giving unskilled workers access to better learning capabilities and promoting the diffusion of learning organizations may thus be combined in the 'New New Deal' referred to above.

WHAT CAN BE LEARNT FROM THE DANISH CASE

In Chapter 14 we indicate what might be learnt from this study of the Danish innovation and competence-building system. There are several specific characteristics of the system that need to be taken into account before one considers the transfer of 'good Danish practices' to other national systems. The model might, however, serve as a prism through which the characteristics of other systems can be seen and as a contrast that brings out their characteristics more clearly. Finally, we hope that the Danish model can work as an inspiration for the development of new institutional combinations that may support the process of European integration on the combined basis of innovation and social cohesion.

WARNING: 'UNSKILLED WORKERS' ARE NOT WORKERS WITHOUT SKILLS!

In this report we make a terminological distinction between 'skilled workers' and 'unskilled workers'. This is a misnomer and a less than satisfactory translation of the original terms in Danish 'faglærte' and 'ufaglærte'. The first category refers to workers who have been through a specific 3–4 years of recognized professional training including theoretical as well as practical elements. The second category refers to workers who have not followed such a program.

The terminology is certainly misleading in Denmark where our case studies show that 'unskilled workers' often have substantial personal skills, as well as technical skills, and often involve in upgrading their competence. It also goes against our emphasis on competence building through experience. Below it will also be shown how 'unskilled jobs' are increasingly taken over by 'skilled workers' and this is reflected in a growing number of students and others with formal training joining the trade union for 'unskilled' workers (SID).

1. The objective: to stimulate a knowledge-based debate about innovation policy

The purpose of this book is to stimulate comprehensive debate about how private firms and public organizations can organize themselves so that they are better able to utilize the technological and organizational possibilities available today. Our aim is to give a picture of the new challenges as well as of the strengths and weaknesses of the Danish economy seen in relation to such technological and organizational changes. On this basis we outline a number of courses of action, which we collect under the term 'innovation policy'.

Thus this is a research-based contribution to policy-making; based on the results we have achieved, it points out some of the critical decisions facing innovation policy today. It is important to establish that there are choices to be made between alternative courses of action which must be made on political grounds; these neither can nor should be based exclusively on scientific analysis. Many of the most crucial decisions must be made on the basis of democratic debate and must take into consideration the evaluations and priorities among the population. A project of this character can contribute by making people aware of new challenges, introducing new angles and pointing to certain characteristics of the Danish innovation system which people were not particularly aware of. It can also contribute to the establishing of a collective vision about the direction in which the social economy is developing, a vision that is both timely and realistic. In this way, the decisions that must be made anyway will, hopefully, become better informed and better coordinated.

THE DISKO PROJECT'S RESULTS AS A POINT OF DEPARTURE

During the period 1996–98 the DISKO project examined various aspects of the Danish innovation system. One of our points of departure was the fact that today we find ourselves in a learning economy, where the ability to acquire and use new knowledge is the key to economic growth and succes for individuals, firms and nations. Another feature is that the Danish economy, to an ever-increasing degree, is becoming integrated in global economic processes.

In terms of method, we have emphasized that the private firm is the breeding ground of technical innovation. This means that the development of the entire economy will be determined to a great degree by what happens in and around the individual firm. On the other hand, in the learning economy firms are dependent on the innovation and competence-building system as a whole. For instance, the development of qualifications and skills within a firm needs to be supported by outside knowledge in the form of an educated workforce and network relationships.

With this background, we organized four sub-projects (modules) to collect new knowledge in relation to the following three questions:

- How and to what extent do technical innovation, organizational change and not least human resource development take place internally in Danish firms? (module 1).
- How and why do firms interact with other firms and knowledge institutions to promote product improvement? (modules 2 and 3)
- What does the Danish innovation system as a whole look like with reference to the production and dissemination of knowledge? (module 4)

We used various methods to collect new knowledge. Among other things we used primary statistics, questionnaires and interviews in connection with visits to firms. A crucial method that helped us to discover connections that have not previously been illuminated by traditional methods was the combination of qualitative data collected via questionnaires with register data from public statistics.

A BROAD DEFINITION OF INNOVATION POLICY

As will become obvious, we view innovation policy as a rather broad concept; we will also argue that it is increasingly necessary to introduce an innovation perspective into areas outside research and industrial policy. Education and labour market policies are essential to innovation and learning. Competition policy and general economic policy affect the economic climate in which firms operate; therefore these policies should to a certain degree be in harmony with innovation policy. Social policy and the institutions of the welfare state also influence people's attitudes toward often risky technical and organizational changes. Environmental and energy policy have great potential in terms of their interplay with technical innovation: the way in which these policies are framed can promote innovation, and conversely innovation can provide a solution to environmental problems. Behind this broad definition of the system and of relevant policies lies the idea that the current division of labour in research and division of labour among authorities has gone too far and that the learning economy calls for new attempts to reunify analysis as well as policy strategies.

THE TOPICALITY OF THE PROJECT – MORE WORK OR MORE EFFECTIVE WORK?

When this project was in the planning stages in the spring of 1995, the economic recovery had begun, but the problem of unemployment still dominated in Denmark. Currently (spring 2001) unemployment has been reduced to a level that is far below what was thought possible five years ago. The politico-economic debate to an ever-increasing degree now concerns bottleneck problems in the labour market, particularly the ways in which a greater portion of the workforce can be mobilized. This change makes the DISKO project's analytical perspective more relevant than ever. Changes in the innovation system that would allow for higher rates of growth in productivity would relieve the pressure on those politicians whose aim is to increase the Danish participation rate further, already high by international standards (see Figure 1.1). It is

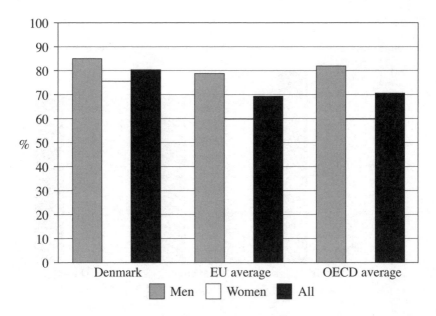

Source: OECD *Employment Outlook* (June 2000), pp. 203–5.

Figure 1.1   Participation rates for men, women and combined in Denmark compared with the average for the EU and the OECD in 1999

surprising that the current debate in Denmark focuses so strongly on mobilizing the final reserves of the labour market as a prerequisite for future prosperity. Figure 1.1 illustrates clearly that the Danish participation rate is already
high by international standards. It reflects in particular the fact that Danish
women are much more active on the job market than their peers in other countries, something they have in common with Norwegian and Swedish women.

   In contrast there is much to indicate that there is less value-added per work
hour in Denmark than on average in EU and OECD member countries. In the
manufacturing sector especially, productivity development within the last 15
years lies well below what we find in other countries (Regeringen 1999, pp.
82–3). Figure 1.2 compares GNP per capita and GNP per work hour in
Denmark with the EU and OECD average. The fact that Denmark is above the
EU average with regard to GNP per capita and far below it with regard to GNP
per work hour is explained primarily by the fact that the Danish population
annually delivers a greater number of working hours per capita. Figure 1.2
demonstrates that the high Danish national income per capita (exceeded only
by Norway and Switzerland) reflects, in particular, the fact that the population
to a large degree is active in the formal sector. Switzerland is the only country

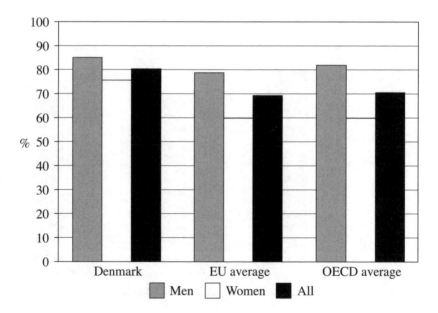

Source: OECD *Science, Technology and Industry Outlook* (1998), p. 100.

*Figure 1.2   Comparison of value-added per capita and per work hour in
            Denmark and the EU in 1996 (total OECD = 100)*

that delivers more work per resident. Thus the Danish population delivered approximately 25 per cent more work hours per adult resident than the EU average for 1996. On the other hand, the value-added produced per work hour is rather modest in Denmark. In this area Denmark ranks near the bottom along with Sweden, Finland and Switzerland.

BOX 1.1   LABOUR SUPPLY AND PRODUCTIVITY

When such great emphasis is placed on expanding the collective labour supply, it is interesting to note that there may be a negative correlation between the larger supply of labour and easy access to labour on the one hand and, on the other hand, strong growth in productivity. In the 1950s and 1960s a clear negative correlation could thus be observed between the aggregate rate of unemployment and productivity growth in the Danish and the Swedish economies (Lundvall 1974); this connection was also present during the inter-war years in the Danish economy (Pedersen 1977). These correlations reflect, among other things, firms' flexible adaptations of organization and technology during periods of scarcity. When firms experience a shortage of manpower, they will seek ways of economizing in its use; this leads to more rapid growth in productivity. In the short term the mobilizing of the least-productive parts of the labour force will, of course, also affect labour productivity in a negative way.

For social reasons it is doubtless a good idea to provide people now living on public benefits who wish to return to the labour force with a chance to regain their foothold. This could be implemented, for example, through jobs with flexible requirements and/or in protective environments or through the relaxation of rules prohibiting part-time work solutions and partial retirement. At the same time, one must not forget that the high Danish participation rate, combined with the high mobility of the workforce, puts greater pressure on the entire population with regard to the structure of everyday life. Some of the elbow-room that has been created, for example through government schemes guaranteeing the rights to paid maternity leave, leave for education and opportunities for early retirement, should be evaluated in this light. A number of essential social functions performed by housewives in other European countries must in Denmark be carried out during the leisure time of men and women who work full time. These aspects of the Danish employment system also need to be considered by policy-makers in other countries in Europe. The common goal of the European Community to increase participation rates in all European countries has recently been confirmed by the meeting organized by the Swedish Presidency at the Stockholm Council meeting. If realized, many of the characteristic features and trade-offs of the Scandinavian societies will appear in a similar form in other parts of Europe.

A reduction in the proportion of the population that relies on public benefits and an increase in the proportion of the population with jobs would certainly contribute to economic growth. One must keep in mind though that such a gain is a one-time gain and that there is a limit to how far one can move in this direction without negative effects on total welfare, for instance through making it necessary to introduce draconian workfare programmes that neglect the needs and wishes of those to be mobilized. This does not hold true for a strategy that focuses on promoting productivity growth. A one per cent increase in annual growth in productivity would provide a permanently increasing standard of living. Nor can we rule out the possibility that the years of low productivity growth in the Danish manufacturing sector have left a backlog that relatively modest efforts could eliminate.

One should be cautious when interpreting international productivity comparisons. There are several problems in measuring productivity and comparing it internationally: a decline in productivity growth may reflect, for example, a shift in demand toward sectors with low productivity. This last argument is, however, less valid when it comes to comparing productivity levels in a sector such as manufacturing, which is exposed to competition and export-oriented. In any case there is cause to examine more carefully the background for the low productivity growth in this sector in Denmark. One hypothesis that should be examined is that weak competition in some service sectors, combined with a monopolistic pricing strategy, gives a distorted picture of productivity development in the manufacturing and service sectors respectively.

It might seem as if the current politico-economic debate is based on a traditional theory of growth, in which growth is seen as something that arises primarily from a greater use of the production factors of labour and capital. The current theory of growth, which is increasingly used as the basis for the analyses carried out by the OECD and the EU, emphasizes that growth is determined to an increasing degree by technological and organizational change as well as by the ability to acquire and use knowledge. In this connection, it is interesting that the OECD refers to recent analyses showing that up to 90 per cent of the combined productivity growth in the private sector can be traced to changes at firm level (OECD 1998a, p. 111). Here, we will focus on the technological and organizational changes in Danish firms, that is, on processes that have a vital impact on the growth of firms' productivity.

BOX 1.2   THE NEED TO CONNECT THE
ANALYSIS OF WHAT IS GOING ON
INSIDE FIRMS TO THE PRODUCTIVITY
OF THE ENTIRE ECONOMY

In the 1998 Business Review the promotion of productivity is emphasized as a future strategy; an 'unfortunate' specialization in production and trade is unequivocally named as the most significant reason for Denmark's low hourly productivity (Erhvervsredegørelsen 98). No analyses of productivity development are given in this light, however, neither in the Business Review nor in the most recent analyses of the productivity problem carried out by the Ministry of Labour (Regeringen 1999, pp. 63 ff.).

Given the importance of productivity growth for the future development of prosperity, it is remarkable how little systematic knowledge there is about the reliability of international productivity data and the underlying causal relations. At the same time Denmark and the other Nordic countries have data sources that have not been fully exploited, including the IDA database, which could be used as the basis for detailed firm-based analyses. This demonstrates the need for a coordinated analytical effort of specialization patterns and productivity in a Danish context. Such an effort should aim at explaining growth in the Danish economy as a whole, but it might begin by examining what occurs internally in the individual firm, the population dynamics of firms and then to link these changes and changes in the sector structure to the observed pattern of aggregate growth (Carlsson 1980).

IS INNOVATION A PANACEA?

It might be particularly tempting for researchers in innovation to become infatuated with the object of their research. 'Innovation' has a seductive sound; it points the way toward enterprise, progress and change. For this reason, a few thoughts on the value of innovation are appropriate here.

If technological and organizational developments in the Danish economy stopped completely for several years, the economy would not just stand still: productivity and the standard of living would actually decline. Danish firms would lose market share, unemployment would increase, and public service at

---

BOX 1.3   STRIKING A BALANCE BETWEEN WORK AND LEARNING

The current focus on the supply side of the labour market also indicates a risk that industrial policy will come to depend too heavily on market conditions. There is a risk that the importance of lifelong learning will be de-emphasized during periods when manpower is scarce. It is vital for long-term growth potential that both public policy and firms' personnel policy is formed in such a way that workers are continuously given the opportunity to attain new knowledge, also in periods of prosperity and labour short-ages.

---

the level we are familiar with would be unaffordable. It is doubtful whether such a standstill is at all compatible with capitalist production methods. It is also difficult to see any realistic solution to the challenge presented by the environmental challenge that does not require a high degree of technical, institutional and organizational change.

Thus innovation is a prerequisite for reasonably stable and sustainable economic development. This does not mean, of course, that all technological and organizational changes contribute positively to the welfare of society. New weapon systems may increase the risk of violence; the Internet may be used by the Mafia; new chemical products may turn out to have unintended effects on the human organism; genetic manipulation intended to fight hereditary diseases raises nearly unsolvable ethical dilemmas. New technology may be abused as well as used, and technological progress will introduce new risk factors into our daily lives.

We should add to this the fact that the actual process of transformation may have direct negative results on economic growth. The innovation process can be channelled into particular areas (nuclear power technologies rather than the search for renewable energy sources) which are not the most promising, economically speaking. And an exaggerated fixation of actors on technology as a patent solution, one that ignores the need to develop human resources and organizational change, may result in declining productivity. Finally, the tempo in the innovation process may be increased so drastically that it prohibits radical change at a deeper level and threatens economic stability – 'intellectual strip-mining' indicates a process where moving rapidly ahead on well-established trajectories may imply that too few resources are used to explore alternative ones.

THE DIRECT AND INDIRECT COSTS OF INNOVATION

Joseph A. Schumpeter emphasized the importance of innovation for economic development more than anybody else did. At the same time he described innovation as a process characterized by 'creative destruction'. The destructive element reflects the fact that every innovation process involves both direct and indirect costs. The direct costs have to do with the development, implementation and use of something new, and these costs are borne primarily by those who are directly involved in the innovation process. The indirect costs, on the other hand, have an effect on people and organizations that have very little influence on the innovation process, for example:

- Employees of non-innovative firms who watch the value of their qualifications declining on the labour market.
- Owners of firms who see the value of their investment declining because their firms are losing market share to innovative firms.
- Taxpayers who see a public infrastructure that has been built using public funds becoming obsolete because of the relocation of production.
- Consumers who experience the loss of value of durable consumer goods they have invested in (computers, for example) when new versions come onto the market.

The transitions that innovation gives rise to in terms of frequent job changes, relocation, new job demands and so forth may be experienced more or less negatively by the people who are affected. Some people (particularly the young and highly educated) will view many of these changes positively, as offering upward social mobility, variety and interesting challenges, while others (especially older people with few, narrow or obsolete qualifications and little say in the decisions that affect them) will primarily experience them in terms of increased stress and new demands that cannot be met.

One fundamental problem related to the rate of innovation is the polarization that has taken place on the labour market in every single OECD country since the early 1980s. It reflects, among other things, that in 'the learning economy' bright people who are quick learners are rewarded, while residual groups tend to be pushed out of production and society (OECD 1994a).

With this in mind, it is obvious that it is neither fruitful nor meaningful to take a general stand, either positive or negative, on technological and organizational transformation. Strategies are needed that consider and take into account both the advantages and the costs involved in the innovation process. How a society organizes the distribution of the indirect costs and benefits of the transformation process is crucial. Who shall bear the brunt of these costs: the entire community, that is, the state and its taxpayers, as in Denmark; the business community, as in Japan; or the individual, as in the United States? The choice made in this respect will affect both innovation and social cohesion. It is of course also a key and highly controversial issue for the European policy coordination now under way.

BOX 1.4   THE DANISH EMPHASIS ON CONSENSUS-BUILDING AND TECHNOLOGY ASSESSMENT

Denmark has developed institutions that systematically and constructively assess technological developments and their impact on everyday life. The Danish Council of Technology and the consensus conferences it organizes have a more central position in Denmark as a forum for instigating debate than corresponding institutions in other countries. Consensus conferences bring together panels of ordinary citizens with experts and the outcome is well reported in the press and used as input for parliament when it designs new regulations and laws.

COMPETITIVENESS, SOCIAL CAPITAL AND LEARNING IN SMALL COUNTRIES

In the National Council for Competence's report (Mandag Morgen 1998, p. 28), an especially interesting diagram was constructed by combining qualitative data from interviews about social relations with the IMD's evaluation of the competitiveness of several countries. The diagram, given here as Figure 1.3, illustrates that most small countries in Europe combine social cohesion with being highly competitive. They are characterized by high scores on both these accounts.

Part of the background for the cohesiveness is that in these small countries, social and political systems have been developed in such a way that the costs of the innovation process are shared on the basis of solidarity principles. Sweden's low placement in terms of competitiveness is interesting. This possibly reflects a somewhat incoherent combination of a rigid system of labour market agreements, concentration on large-scale operations, and the extensive globalization of the largest Swedish firms. It has been claimed that this, combined with factors related to industrial structure, has led to a lack of internal adaptation and the exodus of capital on a large scale (Mandag Morgen 1998, p. 14). Cohesiveness, which can also be said to be one important

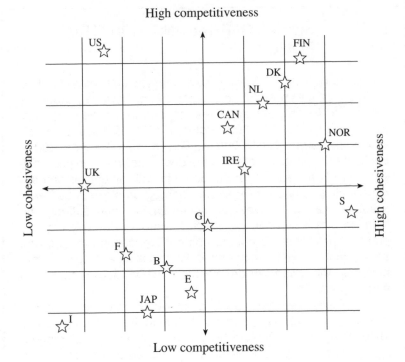

High competitiveness

Low cohesiveness

Hligh cohesiveness

Low competitiveness

Source: Mandag Morgen (1998), p. 28.

Figure 1.3   Competitiveness and social cohesiveness in OECD countries

element of 'social capital', has such great importance in the learning economy because effective learning (unlike the processing of information) presupposes trust and cooperation. While small countries may remain handicapped in some product areas dominated by formal knowledge, they can penetrate in other knowledge-intense areas anchored in interactive learning processes (see Chapter 5).

As we shall see, it is a crucial challenge for a small country such as Denmark to find new ways to tackle the marginalization of those who have difficulty keeping up with the accelerated rate of change in the learning economy. In the next chapter, we will argue that Denmark will never become the breeding ground for epoch-making, radical technical innovations, but that does not rule out the fact that it may remain a pioneer with regard to radical 'social innovations'. And, in a global perspective, there is perhaps a greater need for the latter than for the former.

BOX 1.5   SOCIAL CAPITAL AND INDUSTRIAL POLICY

Social capital, is a relatively new concept first introduced by sociologists and political scientists; it has, however, gradually gained a footing in analyses of economic development (Coleman 1988 and 1990; Putnam 1993; Fukuyama 1995; Woolcock 1998; OECD 2001a; Government Institute 2000). Basically, the concept refers to the degree to which, in civil society, there is a tradition for cooperating with others outside the narrow circle of the family and for solving problems together. If a society has well-developed social capital, transactions and learning processes can be enacted without too many legal or practical problems. To ensure competitiveness in the long run, social capital must be maintained. Russia is an example of what happens to economic development when social capital is undermined.

Historically this type of local resource has constituted a comparative advantage, particularly for small countries (Kuznets 1960; Svennilson 1960). A very important function of modern nation states has been to accumulate and reproduce social capital. This could help to explain the fact that small countries, in spite of not always being able to exploit the advantages of scale in the production of goods and knowledge, have been able to achieve high growth rates and living standards.

Conversely, swindling and fraud in business and in society at large serve to undermine social capital and weaken economic effectiveness. Effective action against economic crime can thus be seen as a measure that promotes innovation. Nor should we underestimate the importance of political processes that are based on principles of honesty, accountability and freedom from corruption.

Growing inequality in terms of economy and power risks weakening growth, particularly in small countries, the competitiveness of which is to a great degree based on cohesiveness. For the project of European policy coordination it is a major challenge to develop institutions that support the reproduction of social capital. The popular resistance to the European project in member countries reflect a strong doubt regarding the capability of Europe when it comes to taking over this function from the nation state. If the European project ends up by neglecting the 'social dimension' and exclusively becomes an Anglo-Saxon-inspired free market zone this resistance will become even stronger.

SUMMARY

The major purpose of this book is to stimulate debate about the challenges and opportunities facing the Danish innovation system. In this connection we will point out various courses of action for individuals, organizations and public authorities. Our point of departure is a comprehensive empirical analysis of the characteristics of the Danish innovation system and an analysis of data from official publications.

In the first half of the book we will introduce the fundamental concepts and perspectives that will be used. Thereafter the innovation system as a whole is analysed. In the second half of the book, the focus is on competence-building within firms. We conclude with a discussion of what can be learnt from the Danish case.

2. Innovation

Innovation takes place when a firm develops a new production process, a new product or a new service and introduces it in the market or into production. The first firm to come out with new developments is a true innovator, while those who implement new developments later can be called imitators. In the real world, the difference between innovation and imitation is not very clearly defined. It is not always easy to copy what others have developed, and often an adaptation takes place so that the innovation fits into the new context. A great deal of the research and development efforts that take place in firms aim toward absorbing new technology and new knowledge that has been developed by others (Cohen and Levinthal 1990).

It is correspondingly difficult to differentiate clearly between innovation and its dissemination. The dissemination of an innovation to a greater number of users is simultaneously a process through which the original innovation is improved, made cheaper and made usable across a broader area. That is why we allow the term 'innovation' to stand for a process that involves both the original new development, its introduction to the market and, as well, its further distribution and use.

INNOVATION AS PART OF DAILY LIFE IN DANISH FIRMS

With this broad definition, innovation is something that forces itself upon every firm that is exposed to competition. In most sectors, it is necessary to develop new products, implement new process techniques and organizational forms and to search out new markets merely to survive. In Figure 2.1 we have illustrated the extent to which Danish firms constantly commit themselves to such forms of new development and change.

More than half of the firms surveyed reported that during a three-year period they carried out non-trivial changes in products, processes and organization. Change and innovation are thus the norm for the majority of firms. At the same time, there are great differences between sectors with regard to the degree to which firms commit themselves to change. In the report on *The Flexible Firm* (Gjerding 1997) we developed an index that gives a

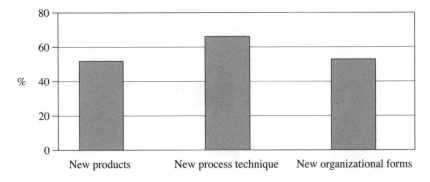

Source: Gjerding (1997).

Figure 2.1 *Percentage of firms reporting that they implemented technical*
and organizational changes during the period 1993–95 (N =
1860 firms in manufacturing, service, construction, and
transport sectors)

comprehensive estimate of firms' degree of orientation to change. We characterized firms that had implemented both organizational change and technical
improvements as 'dynamic', while those who did not implement either type of
change were characterized as 'static'. In Figure 2.2, we have collected the
remaining firms, those who carried out only one type of change, in an intermediate group. As can be seen from Figure 2.2, there are substantial differences between sectors when it comes to engagement in technical and
organizational change.

There are dramatic differences between manufacturing and business
services on the one hand, with a large share of dynamic firms, and transportation and construction on the other hand, where static firms dominate the
picture. The differences in the size structure between the five sectors can only
partially explain these differences (Gjerding 1997, p. 110). Later, we shall
show that these differences have much to do with technological opportunities,
market structure and, not least, the competition conditions.

DANISH INNOVATION ACTIVITIES IN AN
INTERNATIONAL LIGHT

The possibilities of comparing innovation activities in Denmark with those
taking place in other countries are limited. Some of the most adequate data
available go back to the Community Innovation Survey, carried out in a number

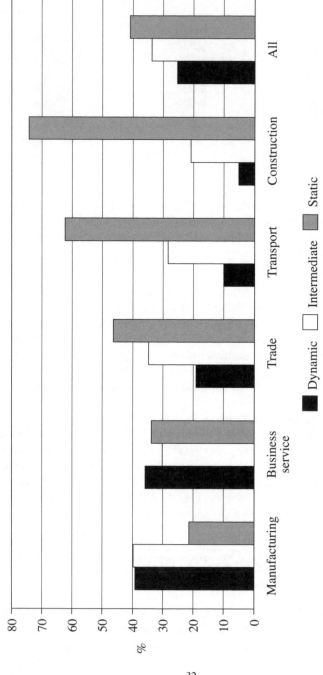

Source: Gjerding (1997).

Figure 2.2 The share of more or less change-oriented firms in five sectors (N = 1860 firms)

Table 2.1   Frequency of innovation: share of firms selling products new to the industry (%)

Size/Country	Netherlands	Norway	Denmark	W. Germany	Average
20–49 employees	10	15	13	4	13
50–99 employees	18	25	23	18	22
100–199 employees	19	31	30	19	27
200–499 employees	27	39	22	32	29
>500 employees	34	52	33	47	40

Source: Christensen and Kristensen (1997).

of European countries around 1993. Here we have only included those countries that used data collection methods similar to those used for Denmark. We shall compare Denmark with the Netherlands, West Germany and Norway respectively with regard to two different measures of innovation activities. One of them measures how frequently Danish firms develop new products (products new for the industry). The other indicator measures the share of turnover made up of new products (again, products new for the industry) in innovative firms.

Table 2.1 demonstrates that there is a pronounced correlation between firm size and the frequency of product innovation in all countries. If one looks at the average for all of the countries, only 13 per cent of the small firms developed products that were new to the industry, whereas the corresponding number for the largest firms is 40 per cent. This great difference reflects the fact that only innovations that are new for the industry, and not imitations, are included. The numbers for Germany do not include firms that only carried out incremental product innovation; for this reason the German numbers are not included in the calculation of averages.

Figure 2.3 summarizes how firms in different size categories deviate from an international average. Small and medium-sized Danish firms are, as we can see from this figure, in an intermediate position in comparison with the other countries (they lie close to the value 1.0). But among the large firms, Danish firms lie below average. It also appears from the paper 'Innovation and industrial development' (Christensen and Kristensen 1995) that a surprisingly large number of Danish firms do not engage in genuine product innovation. This might reflect the fact that there are a large proportion of food industrial companies among the large firms in Denmark. We can thus conclude that the share of large Danish firms that have introduced product innovations is smaller than in the other countries, while the other Danish firms are close to average.

It is also possible to compare the market impact of innovation for the innovative firms. In the European CIS survey firms were asked to estimate how large a percentage of their turnover originated from products new for the

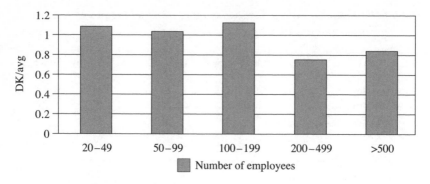

Source: Christensen and Kristensen (1997).

*Figure 2.3   Frequency of innovation: products new for the industry
            (DK/avg)*

industry. Table 2.2 shows the weight of new products in turnover. Here the differences between firms of varying size are less pronounced. The small firms that developed a product that was new for the industry have a percentage of turnover comparable to what we find in large firms.

Figure 2.4 shows that the Netherlands lies markedly below the average for all size groups, while Norway lies close to or above the average. The Netherlands pulls the average down, so that Denmark ranks above average in all size groups, particularly in the group of large firms.

The information available on the relative position of Danish firms relative to that of firms in other countries with regard to product innovation gives a somewhat mixed picture. With regard to small and medium-sized firms, Danish firms do not deviate significantly from what one finds in other small,

*Table 2.2   Degree of improvement in the innovative firms: share of turnover
            from products new to the industry*

Size/Country	Netherlands	Norway	Denmark	Average
20–49 employees	13	17	18	16
50–99 employees	11	30	23	21
100–199 employees	10	20	18	16
200–499 employees	8	16	16	14
>500 employees	12	17	25	18

Note: Comparable data were not available for Germany.

Source: Christensen and Kristensen (1997).

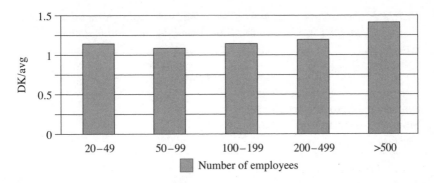

Source: Christensen and Kristensen (1997).

Figure 2.4 Degree of change: products new for the industry (DK/avg)

highly developed countries. The larger firms, however, do deviate in two respects. On the one hand, a relatively large number of the larger firms do not introduce new products at all. On the other hand, the large firms that do implement product innovations are more dependent on new products for their turnover than firms in other countries. One possible explanation for this pattern could be that the population of large firms in Denmark is polarized. A big proportion belongs to the low-tech group (foodstuffs), while the relatively small percentage of big high-tech firms (pharmaceuticals and electronics) compete to a high degree through developing and bringing to the market new products. These numbers thus suggest a Danish industrial structure that is polarized with regard to innovative capability. Such a structure makes special demands on innovation policy to be selective and differentiated.

THE DANISH ECONOMY IS CHARACTERIZED BY INCREMENTAL INNOVATION AND BY IMITATION

In the international comparison we focused on innovations that were new for the industry. These make up only a small percentage of the total number of innovations in Danish firms. As a rule, new developments occur in the individual firm when that firm imitates or adapts what others have already developed elsewhere.

Innovations generally appear when someone combines familiar elements in a new way. Some innovations are technically radical and involve the construction of completely new technical systems. This was true, for example, for the implementation of the steam engine as a new source of power in the nineteenth

Table 2.3   Percentage of product-developing firms that reported that their product was new to the Danish and the international market

	New to the Danish market	New to the foreign market
Percentage of product-developing firms who answered yes to the question	20.2%	10.8%

Source: Lund and Gjerding (1996), App. 1, p. 9.

century and of the computer as a means of communication in the twentieth century. But the vast majority of innovations are gradual ('incremental'). This type of innovation is totally dominant within industries such as foodstuffs, furniture and clothing (Maskell 1998a). Radical innovations are seldom developed in Denmark, and when they are, it cannot always be assumed that the skills exist to successfully exploit them locally. However, the import of knowledge and technology from other countries and the gradual improvement of products and processes play a decisive role for the competitiveness and product development of Danish firms.

In order to illuminate the degree to which product innovations were radical, firms were asked in the survey whether the new product was new to the Danish and the international markets respectively. The answers to this question appear in Table 2.3, which shows that only about one out of 20 Danish firms introduced a product that was new to the world market in the course of a three-year period (Table 2.3 includes only the firms that have introduced a new product – that is around 50 per cent of all the firms that have responded to the sample). There is no perfect relationship between the radical nature of a technical innovation and its novelty to the market, but one can reasonably assume that there is a certain correlation between the two aspects. While incremental innovation and change are part of the daily routine for most firms, only a small percentage of firms engage in radical innovations. But as we can see from the international comparison, Denmark is not any worse off with regard to products 'new for the branch' than other small countries such as for example the Netherlands or Norway. (See also Christensen and Kristensen 1997, pp. 17 and 21.) Thus it is a general characteristic that gradual innovations dominate in small countries.

We will place great emphasis on incremental change on the grounds that in a small open economy continuous gradual renewal is more crucial to its growth potential than dramatic breakthroughs. An innovation policy that focuses one-sidedly on being at the absolute technological forefront, for instance by promoting centres of excellence in research with weak linkages to the broader production system, may in the long run undermine the competitiveness of a small open economy (see also Box 2.1).

BOX 2.1 A WARNING AGAINST GLAMOROUS INNOVATION POLICY IN SMALL AND LESS-DEVELOPED COUNTRIES

In international organizations that concern themselves with innovation policy, large countries will often set the agenda. With good reason, they will be more oriented toward research-based, radical innovations than small countries and less-developed countries. It is tempting to import such policy models to countries with totally different economic structures.

One important task of research policy is to support growth in the science-based parts of the Danish economy. This portion of the economy is of great social importance seen over a longer period, because it is characterized by high and rapidly growing productivity as well as by more rapid employment growth than more traditional sectors. This might explain the current focus of research policy on patents and university-based innovations as essential tools in innovation policy. This policy is of particular relevance for industries based on scientific research, especially firms producing biotechnology, pharmaceuticals and electronics.

At the same time it is clear, given the specific Danish industrial structure and the innovation patterns that characterize the Danish economy, that such initiatives cannot stand alone in the area of innovation policy. In industrial areas with higher proportions of total employment, such as construction and transport, the main policy objective should be to break with old-fashioned routines and rigid divisions of labour. In other traditional manufacturing and service areas dominated by small firms the aim is to establish rather modest connections to institutions of knowledge; for example, by employing at least one or more highly educated expert(s) or generalist(s) in each firm. Finally there is an intermediate group of firms that have attained a technical level enabling them to use older and more recent research results in their own innovation processes but which do not currently have adequate access to academic environments. In this situation incentives for personnel exchange between industry and universities would presumably be an important solution.

Recent initiatives aimed at promoting mobility need to be developed.

A completely different, fast-growing group of firms can be placed in the category of 'knowledge-intensive business services'. They make their living through the production, sale and use of knowledge. Innovation and research policy in this area needs to be rethought. Very little basic research exists about how this type of firm enters into innovation processes. It is something of a paradox that we possess detailed knowledge about the production of pigs and computer hardware but know so little about the production of knowledge and about how learning affects economic development. A number of new initiatives are needed in order to take into account the growing importance of these kinds of activities, from basic research to standardization and quality control of business services.

FROM RESEARCH-BASED TO KNOWLEDGE-BASED INNOVATION

The knowledge base for technical innovation varies between different areas and sectors. It can be established through scientific research, but it can also spring from practical experience. For the new techniques and products developed in the areas of pharmaceuticals and biotechnology, the research that takes place at universities is crucial to the technical progress achieved. The distance from scientific research to technical innovation is very small in this instance. In other sectors, such as furniture, clothing and to some degree the machinery industry, most innovations reflect the combination of technological insights with practical knowledge and experience that stem from the daily activities of the firm, not least, the daily contact with customers.

It is often the case, however, that a combination of theoretical and practical knowledge is necessary in order to carry out an innovation with market success. When designing a factory for the production of a drug developed through scientific research, one needs to draw upon practical experience. Conversely, the development of new materials for use as the basis for developing new types of clothing and furniture often takes place in the chemical industry. But the relative emphasis placed on theory and practice may differ dramatically between industries (Kline and Rosenberg 1986).

These distinctions between different types of innovations are important because they illustrate the limits to discussing innovation and innovation policy 'in general'. When we speak about 'the Danish innovation system', the focus is on the interplay between technical innovation and organizational change, regardless of whether the innovations in question are based on research or more rooted in practice. At the same time, it is important to determine the particular types of innovations that characterize the Danish innovation system in particular, as well as whether the relative positions of theoretical and practical knowledge that characterize innovations today will remain appropriate and relevant also in the future.

PRODUCTIVITY GROWTH AND KNOWLEDGE CREATION IN VARIOUS AREAS OF THE DANISH ECONOMY

In connection with a Master's thesis in Economics at Aalborg University, calculations were made about the particular types of knowledge input that most strongly affected the rate of growth in total productivity in various sectors. In Table 2.4, some of the major results of this analysis are summarized. The table

Table 2.4   Knowledge input and growth in five primary sectors

	Main source of technology content	Factors influencing productivity*
Supplier-dominated (e.g. clothing, furniture)	Purchase of technology	Own R&D, Purchased R&D, Unskilled labour
Scale-intensive (e.g. meat, dairy)	Purchase of technology	Unskilled labour
Specialized supplier (e.g. machines, measuring instruments)	Own R&D	Unskilled labour, Skilled labour
Research-intensive (e.g. pharm., electronics)	Own R&D	Own R&D, Purchased R&D, Skilled labour
Service-intensive (e.g. trade, telecom)	Own R&D	Unskilled labour, Skilled labour.

Note: *Significant variable in regression analysis with total productivity as dependent variable.

Source: Hansen and Nielsen (1997).

shows that different types of knowledge input have different effects on economic growth in the different sectors.

There are a number of problems with this type of analysis in which, among other things because of a limited data set (observations for all of the sectors exist only for the period 1987–92), time series data must be combined with cross-section data, but it is interesting that similar patterns occur in recent OECD publications on the particular types of knowledge input that determine competitiveness in the various sectors (OECD 1996, pp.120–1). Together the two analyses indicate that different types of knowledge input are crucial for growth and competitiveness in different areas of the economy. While R&D is important to growth both in supplier-dominated and research-intensive firms, skilled and unskilled labour is more important for specialized suppliers and service-intensive firms.

These observations are important when appraising the effects of any innovation policy. No matter what knowledge resources one decides to make more abundant or less expensive for firms, the policy will have a different effect on different parts of the economy. On the face of it one would think that support for universities and for the education of skilled labour are examples of a general policy. None the less this kind of policy will have selective effects. The task facing innovation policy is to find those instruments and areas in which one can attain the best results at the lowest cost.

ORGANIZATIONAL CHANGE AS A PREREQUISITE FOR PRODUCTIVITY GROWTH

The DISKO project took as one of its springboards some earlier analyses of the interplay between technical innovations and productivity. In the PIKE project (the acronym stands for the Danish for 'Productivity and International Competitiveness'), we were able to demonstrate that the firms that implemented information technology but failed to supplement it with organizational change and upgrading their employees' qualifications had meagre or even negative productivity development (Gjerding et. al. 1990). This was later confirmed by a much more comprehensive study carried out in connection with the analyses of the Danish Welfare Commission (Ministry of Business and Industry 1996). Information technology plays an important role in nearly every firm in the production and service industries, and therefore this was a very important result. It showed that the implementation of new technology in itself does not guarantee greater productivity growth. Organizational change is often a prerequisite for attaining improvement in productivity development.

Organizational conditions are also important for the ability to develop new products and services successfully. There are many studies showing that collaboration with customers, suppliers and knowledge institutions is a prerequisite for the development of attractive products. These findings are supported by the analyses we have undertaken in this project (see also Box 2.2).

BOX 2.2   TWO STUDIES OF THE IMPACT OF ORGANIZATIONAL FORMS ON INNOVATION PERFORMANCE

Laursen and Foss (2000) demonstrate that the use of Human Resource Management (HRM) practices positively influences innovation performance and that there is a complementarity between the different practices (using one more practise increases the returns of using another one). The relationship is analysed by estimating an empirical model of innovation performance using data from the DISKO survey. Using principal components analysis two HRM systems, which are conducive to innovation, are identified. The first is one in which all nine (HRM) variables in the analysis matter (almost) equally for the ability to innovate. The second system which is found to be conducive to innovation is dominated by performance-related pay and to some extent by in-house training. The nine HRM practices included are: interdisciplinary workgroups, quality circles, systems for collection of employee proposals, planned job rotation, delegation of responsibility, integration of functions, performance-related pay, firm-internal training and firm-external training.

Lund Vinding (2001) investigates the importance of human capital for the firms' absorptive and innovative capacity. The estimation of an ordered probit model including 1544 DISKO firms from the manufacturing and service industry shows that application of human resource management practices within the firm and development of a closer relationship with both vertically related actors and knowledge institutions, not only promotes the ability to innovate but also increases the degree of novelty of innovation. Finally, work experience among managers, heads of departments, and employees at the managerial level does actually show a negative effect on the ability to innovate for science-based and information and communication technology ICT – intensive firms, thus indicating the importance of updating the skills of the employees in these high-tech sectors.

Thus one can generally ascertain that the ways in which firms are organized both internally and with relation to external actors are crucial to what they can attain in terms of competitiveness, employment and productivity when introducing new technology. Technical change without organizational change and human resource development has been shown to be counter-productive. Therefore, when characterizing innovation systems, we see the specificities of the interplay between technological and organizational change as essential.

SUMMARY

In this chapter we have shown that innovation can take various forms. Incremental innovations and imitation are especially important for growth and competitiveness in a small open economy like Denmark's. We have also shown that different types of knowledge affect productivity growth and competitiveness in different areas of the Danish economy differently. This provides innovation policy with a complex and compound task. There is a need to stimulate the science-based industries, but this must not lead to the neglect of stimulating innovation and change in less glamorous firms in sectors such as construction and transport. Also, there is a need to rethink innovation policy so that it also takes into account the growing importance of knowledge-intensive business services for industrial dynamics.

3. The innovation system

The general background for the concept 'innovation system' is the comprehensive theoretical and empirical research on technical innovation that took place in the 1970s and 1980s. The most important result of this research was a rejection of a linear understanding of the innovation process, in which it was assumed that basic research was automatically converted to new technology and new technology was converted to innovation. On the contrary, the new research showed that innovation is generally an interactive process in which later steps in the process are linked back to earlier ones. Also, innovations are not usually singular events that result from the genius of individuals. Rather, innovation comes about as the result of a social process involving an interplay between many individuals and organizations over a longer period of time in which cumulative learning processes take place. The fact that innovation is a cumulative and interactive process means that the ability to innovate will reflect the relations and the interplay that exists between individuals, organizations and institutions. This shift in the understanding of the innovation process made its first policy breakthrough in 1992, when the OECD published the TEP (Technological and Economic Policy) report (OECD 1992).

The term 'innovation system' was introduced in 1985 in Lundvall (1985, p. 55) as referring to the interplay between firms and institutions involved in knowledge production. The main theme of that paper was the interplay between producers and users in connection with the development of new products. The term 'innovation system' aimed at making people aware that this interplay also took place between basic research (as producers), applied research (as users), universities (as knowledge producers) and industry (as knowledge users). One important consequence of such a shift in perspective was to make obvious the fact that the demand side plays a crucial role with respect to the innovation process. This reflected empirical research in Aalborg, which had shown that 'competent users' and qualified demand in the home market often appeared as essential explanations of technological positions of strength in export specialization (Andersen, Dalum and Villumsen 1981).

Another aim of the system concept was to draw attention to the importance of the degree to which different elements fit together (Lundvall 1998, Lundvall et al. 2001). The concept is critical of naive notions of 'benchmarking', where it is assumed that one can discover the best practice in a single area and then introduce it into a broad area without considering the context (the system) in which it will operate (Lundvall and Tomlinson 2001). This does not imply that an innovation system always consists of elements that fit well together. Established elements and institutions are constantly challenged by new developments in the system's surroundings, and a system that functions well today may in a short while lose its efficiency and become obsolete. A topical example is the Japanese system, which until recently appeared as a sort of ideal in a number of respects but which seems to be much less adequate in the current global context.

DEFINING THE INNOVATION SYSTEM

What types of activities and organizations make up the core of the innovation system, and what framework conditions are fundamental for an understanding of the system's mode of operation and efficiency? We will begin with the following definition.

The innovation system is made up of organizations that, through their resources and activities, affect the speed and direction of the innovation process; it also includes the relationships and interactions between these organizations. The system can be characterized by its specialization, its institutional set up and its connection to its environment. Innovation systems are open systems, but at the same time they have some degree of autonomy from their environment with regard to their development, way of functioning, and specialization.

In the previous chapter we saw that innovations take place primarily in private firms. As a result of this, firms are the organizations that are most centrally placed in the innovation system. For example, it is very important that a close collaboration exists internally between different departments in the same firm. Other types of important organizations are knowledge institutions and educational institutions. Of particular importance are the relations between firms, and between firms and knowledge institutions, that characterize a system. The labour market, the education and training system, and the investment capital market all constitute an important framework for innovation systems.

THE INNOVATION SYSTEM IN A NARROW SENSE

Most researchers will be able to accept a definition that corresponds somewhat to the one above, but they would not necessarily agree on how to apply it more concretely in pursuing empirical work. In the United States, especially, there is a tendency to focus exclusively on the interplay between universities, research departments of firms and technological policy. The institutional conditions emphasized in the US are typically patent laws and other ways of regulating intellectual property rights. This perspective reflects to a certain degree the fact that the United States is in fact a breeding ground for radical science-based innovations and that these do have tremendous influence on the dynamics of the US economy. It also reflects the fact that high-tech products make up a great percentage of production and exports in the US and that it is an economy dominated by huge corporations many of which operate on the basis of science and research.

The organizations and activities outlined above enter as one part of what is going to be studied, but our definition of the innovation system is broader. This reflects to a certain extent the fact that we are examining a national innovation system with a completely different make-up than the US one. But it also reflects our theoretical and historical perspective, in which we place great emphasis on the learning processes that stem from practice (see Chapter 7). It is also compatible with the broad definition of innovation given above, as well as the significance we assigned to the interplay between technological and organizational change. Finally, the recent NASDAQ crisis in the US and similar developments in the rest of the world have demonstrated the risk of a high-tech bias and the instability that is connected to high-tech sectors. Even in big economies it might be more adequate to design innovation policy within a broader definition of the innovation system (Lundvall and Maskell 2000; Amable et al. 1997).

THE INNOVATION SYSTEM IN A BROAD SENSE

The narrow delimitation of the innovation system is problematic for a number of reasons, among them the fact that the link between science and innovation – with certain exceptions, such as biotechnology – is anything but direct. Firstly, only a small percentage of basic research results are translated into new technology, and when that happens it is usually after great delay. The main economic effect of the research carried out at universities is indirect and goes through the education of graduates who when hired by firms enhance the ability of firms to cope with complex problems.

Secondly, only a small portion of all innovation springs directly from research. Innovation takes place in all sectors of the private economy. Small and medium-sized firms in industries with a low level of research and development are continually implementing new technology in order to make production more efficient; they add new products to their line at regular intervals. They also develop new organizational and marketing techniques. These innovative activities are crucial to their competitiveness and survival. In an economy such as the Danish one, this dynamism, which takes place with very little connection to research, is essential for economic growth.

INNOVATION SYSTEMS AT DIFFERENT LEVELS

This book focuses on the national innovation system. During the last few years there has been a development of innovation system concepts linked to other levels in the economy (Edquist 1997; Freeman 1997; Lundvall and Maskell 2000). Franco Malerba has analysed the differences between sector-specific innovation systems (Breschi and Malerba 1997). Bo Carlsson has analysed technology-specific systems (Carlsson and Jakobsson 1997). Michael Storper has delimited regional innovation systems and related the dynamics of these to economic globalization (Storper 1998). In principle, the individual firm and its interaction with its surroundings can also be seen as a 'corporate innovation system'.[1] Common to these analytical approaches is a perspective in which innovation is seen as an interactive process and the respective systems are characterized by a certain degree of inherent autonomous dynamics.

Analyses of such systems can contribute to an understanding of the national innovation system. National specialization will often reflect that within nations, there are regions that are specialized in specific sectors. In Denmark, for example, we find regional clusters such as 'Medicon Valley' in the Copenhagen metropolitan area, a 'Mobilecom Valley' in northern Jutland, and regions specializing in the furniture and clothing industries respectively (the Herning area).[2]

Other partial systems are delimited by their technology or sector within national boundaries. In the OECD project on national innovation systems, analysis has been carried out of how different national economies are dominated by a few 'innovative clusters' (OECD 1999b). In connection with DISKO's analysis of knowledge flows in the Danish innovation system, two such partial systems were focused on. These systems are characterized by a particularly intense interaction related to the development of new products (Drejer 1998, pp. 71–5).

The first cluster reflects the interaction of producers and users in the development of new packaging technology. The cluster includes firms in the paper industry and the foodstuffs industry respectively. The second cluster is made up of firms in telecommunications and electronics respectively.

Our analysis shows that the food industry is an important recipient branch of product innovations from the paper industry, as 80 per cent of firms within the paper industry report that they have delivered product innovations to firms within the food industry. At the same time, 50 per cent of the firms in the paper industry report that firms in the food industry participated actively in the development process. The close relationship between paper and food is supported by a study done by Christensen et al. (1996); this study also shows that the development of packaging plays an important role in product development in the food industry.

The relation between paper products and foodstuffs is one example of a vertically organized partial system that includes the suppliers of innovations and their most important users. The relationship between firms producing telecommunications equipment and electronics firms represents another example. In this case, 90 per cent of telecommunication firms have supplied product innovations to electronics firms, whereas 40 per cent of telecommunications firms report that electronics firms have participated actively in their product development process.

These two partial innovation systems point to the fact that relations between firms are important for innovation both within the high-tech sector and in middle- to low-tech industries. This is yet another illustration of why innovation activity cannot be equated with technological activity in high-tech industries. At the same time the two examples illustrate that innovation is largely an interactive process. In reality we are not dealing with a one-way flow; rather, the supplier, instead of innovating for the recipient firm, innovates with it.

INNOVATION AS AN INTERACTIVE PROCESS AS ILLUSTRATED AT THE FIRM LEVEL

The previous example was based on data that at a more aggregate level connected firms in different sectors with each other. We also have access to data that allow us to give a general assessment of the importance of collaboration for the innovation process at the level of the individual firm.

The results from the DISKO sub-project on inter-firm collaboration emphasizes the importance of using a systemic perspective. It turns out that nearly all of the production firms that have developed one or more new products during the last few years have collaborated with other firms to do so. Figure 3.1 shows that a majority of firms normally collaborate about product development.

Firms also point out that the collaboration that takes place is as a rule very useful for the successful completion of the project. They were asked about the importance of various partners seen in relation to what they themselves indicated as their most important project. The pattern of responses appears in Figure 3.2.

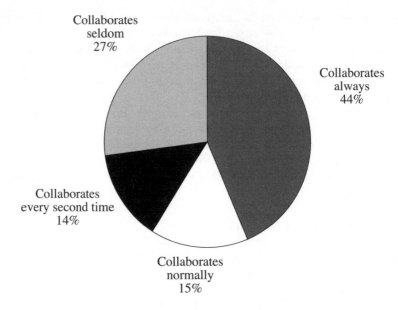

Collaborates
seldom
27%

Collaborates
always
44%

Collaborates
every second time
14%

Collaborates
normally
15%

Source: Madsen, P.T. (1999), *The Collaborating Firm*, Industry and Trade Development
Council.

*Figure 3.1   Frequency of collaboration in connection with the development
of new products (N = 250)*

THE INCREASING IMPORTANCE OF THE SYSTEM
PERSPECTIVE

There is much to indicate that a system perspective is becoming increasingly
important for understanding the processes of change that are taking place.
When competition intensifies, there is actually a tendency to intensify collaboration with various partners. In Figure 3.3 we summarize the responses of
1860 firms in the fields of manufacturing, transport, construction, trade and
business services.

Figure 3.3 shows a growing 'density' of the innovation system particularly
with respect to customers and suppliers. The image of the individual firm as
an isolated unit carrying out innovations alone is becoming less and less relevant. The strengthening of collaboration with other firms does not occur in
conflict to the intensification of competition. On the contrary, it is particularly those firms that report a strong intensification in competition (K-firms)
that strengthen their collaboration with their surroundings. They do
strengthen their relationship to a much higher degree than firms experiencing

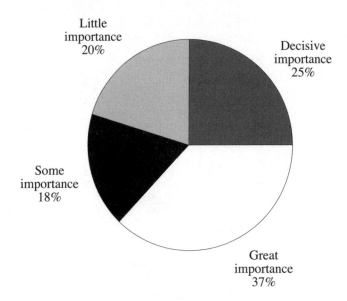

Little
importance
20%

Decisive
importance
25%

Some
importance
18%

Great
importance
37%

Source: Madsen (1999).

Figure 3.2   *The importance of the collaboration partner for the completion
of the project (N = 283), (set responses with respect to 431
partners, specified in relation to 283 projects)*

moderate intensification (M-firms) and than firms not experiencing any intensification at all (B-firms).

Figure 3.4 shows that the firms that did not experience intensified competition (B-firms) were the ones least likely to form closer relationships with
others, while those that reported a mild intensification in competition end up
in an intermediate position.

SUMMARY

The basic hypothesis behind a systemic approach is that the innovation
process is interactive. This basic hypothesis is supported by all the various
data we have available. There are also strong indications that the interaction
and mutual dependence between firms is increasing in importance. Even so
there is a constant temptation to fall back on the linear perspective of the innovation process, in particular in the formation of policies and practical strategies. A linear model is simpler and more easy to apply. It is often easier to see

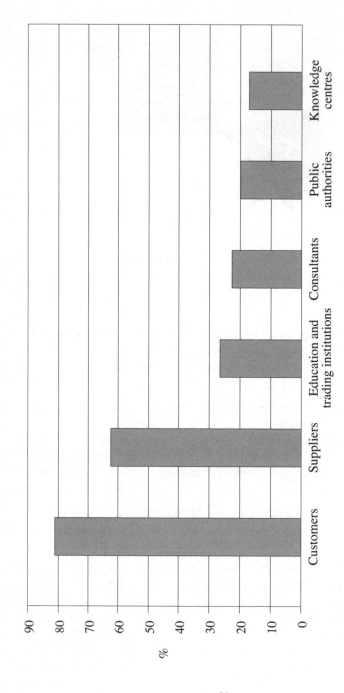

Source: Gjerding (1997).

Figure 3.3   *Share of firms that answered the question, 'To what degree did your firm develop a closer relationship with the following agents during the period 1993–95?' with the answers 'to a great extent' or 'to a certain extent' (N = 1860)*

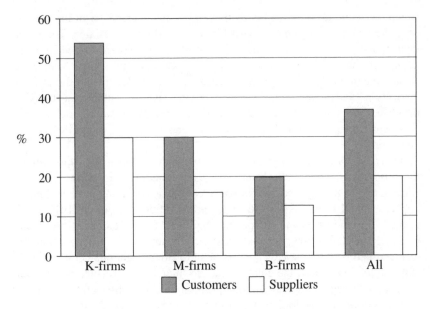

Source: Gjerding (1997).

Figure 3.4 *Share of firms that answered the question, 'To what degree did your firm develop a closer relationship with the following agents during the period 1993–95?' with the answer 'to a great extent' (N = 1869)*

how to stimulate the advancement of new knowledge than it is to see how to improve the abilities of the users of both old and new knowledge to locate knowledge, decide what is relevant, acquire the knowledge and finally put it to use.

A highly developed and sharp inter-ministerial division of responsibility with regard to innovation policy areas risks further cementing this linear understanding. One can also speak of two somewhat different tasks facing industrial policy: one is to do with promoting a research-based production sector and the other is to raise the level of knowledge in the entire economy. In principle one could imagine that the first task would be central to the Ministry of Research and IT, while the second would be placed primarily in the Ministry of Business and Industry.

It is hardly expedient to create too sharp a distinction of this kind. And further it is essential to ensure a coordination with two other ministries who are responsible for the development of human resources, namely the Ministry of Education and the Ministry of Labour. One possible institutional solution, which takes into account the interactive and systemic character of innovation processes, may be inspired by what Finland has done in this area. There, an inter-ministerial council with direct responsibility for policy related to technology and innovation has been set up directly under the Prime Minister's chairmanship. In Denmark, given the distinctive characteristics of the Danish innovation system, one could consider giving such an authority a broader mandate, thus ensuring the connection between the development of qualifications and labour market policy on the one hand and research and innovation on the other.

This need for coordinating all the different sector policies that contribute to the promotion of innovation and competence-building, including policies contributing to the reproduction of social capital, is becoming more and more important at all levels. Therefore I have proposed the creation of 'High-level councils for innovation and competence-building' at the regional, national and European level. The idea is to establish new centres for policy coordination that take into account the new context of a globalizing learning economy and, at the same time, constitute a counterpart to ministries of finance and central banks that pursue policy coordination primarily based on financial (and therefore short-term) considerations (see Lundvall and Archibugi 2001, p. 16).

NOTES

1. This perspective forms the basis for Whitley's analyses of 'national business systems' (Whitley 1994). For a comparison between the business system and the innovation system approach see Lundvall (1999).
2. If we examine the distinctive pattern of education and labour market mobility, we find indications that the Danish innovation method is particularly conducive to the establishment of 'industrial districts', that is, regions with a high level of specialization in the production structure (see the analyses of education and the labour market in Chapter 6).

4. A national innovation system?

Here we will deal with the Danish innovation system as one of a number of national innovation systems. In the previous chapter we saw the close connection between an understanding of the innovation process as interactive and the development of the systemic approach. In this chapter we shall illuminate the degree to which one still can identify national innovation systems in a world characterized by gradually increasing globalization.

The concept of a 'national innovation system' has roots that go far back (Freeman 1995a refers particularly to List 1841), but in its modern version it is relatively new. It was first used in Freeman (1987) and was further disseminated through Lundvall (1992) and Nelson (1993), among others. In 2000, nearly a decade after the concept was presented to an international audience, it has become a common analytical tool in such international organizations as the EU, UNCTAD and the OECD as well as in a number of countries. For example Finland, Ireland, Taiwan and Korea use it as the basis for the framing of national innovation policy strategies. Recently Sweden established a new central authority named the Authority for Innovation System Policy.

The aim of the concept is to explain historical processes, and to establish a theoretical basis for policies related to economic growth. The old neoclassical theory of growth (Solow 1957) showed that a large part of actual economic growth could not be explained by growth in the production factors of labour and capital. This residual was named 'technical progress'. The 'new theory of growth' demonstrates in general terms how investments in research and education can yield greater growth because there are externalities and dynamic scale advantages in the production of knowledge (Romer 1990).

This is, of course, interesting in itself, but it provides only the most basic guidelines as to what type of innovation policy that is preferable. Should more resources be allocated to basic research or to applied research? Should academic or more practically oriented education be favoured? An especial problem for the new theory of growth is its presumption that all firms are identical (close to 'a representative firm') and that they under normal circumstances (as long as the market is functioning) are optimizing agents. This precludes for instance the consideration of policies that aim to enhance economic competence within firms, and for the same reason there is very little to say about the importance of both the internal and external structure of firms for economic performance. Analyses of national innovation systems are justified because they recognize that firms differ and that institutional factors are important for the outcome in terms of innovation and economic growth.

The fact that innovation systems could be national was first rendered probable through empirical research (Freeman 1987; Nelson 1988). The industrial decline of the UK and the success of the Japanese economy in the post-war period apparently had something to do with the ability to develop, absorb and use new technology. Further analysis showed that the crucial differences were 'systemic' in that they could hardly be separated from other conditions. In Japan, for example, there was a mutual dependence between internal firm flexibility in job functions, life-long employment, wage systems that provided a share of the firm's profits, mutual forms of ownership and strong and long-term network relationships with suppliers. Taken together this combination reflected a more long-term perspective and a knowledge structure with particular emphasis on collective and tacit knowledge (knowledge that cannot be written down, often the ability to do something – the ability to ride a bicycle is a classic example; see Polanyi 1966). Correspondingly one finds strong connections between the way the educational system and the labour, financial and commodity markets are organized in the UK. Together these reflect a short-term perspective and a knowledge structure that emphasizes individual, formalized knowledge (Lam 1998).

NATIONAL SYSTEMS IN A HISTORICAL LIGHT

Researchers who have concerned themselves with the role and function of the nation state have pointed out that the modern nation state, which was socially constructed and is typically only about 200 years old, has functioned as an ideal framework for industrialization and economic growth. This is particularly true for the small homogeneous nation states in Europe (Gellner 1983). Here the development of a national system of education, governmental regulation of the labour and capital markets, and not least a social policy based on solidarity have made possible an extremely rapid transition from an agricultural society through an industrial society and on toward a service-oriented society.

For the small countries in particular (the Nordic countries, the Benelux countries, Austria and Switzerland), the framework of the nation state has been important to economic growth (Katzenstein 1985; Kuznetz 1960). This is a paradox since theoretical analyses indicate that there are large-scale advantages associated with the production of knowledge – advantages that ought to restrict growth in these countries compared to larger countries (this is one conclusion emanating from the new theory of growth). It also appears that the majority of these countries specialize in products containing relatively little knowledge and research.

Despite these handicaps these countries have managed to attain a standard of living that is above the average for the medium-sized countries. Part of the explanation is that their close social interaction has enabled them to build up a foundation for economic development partially based on experience-based and production-based knowledge combined with the capability to absorb knowledge produced in other countries. Thus historically, small countries have built up 'social capital', which has enabled them to compete with large countries especially in areas where qualifications other than those arising from academic research are needed (compare Figure 1.3 above).

The historical function of the nation state is being challenged today both by the internationalization of the economy and by the process of European integration. A larger proportion of production is organized by foreign ownership and, especially in the most rapidly changing sectors, international networks of firms collaborate in the development of new technologies. A number of the classical government functions that were formerly concentrated at national level tend to be moved upward to a European level, while others (this is less true for small countries) have moved downward to a state or regional level. This raises the question if it remains meaningful to operate with an analytical tool such as 'a national innovation system'. Is there a need for a national innovation policy, or can the responsibility for this be handed over to the EU – for instance through the consecutive framework programmes for research and technology? In this context it is also relevant to ask to what degree the European integration process risks to undermine the social capital that has been built up in the small countries.

WILL GLOBALIZATION UNDERMINE THE NATIONAL INNOVATION SYSTEM?

Since the concept of a national innovation system was introduced, it has been critically re-examined from the perspective of globalization. Archibugi and Michie (1995) have attempted to summarize these considerations, reaching the following conclusions:

- The application of technology across national borders is extremely widespread.
- New technology is still developed primarily in the homeland of international corporations, but there is a tendency toward increasing localization of R&D activities in other countries.

Maurseth and Verspagen (1999) examine patenting in various European regions with a view to discovering the role that national innovation systems play in Europe today. They conclude that distance is still a barrier to the transfer of technological knowledge and that national borders still play a significant role as barriers.

These results relate primarily to formalized knowledge and to what we described above as 'the innovation system in a narrow sense'. If we look at the broad definition of the innovation system, there is reason to believe that the national system is even more crucial. The type of competence that it builds into the workforce and organizations will be unlikely to flow freely across national borders. Labour is still the factor of production with the least mobility across national borders.

There is a tendency that an increasing number of young people choose to be educated abroad, and this can result in both 'brain drain' and 'brain gain' for their home countries. In later chapters we shall warn against policies that a priori treat education and the labour market as closed national institutions. The most dynamic Asian countries have typically been able to combine national strategies with an openness regarding human capital. But for most countries these movements remain marginal as compared to the whole labour force.

NATIONAL AND INTERNATIONAL COLLABORATION BETWEEN FIRMS

Of course this does not imply that national innovation systems are closed to the outside world. The analyses we carried out in module 2, in which we looked at firm collaboration, can be used to illustrate the degree of internationalization in Danish industry (this specific study includes only manufacturing firms).

Figure 4.1 shows that there is still a stronger tendency to collaborate with domestic than with foreign customers and suppliers in connection with product development. The difference is most marked with regard to suppliers. When firms are asked what importance they place on their collaboration with various partners, a more balanced picture appears.

Figure 4.2 shows that customer collaboration and collaboration with foreign partners when it occurs is given greater emphasis than collaboration with Danish suppliers of material and components. Seen in relation to globalization this implies that 'important collaborations' in product development with customers and suppliers take place with partners abroad to almost as high a degree as Danish collaboration. This is especially interesting when one considers the many relatively small firms that participated in the study.

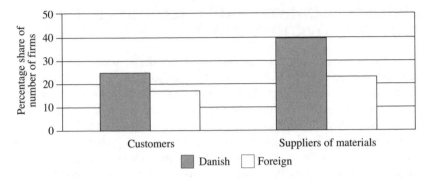

Source: Madsen (1999).

Figure 4.1 *Product development collaboration with Danish and foreign*
customers and suppliers respectively in connection with the
most important project

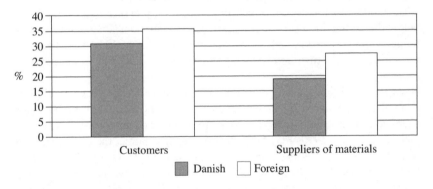

Source: Madsen (1999).

Figure 4.2 *Importance of collaborators – percentage reporting that*
collaborators were of 'crucial importance'

These observations and other analyses carried out under the auspices of the
Danish Agency for Trade and Industry (Andersen and Christensen 1998) indicate that what holds the national innovation system together is to a decreasing
degree an interaction between customers and suppliers in connection with product development, and to a growing degree a joint system of education and labour
market dynamics. We shall examine these other factors in Chapter 6; in this
connection, we merely wish to show that these areas have distinctive Danish
characteristics that help to constitute a particularly Danish innovation system.

THE DEGREE OF INTERNATIONALIZATION IN THE DANISH INNOVATION SYSTEM

If one takes into account the size and make-up of the economy, the degree of internationalization in the Danish economy is not particularly high. This is true for foreign trade (Regeringen 1999, p. 174) and to an even higher degree for the amount of direct investments to and from Denmark (ibid., p. 180). Sales from Danish firms located abroad make up only a modest portion of direct export of goods. This relatively controlled degree of globalization in the Danish economy reflects among other things the fact that Danish firms on average are smaller than for example Swedish and Dutch ones. More specifically it reflects the fact that there are few large multinationals in the Danish economy when compared with Sweden and the Netherlands (Edquist and Lundvall 1993).

The limited degree of internationalization may have both advantages and disadvantages with regard to the potential for economic development. Competition in export and import markets encourages firms to make changes, since export and import contribute to competition pressure. As we shall see below the competition pressure necessitates a continuous adaptation of technologies and organizational forms. International competition also helps to keep price levels down and to avoid monopolistic conditions in the national economy.

At the same time, it may constitute an advantage to have a population of firms that is primarily dependent upon the national innovation system. For example the massive export of capital from the Swedish economy that took place in the early 1990s may be seen as a way of avoiding the transformation pressure that the Swedish firms were experiencing. In Denmark firms that have experienced a corresponding transformation pressure have had to make changes both with regard to technology and organization, because they did not have the same opportunity to move abroad. To put it another way, it is a question of finding a balance between 'exit' and 'voice' (Hirschman 1970). If the trendsetting firms find it too easy to move abroad (exit), their interest in influencing policy (voice) with the aim of maintaining the national innovation system, including social capital, would be correspondingly limited.

SUMMARY

All indicators point to the conclusion that economic interaction across national borders is increasing. This does not mean, however, that the significance of the national innovation system will decrease. Ever-increasing global competition involves the building up of local and national positions of strength that can maintain and attract resources in international competition; in the future this will become more and more crucial. Firms holding such positions of strength will to an increasing degree possess knowledge that cannot easily be removed from the organizational and geographical context in which it is rooted. This knowledge may lie internally within firms, in their mutual relations with other firms, in their contact with public organizations or in the local labour force. Later we shall examine how 'industrial districts' may play an essential role in an economy like the Danish one, where the mobility of the workforce between firms is great, while mobility between geographical areas and sectors is more limited. One answer to the challenges of globalization is paradoxically a more conscious attempt to promote industrial development and knowledge creation at a regional and national level.

At the same time it is clear that globalization presents challenges to many of the established institutions and routines in the national economy. In Chapter 6 we shall look more closely at the extent to which this holds true with regard to education, the labour market and the financing of investments.

5. The specialization of the Danish innovation system

One essential aspect of a national innovation system is its specialization in relation to other national systems.[1] This specialization reflects the types of activities that take place more intensely in Denmark than in other countries. There is a close connection between specialization patterns in production and specialization in the system's knowledge foundation. On the one hand, a national economy will attract activities that utilize the specialized knowledge embodied in the workforce and in the regional networks within the country's borders. On the other hand, the experiences made within a particular area of production will feed back into and strengthen the knowledge foundation in that area. This explains why specialization patterns in production and export change very slowly and why globalization has proven to be compatible with unchanged or even growing specialization between national economies (Archebugi and Pianta 1992).

The specialization of the innovation system is particularly interesting for two reasons. Firstly, it gives a hint of what are the areas of strength and weakness within the economy. An innovation policy has to take this as its point of departure. Secondly, considerations have been voiced about the extent to which fundamental weaknesses exist in the Danish specialization pattern, weaknesses that could argue for the development of strategies intended to change the pattern (see Box 1.2) As we shall see, some of the weaknesses ascribed to the industrial structure are something Denmark shares with several other small highly developed countries (Andersen and Lundvall 1988; Freeman and Lundvall 1988).

THE DANISH INDUSTRIAL STRUCTURE

We can illuminate specialization using different variables, from production and foreign trade to patents. One weakness common to all these indicators is that they shed light on production, foreign trade and patenting only in connection with manufacturing products. The increasing importance of services, including knowledge-intensive business services, means that analyses of specialization need to be expanded so that they take this into account. This is reflected in the most recent OECD analyses, in which analyses of high-tech manufacturing are beginning to be supplemented with analyses of 'knowledge-based sectors', which include business services (OECD 1998b, p. 36). By way of introduction, therefore, we will provide an overview of the composition of the entire Danish economy with regard to industrial structure and compare it with what we find in other small OECD countries.

The relative importance of a particular sector can be measured through the creation of value that takes place in the sector; we measure this value-added as a share of the entire economy. On this basis we summarize the development of the industrial structure in four small countries in Figure 5.1. Common tendencies in these four small countries are that the importance of agriculture in the economy declined, and the importance of private services increased. Manufacturing and the public sector retained their shares virtually unchanged. For the period 1985–95 this pattern is true for Denmark as well. At the same time, it is worth noting that the transition process took place more slowly in Denmark with regard to both the decline of agriculture and the expansion of private services. With respect to the following specialization analysis it is essential to note that manufacturing as a whole makes up only about 20 per cent of the total economy in terms of value-added, while a single sub-sector of private services, for example business services, makes up 18 per cent.

LOW-TECHNOLOGY SPECIALIZATION IN THE DANISH ECONOMY

One theme that has characterized the Danish discussion is the low-tech specialization in production and foreign trade. In other words, sectors that depend intensively on R&D carry less weight in Danish production and export than in most other countries. This becomes apparent when industry is broken down into sub-groups and the different industrial sectors are grouped together according to the respective intensity of their R&D.

All of the three Nordic countries listed in Figure 5.2 produce a smaller share of high-tech products (this includes aeroplanes, pharmaceuticals and electronics, for example) than one finds in larger countries and in the Netherlands and Korea. Denmark and Finland in particular stand out because of their specialization in low-tech industrial products (such as paper, clothing, furniture and foodstuffs).

In the case of export specialization, a similar picture of the Danish situation emerges. In Figure 5.3 a numerical value greater than one indicates that a particular country has specialized in export in that particular product group. Numerical values less than one demonstrate that the particular product group makes up less of that country's export than the OECD average. In Figure 5.3 a

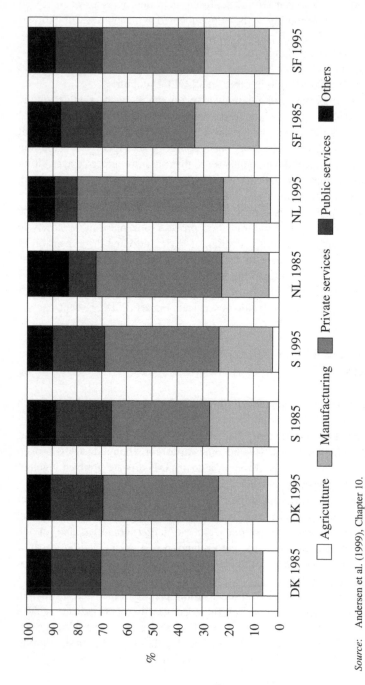

Source: Andersen et al. (1999), Chapter 10.

Figure 5.1 *Comparison of industrial structure 1985 and 1995 in Denmark, Sweden, the Netherlands and Finland (measured as a percentage of the entire economy's value-added during those years)*

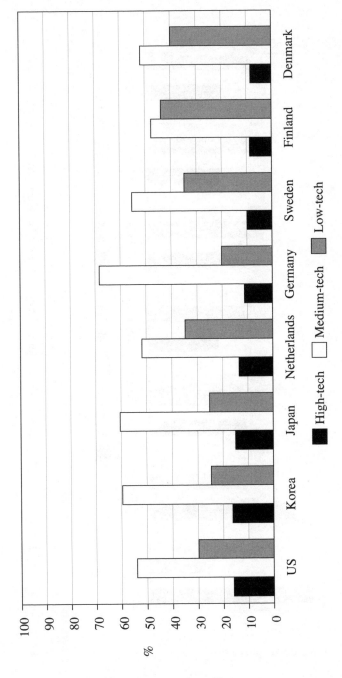

Source: Andersen et al. (1999), Chapter 10.

Figure 5.2 The make-up of industry in respectively high-, medium- and low-tech sectors in 1995 (measured as a percentage of value-added in industry as a whole)

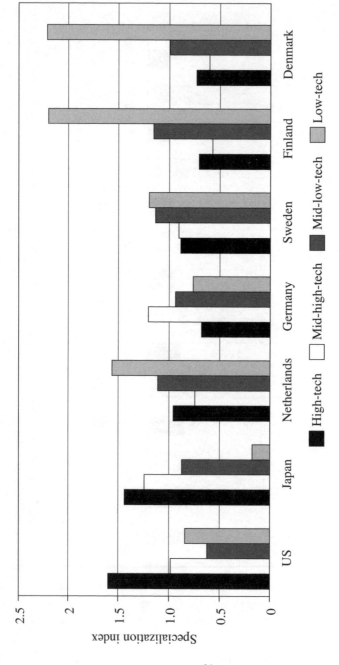

Source: Andersen et al. (1999), Chapter 10.

Figure 5.3 Export specialization for products with various technology content for seven OECD countries, 1994

subdivision has been made of products in the mid-technology group into mid-high-tech (for example automobiles, the chemical industry and machinery) and mid-low-tech (for example shipyards, oil refineries and metal products.

Figure 5.3 shows that none of these four small countries has specialized in high-tech or mid-high-tech products. They have however specialized in mid-low-tech and low-tech products. Once again Denmark and Finland appear as having an extreme degree of specialization in low-tech products.

On the basis of this analysis, it is of interest to examine the Danish pattern of specialization more closely from another angle, namely a division that focuses directly on the degree to which the economy is specialized in high- or low-growth products respectively. The aim of Figure 5.4 is to shed light on the extent to which the Danish economy has been hampered during the last 30 years by an export specialization in low-growth products. In the figure a number greater than one for high-growth products indicates that firms in that particular country have specialized in the export of products characterized by above-average growth on the global market.

Once again we find a difference between large and small countries similar to the one we found when high-tech products were in focus. Thus Figure 5.4 shows that at the end of the period in question (1994) the three large countries had specialized in products for which the export market had above-average growth (for the period 1961–94), while this was not the case for the four small countries. All other things being equal we must allow that greater effort was needed to achieve growth in the entire economy in the small countries, not least in Denmark and Finland, the countries with the most intense specialization in low-growth products.

One reason that low-tech specialization has been perceived as a problem is that the market for products demanding a high level of R&D has grown more quickly than other markets. These sectors have also had a faster rate of growth with regard to both employment and production (see Box 5.1). Therefore, in countries specializing in high-tech products, there will be a positive effect on exports even with an unchanged market share. Another argument might be that high-tech products are less affected by price competition and that the producers can realize higher real income without a negative effect on market shares.

Fagerberg (1995, p. 21) has demonstrated that, in general, small, highly developed countries seem to be handicapped with regard to the production of high-technology products. Because of the advantages of scale in production and the close connection of these technology areas to strong military demand, large countries have an advantage. At the same time, Fagerberg points out, that there is great potential for knowledge-based competitive advantages in product areas that are not as intensive in their use of R&D. One problem with these areas is that they may be more cost-sensitive than high-tech products. On this basis, he claims that small countries, in order to withstand competition, must

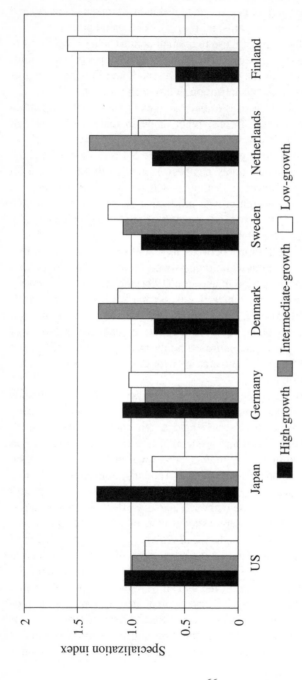

Source: Dalum et al. (1997).

Figure 5.4 *Export specialization for products with different world market growth for the period 1961–94 for seven OECD countries*

BOX 5.1   PRODUCTIVITY AND HIGH
             TECHNOLOGY

A number of OECD analyses have shown that the R&D-intensive activities that are collectively called 'high technology' are growing at a faster rate than the rest of the economy, both in terms of employment and productivity (see for example OECD 1994b, Chapter 4). DISKO data enable us to divide 1600 Danish workplaces into four different categories; these have been used earlier in Danish innovation analyses and originate in the work of Keith Pavitt (1984):

- Science-based (such as electronics and pharmaceuticals, 98 units).
- Specialist suppliers (such as the machine industry, 137 units).
- Scale-intensive (such as dairies, 178 units).
- Supply-dominated (such as clothing, 153 units).

The analysis shows that productivity is highest in the science-based firms and that productivity growth in these firms is above average for the period 1990–95 (8.9 per cent versus 5.9 per cent) (Dahlgaard and Reichstein 1999).

be correspondingly more innovative and aim to achieve a much more rapid dissemination of technology within sectors that are less demanding in terms of research and development.

SPECIALIZATION AND GROWTH

Is the Danish specialization pattern tenable in the long run? Or conversely, is it a problem at all? It is a fact that many of the countries with low-tech specialization do very well both in terms of standard of living and employment. This is particularly true for the economic development over the last decade in Denmark and in the Netherlands.

In order to further illuminate this problem, in Table 5.1 we have compared the degree of high-tech specialization in export and production with per capita

Table 5.1   Key data for countries of varying size, 1992

	Large countries	Medium-sized countries	Small countries Non-Nordic	Small countries Nordic
GNP per capita (US$)	22.887	18.910	16.725	25.843
High-tech prod.	26%	13%	9%	11%
Mid-high prod.	50%	48%	38%	33%
Export				
Mid-low prod.	10%	15%	15%	16%
Low-tech prod.	14%	24%	38%	40%
High-tech prod.	13%	7%	6%	6%
Mid-high prod.	32%	31%	19%	22%
Production				
Mid-low prod.	18%	22%	25%	21%
Low-tech prod.	37%	40%	50%	51%
R&D expense as % of GNP	2.8%	2.1%	1.6%	2.4%

Source: Lundvall and Maskell (2000).

income in groups of countries of varying sizes. The table shows that the Nordic countries, despite being dominated to a greater degree than the other small countries by low-tech products, have an income level well above that found in the other three groups of countries. This illustrates that there is no direct connection between a specialization in high technology and a high level of income. At least, it is possible to conclude that there are other factors that may overcome the negative effect of a low-tech specialization.

More ambitious attempts to demonstrate a systematic connection between the degree of high-tech foreign trade specialization and growth confirm the fact that there is no simple, direct connection between the two. One reason for this is that changes take place over time in what product groups are the most rapidly growing in global market (Laursen 1998, s. 157ff.; Dalum, Laursen and Verspagen 1999).

WHAT LIES BENEATH THESE PATTERNS?

High-tech and high-growth products are aggregate categories, and underlying them there is, of course, a specialization in concrete sectors and technologies. It is essential to know this concrete specialization, since it will make specific

Table 5.2   *Comparison of export specialization for Denmark, Sweden, Holland and Finland for different industries in 1980 and 1994**

	Denmark 1980	Denmark 1994	Sweden 1980	Sweden 1994	Holland 1980	Holland 1994	Finland 1980	Finland 1994	OECD weight 1980	OECD weight 1994
Foodstuffs	**4.1**	**3.7**	0.2	0.3	**2.3**	**2.7**	0.4	0.4	8.1	7.4
Textiles	0.9	1.0	0.5	0.3	0.8	0.9	**1.3**	0.4	6.5	5.7
Furniture	**2.2**	**3.1**	**3.3**	**3.0**	0.4	0.6	**7.1**	**4.3**	2.1	2.1
Paper	0.6	0.7	**4.1**	**3.4**	0.7	0.9	**8.1**	**7.5**	3.8	3.7
Chemical	0.8	0.9	0.6	0.8	**2.1**	**1.6**	0.6	0.6	18.8	17.1
Pharmaceutical	**1.8**	**2.5**	0.9	**2.1**	0.9	**1.1**	0.3	0.3	1.1	1.9
Non-metallic minerals	1.0	1.0	0.6	0.5	0.6	0.7	0.6	0.8	1.9	1.6
Metals	0.4	0.4	**1.1**	**1.5**	0.7	0.9	0.8	**1.7**	9.2	9.5
Metal prod./Machine	0.7	0.7	**1.1**	1.0	0.5	0.7	0.5	0.7	47.3	55.2
Computer	0.3	0.6	**1.1**	0.3	0.5	**1.4**	0.2	0.7	2.2	4.6
Consumer electro.	0.7	0.6	**1.1**	**1.2**	**1.1**	0.8	0.5	**1.1**	4.0	7.3
Flight industry	0.2	0.2	0.1	0.4	0.5	0.5	0.0	0.1	2.7	3.0
Automobile industry	0.2	0.2	**1.1**	**1.1**	0.2	0.3	0.2	0.2	11.6	14.1

Note: *To facilitate reading of the table, observations denoting specialization (n>1) are specifically marked.

Source: Andersen et al. (1999), Chapter 10.

demands on policies relating to, for instance, the labour market and the education system. In Table 5.2 the focus is on export specialization in categories corresponding to 13 different industries within manufacturing.

It appears in Table 5.2 that Denmark is highly specialized in the export of foodstuffs, furniture and pharmaceuticals respectively. During the period 1980–94, this specialization intensified with regard to both furniture and pharmaceuticals, while specialization in foodstuffs declined. The weights given to the respective industry in the far right column are important because they suggest the weight of the export market in question. Thus the great weight in metal and machinery category implies that Danish exports of metal and machinery products is larger in terms of value than are the three areas of intense specialization. The weights also demonstrate that the share of export to OECD countries made up by foodstuffs is declining and furniture export is stagnant, while pharmaceuticals is the only Danish specialization area in which the market is growing faster than the total OECD export.

If we examine the other areas – that is, if we exclude the three Danish areas of strength – the Danish specialization pattern appears to be very stable. For example there is no indication that there have been Danish breakthroughs in the electronics-dominated market or on the automobile or aeroplane markets during the last decade.

*Table 5.3   Ranking of Danish manufacturing industries according to degree
            of specialization in terms of production, employment and R&D,
            1990*

Production (% of DK total)	Employment (% of DK total)	R&D (% of DK total)
1. Food, drink and tobacco (28.4)	1. Food, drink and tobacco (21.0)	1. Pharmaceuticals (23.8)
2. Machine industry (11.6)	2. Paper and printing (12.1)	2. Machine industry (15.6)
3. Paper and printing (10.0)	3. Metal products (11.6)	3. Instruments (11.6)
4. Metal products (7.5)	4. Wood and furniture (8.8)	4. Communication and semiconductors (9.9)
5. Wood and furniture (5.3)	5. Textiles and clothing (7.9)	5. Other industry (8.3)

Source: Drejer (1998).

Another way of illustrating Danish specialization is to rank industries with
respect to a number of criteria. Such a ranking has been made in Table 5.3 and
includes specialization in terms of production, employment and R&D respectively. Table 5.3 illustrates that the production of foodstuffs, machinery, metal
products and furniture carries a great deal of weight in Danish production and
employment, but with the exception of the machinery industry these areas do
not appear as important in connection with research and development.
Conversely, some of the sectors that represent the majority of investments in
research and development (pharmaceuticals, communication and instruments)
carry little weight in terms of production and employment. This is also true to
a certain degree for exports, where the pharmaceuticals industry makes up
only 5 per cent of total exports, while the low-tech industry of wood and furniture makes up 6.5 per cent. The total picture is one in which the industrial
structure appears polarized, with a few small very high-tech islands (pharmaceuticals and mobile communication) standing out in a sea of mid-tech (metal
products and machines) and low-tech (food and furniture) products.

PATENTING AS AN EXPRESSION OF TECHNOLOGICAL SPECIALIZATION

Patenting data are being used to an increasing degree as a measure of technological specialization. Unlike R&D data, which provide us with knowledge

about the investment in formalized knowledge production, patent data express outcomes of an innovation process. They also have the advantage of giving detailed information both about the parties who take out patents and the content of those patents in terms of new technology. But there are also a number of problems with using patents as indicator. The most crucial problem is that they are used much more frequently in some sectors than in others even when the innovation activity is at the same level. Seen in relation to a given innovation tempo, the chemical industry, for example, uses patents to a much greater degree than the electronics industry. Thus one cannot always conclude directly from the fact that there is only a modest patenting activity within a sector that technical change is occurring at a modest rate within that sector.

If one examines the patents of Danish firms in the US, there are three areas where Danish firms appear with relative strength. These areas are primarily pharmaceuticals (0.9 per cent of the total patents in 1996) and secondarily industrial chemicals and non-electric machinery respectively (0.4 per cent of the total patents in 1996) (OECD 1998b, p. 287). This confirms that Denmark holds a strong knowledge position in the pharmaceutical industry. This can be further illustrated by examining the patenting patterns of Danish firms over a longer period. As Figure 5.5 shows, NOVO and Danfoss have a special status among Danish firms with regard to patenting.

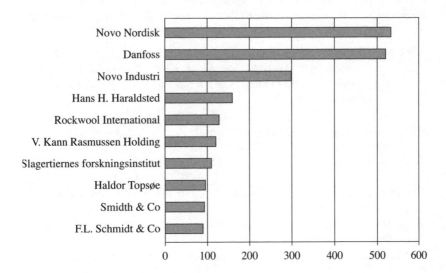

Source: Danish Patent Database/Mette Præst.

Figure 5.5   Overview of the ten Danish firms with most patent applications, 1982–95

REGIONAL SPECIALIZATION ILLUSTRATED BY PATENT DATA

As a rule, there is a connection between the international specialization of a national economy and its internal regional specialization. One often finds that the positions of strength in export specialization correspond to the fact that one or several areas in the country have specialized in that particular product area. For sectors with a stronger knowledge basis, this can be illustrated with the help of patent data. Here we shall examine how relative positions of strength within the export areas of pharmaceuticals, telecommunication and the machinery industry reflect a regional concentration of patenting activities concentrated in Copenhagen, Northern Jutland and Southern Jutland respectively.

Table 5.4 shows that the three regions have very different knowledge foundations. The Copenhagen metropolitan area is particularly strong in the area of chemical and biological processes. Northern Jutland's strength lies in 'process engineering' connected to the food industry and other manufacturing industries. However, Northern Jutland also has a specific position of strength within mobile communications. The specialization of Southern Jutland is completely dominated by Danfoss and lies in the areas of electrical and mechanical engineering. Another regional area of strength that is not directly apparent in this arrangement is the area of Northern Zealand, north of Copenhagen, which has

Table 5.4   *Overview of the areas of technology (30 in all), where the firms in the region in question are highly specialized in terms of patent applications (the numbers in parentheses are specialization figures)*

Greater Copenhagen	Northern Jutland	Southern Jutland
1. Biotechnology (1.9)	1. Materials (2.6)	1. Thermal technology (3.5)
2. Organic chemistry (1.8)	2. Telecom (2.2)	2. Mechanical elem. (3.4)
3. Pharmaceuticals (1.8)	3. Machines tools (1.8)	3. Aerospace tech. (2.8)
4. Nuclear tech. (1.7)	4. Civil engineering (1.7)	4. Electrical mach. (2.6)
5. Materials (1.5)	5. Chemical engin. (1.6)	5. Engines (2.2)

Source: Danish Patent Database Mette Præst.

a high concentration of firms producing electronics and measuring instruments. In the next chapter we shall examine some of the mechanisms connected to the labour market that may explain why Denmark's knowledge foundation has a highly developed regional specialization; we shall also discuss what impact this will have on challenges to innovation policy.

SUMMARY

In this chapter we have shown that although low-tech sectors dominate Danish industry, there are a number of knowledge-based areas where Denmark is at the forefront internationally. This is especially true for the pharmaceutical industry, but it also holds true to a certain extent for wireless communications, biomedical electronics, and portions of the mechanical and electromechanical industries. But these scientific activities do not carry much weight from an economic standpoint, neither with respect to production nor to export (knowledge-intensive activities have been calculated to make up only eight per cent of total production in Denmark – see Drejer 1998). The Danish industrial structure is to a high degree dominated by production areas that, internationally speaking, are characterized by both low wages and low levels of research-intensity. To a certain extent Denmark shares this fate with other small countries. However, Denmark and Finland appear on the low side, even compared with these other small countries. While recent data show that Finland in the 1990s became more specialized in high-technology products the degree of specialization in this area was actually further weakened for Denmark (Andersen et al. 2001, p. 75).

Sector-level data indicate that a strong presence of high-tech sectors in the national economy and in export ought to promote economic growth. In analyses examining the development dynamics of the entire economy, it has not been possible to demonstrate any clear connections in this direction. In any case, it will take a long time to build up new research-based positions of strength in the industrial structure, and it is hardly realistic to change the prevailing specialization patterns to any significant degree within the near future.

Until now this handicap has been compensated for by a high participation rate and a high degree of change and flexibility in firms' use of resources, including rapid diffusion of new technologies. One should not allow oneself to be led astray by the term 'low technology' in this context. The production equipment and manufacturing methods used in the production of foodstuffs, furniture and clothing are highly advanced. They are often combined with a high level of competence in industrial design and with advanced marketing methods.

This type of knowledge foundation is not strongly correlated to the extent of research and development, but it is fundamental to competitiveness within these sectors. The economic standard of living reflects among other things the fact that Danish firms have been able continuously to attain a particularly effective creation and utilization of experience-based knowledge in more traditional product areas. This relative success has to do with a close social interaction across the boundaries of organizations, departments and management levels. This interaction is supported by a system of education and a labour market, each with its own national idiosyncrasies. We shall look more closely at these aspects of the Danish innovation system in the next chapter.

NOTE

1. This chapter is largely based on empirical material provided by Bent Dalum, Mette Præst, Ina Drejer and Michael Dahl.

6. Education, labour markets and capital markets as fundamental components of the Danish innovation and competence-building system

One important dimension of the Danish innovation system is its specialization. Another is its institutional set-up, particularly the construction of the institutions and markets that are responsible for communicating strategic resources to companies. In this chapter we will delineate the characteristics of the system of education, the labour market and the capital market from the perspective of innovation policy. In the second half of the book, we shall examine more closely some specific aspects of these markets and institutions, especially the organization and content of vocational training. In Chapter 12 we shall look more closely at the system of adult vocational training, while in Chapter 13 we analyse the impact of firm behaviour on labour market dynamics and vice versa.

The following discussion of education is almost entirely based upon a perspective of industrial development. It is obvious that this is a limited perspective and that education has much broader social and cultural functions. Education is also about the self-realization of individuals and this is a perspective that has always been given high priority in Denmark.

DANISH COMPREHENSIVE SCHOOLS

In connection with the increased awareness that knowledge is a strategic resource in economic development, the system of education has undergone close scrutiny, not least by economists both internationally and in the course of national debate. It is thus characteristic that the 1997 OECD report on the Danish economy gives high priority to a critical analysis of the system of education (OECD 1997b). The Danish Ministry of Finance has also began to focus on what is taking place in the system of education. The establishment of the National Council for Competence, on the basis of private initiative, and the Council's first report, have also focused on the Danish system of education (Mandag Morgen 1998).

These reports and analyses give a complex picture of the expediency and efficiency of the system. Nor is there agreement about which policy measures are most urgent. This disagreement is perhaps best illustrated by the fact that the OECD has written reports giving a very negative impression of the Danish education system while at the same time publishing analyses praising the same system. To a certain degree these nuances reflect differing value systems and perspectives, but they particularly reflect the fact that more rigorous and to some degree opposing demands are signalled to the education system.

THE CHARACTERISTICS OF DANISH COMPREHENSIVE SCHOOLS

It is somewhat banal to state that there is a mutual influence between a nation's culture and its schools. Actually, the school system from the very beginning played a crucial role in the formation of modern nation states. In countries such as France this role of the school remains fundamental and explicit when considering reforms. The history of education in Denmark has its own unique features. It is characterized by a combination of state responsibility for funding and the quality of the school and a high degree of freedom when it comes to organizing education according to different cultural values and pedagogical methods. The philosopher Grundtvig and his emphasis on popular learning among adults without formal degrees as the outcome still play a role in shaping the debate about the school (see also Chapter 14).

With respect to innovation and economic development there are thus certain Danish cultural attributes that deserve particular notice. Danish citizens and wage-earners are as a rule more flexible, more open to new ways of doing things and more disposed to participating in courses characterized by 'lifelong learning' than citizens of other countries. However, Danes are not particularly work-oriented. Leisure time and family time are higher priorities (Mandag Morgen 1998, pp. 61–4). These fundamental attitudes are reflected in the Danish system of education – it is here that they are produced and reproduced.

Among other things, this means that young people do not feel any particular compulsion to do schoolwork during their leisure time, nor do their parents strongly encourage them to do so. Danish schoolchildren spend markedly less time on home preparation than children in other countries. However, instead they work and earn money to be used for their own consumption at a level that far exceeds that of children in other countries. One can say that to a certain degree they have appropriated the wage-earner role while still schoolchildren. They are to a certain degree self-supporting while attending school for the required number of hours. They achieve early independence, also economically, from their parents. (In the public debate there has been much more focus placed on women's liberation than on this 'youth liberation', despite the fact that it is perhaps just as radical when it comes to understanding the very individualistic character of Danish society.)

It is becoming more and more common for young people, after completing the mandatory nine years of state schooling (corresponding to British O-levels) or an additional three years of upper-secondary education (corresponding to A-levels), to spend one or more years travelling abroad, not for study purposes but rather for the experience. In other countries such career interruptions are perceived negatively because they delay students' careers relative to their peers. But the experience that this period of travel provides gives the young person independence and perspective while also equipping him or her with social, linguistic and cultural skills.

In the Danish school itself the atmosphere is more democratic and informal than in larger European countries such as France, Germany and the UK. Pupils become accustomed at an early age to the legitimacy of discussing with and questioning teachers and other authorities; they also become accustomed to cooperating within groups. Taken together, these elements in the framework of youth education provide a number of general personal qualifications: the abilities to accept responsibility, to communicate and to work with others. These qualifications correspond quite well to those required in modern firms, which must operate in an extremely turbulent environment (for an account of the DISKO data that support this, see Chapter 12). Here lies perhaps the most essential part of the explanation of the success of the Danish economy, which paradoxically combines a high wage level with a strong specialization in low-wage industries.

THE QUALITATIVE WEAKNESS

Danish pupils seem to do poorly at certain age levels with regard to reading, mathematics and science skills (OECD 1997b, pp 89–90). Their difficulties are typically in subjects that have a more formal structure in which intuition and the ability to communicate are not sufficient. This is also reflected in the young people's choice of study, where study programmes with a heavy concentration on mathematics are rejected in favour of programmes requiring social interaction and creativity. In a way, this pattern corresponds to the Danish specialization pattern in production and innovation. As we showed in Chapter 5, only a relatively small portion of Danish production and export originates in sectors with strong, direct roots in science.

This orientation of the study choices of young people should not, however, be perceived one-sidedly and negatively. The two fastest-growing sectors in OECD countries are business services and personal services;

knowledge-intensive business services in particular will come to play an increasingly important role in international competition. For this reason there will be a need for a great number of highly educated people with backgrounds in the humanities and social sciences; there will also be a need for experts able to communicate complex knowledge in a multicultural context.

In general, however, there is much to indicate that in the future it may prove problematic simply to reproduce this pattern in the school system. Change will take place at a faster rate and there will be increasing demands to enter into social, interactive learning processes. This is where the Danish competencies may prove especially useful. At the same time, however, there is a tendency that the knowledge base is becoming more formalized in the area of the production of goods and services. This formalization places greater demands on employees in these sectors: they must have basic skills in the areas of reading, writing, arithmetic and computers. In some of the case studies carried out in DISKO we were able to demonstrate that firms had faced the decision of either having to dismiss their unskilled workers or provide them with special training in connection with reorganizations, namely because workers did not possess such basic abilities (Voxted 1999a).

Thus a double challenge faces the school system. On the one hand its present orientation toward fostering independent, critical citizens who are positive toward change harmonizes with the demands of the future labour market. On the other hand there is a need for more effective teaching and learning of formal abilities such as language, mathematics, science and computers. It may prove that the conflict between these two goals is not as irresolvable as it may seem. A modernization of teaching methods in the more formal subjects could, for instance, be part of the solution. Creative use of IT and practically-oriented learning methods, in which pupils can see how the tools they learn in various subjects help to solve practical problems, are examples of what such modernization might involve.

In this area, as elsewhere in the educational system, incentives for experimentation – and follow-up of initiatives in the form of analysis and the sharing of experiences – should be provided. A current OECD project has shown that very little applied research takes place in the area of education; it also showed that, unlike in the area of health care, for example, there are few effective mechanisms for the transfer of experience among schools and between schools and researchers (OECD 2000b).

THE QUANTITATIVE WEAKNESS

Another crucial weakness is that the Danish system of education still leaves too many pupils without an upper-secondary education. The percentage of the workforce in Denmark with an upper-secondary education is about 60 to 65 per cent, near the bottom when compared to other countries with similar income levels. This relatively weak placement will be weakened further in the future unless priorities are reconsidered. Nor is the number of citizens with university degrees including PhDs particularly high in Denmark seen internationally (National Council for Competence 1998, p. 21).

It is especially important – and we shall return to this a number of times as our analysis continues – to reduce the number of young people who leave the educational system with no qualifications beyond basic schooling. This group will be even more vulnerable in the labour market of the future. Special resources need to be earmarked for this purpose, but it is also necessary to further develop pedagogical methods that will enable a larger percentage of each age cohort to complete a meaningful and attractive upper-secondary education.

PEDAGOGICAL CHANGE REQUIRES THAT TEACHERS TAKE THE LEAD

The types of teaching used at various educational levels have undergone considerable changes throughout the last several decades. Universities in particular have succeeded in improving teaching methods and the percentage of degrees completed by using project-based learning methods and group assignments. Despite the fact that these teaching methods have been documented as more effective than the old ones in providing the competencies that are demanded in the labour market, particularly for engineers and business economists, there is a certain hesitation about accepting the 'new' methods, both in academic circles but also surprisingly enough in certain employers' organizations. The need for interdisciplinary practice is constantly increasing, but is still having difficulty finding acceptance in the academic system. In the academic community, incentives for success (hiring and advancement criteria as well as research and teaching evaluations in a single narrowly defined academic discipline) seem to foster a restrictive organization of both research and teaching into single disciplines. Universities, too, are facing the double challenge of on the one hand strengthening traditional areas of specialization while on the other hand developing new interdisciplinary areas of knowledge that match the new problems raised by technological and social change.

There is a corresponding need for radical changes at earlier levels of education. It is difficult to see any rationale, for example, for splitting up the school day into 45-minute lessons for different subjects, a condition we see not only at secondary level but also earlier. Experience-based pedagogy needs to be given more room, as it takes advantage of the fact that many Danish pupils today have part-time jobs. Put in everyday terms, we could say that upper-secondary education needs to change so that it focuses even more than before on teaching pupils to learn. This theme will be further substantiated in the next chapter, which will treat the 'learning economy'.

BOX 6.1   IN THE LEARNING ECONOMY ONE OF THE KEY COMPETENCIES IS THE ABILITY TO BUILD BRIDGES BETWEEN PEOPLE

In current debates about education and research policy, there is a tendency to return to a perspective that focuses entirely on physical production, despite the fact that this area today makes up only a relatively small portion of the entire economy. This leads to a situation in which technical and scientific knowledge is seen as the main essential input of competence into the economy. There may, of course, be good reasons to be worried about the short-term and mid- to long-term lack of electronics engineers. However, the complaints that more students are specializing in pedagogical and sociological areas may be exaggerated. In an economy where it is becoming more important to build bridges between people than to build bridges between Danish islands, these groups will be just as essential to competitiveness as traditionally educated engineers. The problem is not that more people are choosing careers with communicative functions, but rather that the educations they choose are too often, by tradition, aimed at a career in the public sector. For the same reason, it is unwise to treat research in the humanities and social sciences as being of secondary social and economic importance and to continue to allow natural science traditions and criteria to dominate research policy.

It is important to establish a realistic strategy for change, particularly when radical changes are to be made within a system as dependent on its history as the school. Restrictive economic approaches, which measure quantitative indicators and give grants according to some kind of 'benchmarking' of performance, might seem rational to the logic of the Ministry of Finance, but they will more than likely increase the schools' unwillingness to implement change. In other areas of the DISKO project we have seen how organizational change in the business sector requires participation across the board by middle management, labour representatives and employees. This will also hold true for a restructuring of the educational system. It is crucial that the people within the system who are interested in promoting change – among other things because they want to have more interesting, meaningful work to do – play the major role in the process of change. Besides, there are many other reasons to be critical to attempts to benchmark public sector activities (Lundvall and Tomlinson 2001).

Openness to incentives that support local experiments – perhaps even in the form of 'green-field investment', in which new units are built up from ground level – is crucial for progress in this field. Collaboration between researchers, teachers, pupils and parents in connection with such experiments is presumably also a requirement for moving ahead. Educational research is generally an area that should be given higher priority. It is thought-provoking that the pharmaceutical industry uses close to 10 per cent of its turnover on research and development, while the resources set aside for educational research make up less than one per cent of the funds allocated to education. It is not apparent that this reflects a wise social weighing of priorities.

SUMMARY OF THE CHALLENGES FACING THE SCHOOLS

Denmark has an education system that, internationally speaking, is better adapted to the development toward the learning economy than that of most other countries. At the same time, the system is put at risk by partially conflicting demands. On the one hand there is a demand for measurable efficiency with regard to formal qualifications and on the other hand a demand for the production of change-oriented individuals with the ability to co-operate and communicate. Elements in the policy process of change that can meet these requirements will be:

- Continued and increased use of forms of learning that promote independence and the ability to collaborate – also with those in other disciplines, subjects and functions – at all levels of study.
- Consistent attempts toward the teaching and learning of basic competencies in Danish, mathematics and foreign languages at earlier levels through the use of new teaching methods that place particular emphasis on helping a large share of the total number of pupils to develop these skills to a reasonable degree.
- Greater emphasis throughout the entire education process on activities that are practice-related and problem-oriented; in study levels near the

transition to the world of work, the implementation of compulsory practical elements.

In order to put these changes into practice, positive incentives are needed for local pedagogical improvements by teachers in collaboration with researchers, parents and students. In this reform process we must remember that school is about more than preparing students for the world of work. Human beings are more than a source of labour, and the school has other aims that must be weighed against those that are focused on here.

THE DANISH LABOUR MARKET AS A FRAMEWORK FOR KNOWLEDGE CREATION AND LEARNING

Denmark's labour market, like its education system, has particularities that make it unique from an international perspective, and are essential in explaining the existence of a particular Danish mode of innovation. The labour market is characterized by great flexibility with regard to job changes between workplaces. In this regard the Danish labour market resembles the US one. To a certain extent this high labour market mobility reflects very liberal legislation with regard to the right of employers to dismiss their employees. In this area Denmark holds an extreme position in the European context (Smith 1997).

At the same time, there is a publicly organized system of unemployment support. In an international comparison it has a high level of compensation and a long period during which benefits can be drawn. This is the reason why Danish wage-earners, despite frequent job changes and without legally mandated employment security, feel a low level of insecurity about their job situation when compared with other European wage-earners (OECD 1997a, p. 132 ff.).

We also saw in Chapter 1, that the Danish population participates in the labour market to a much higher degree than the EU average. At first glance, this seems paradoxical, since the combination of a high tax burden and public subsidies should encourage people not to participate actively in the workforce. Economists who specialize in the labour market have shown that a large proportion of workers receive very little economic gain from being active in the labour market. This reflects, presumably, that Danish workers, and women in particular, place a positive value on having a job and the individual independence it brings. The fact that unemployment compensation is at a reasonable level and lasts for a certain length of time presumably contributes to the attraction of achieving and maintaining a permanent connection to the labour market. The motivation for active participation in the labour market is generally high in Denmark.[1]

MOBILITY, CONTINUING EDUCATION AND LEARNING

This extremely high mobility also reflects the fact that the Danish industrial structure is made up of a larger share of small workplaces and firms than one finds in other countries. One consequence of this combination of high mobility and small workplaces is that there are relatively few incentives for employers to invest in the education of their own employees.

Conversely, though, Denmark has established a public system of continuing education that is unique in comparison to the outside world (see Chapter 12 for an analysis of this). A greater proportion of the adult workforce than in other countries participates in continuing education, and a greater share of GNP is spent on continuing and adult education than is the case anywhere else in the world. The public sector has thus taken on a role that the small Danish companies would have difficulty fulfilling on their own.

This seems to have affected the way in which large companies develop human resources. It appears that Danish firms, also when compared on the basis of size, invest less in the education – including continuing education – of their own employees than in most other countries (Dansk Management Forum 1996, p. 63). There is also less systematic planning in the development of human resources in Danish firms (ibid., p. 64).

THE CONSEQUENCES FOR LEARNING AND THE MODES OF INNOVATION

A picture emerges in which the development of competence in Danish business life takes place primarily through recruitment and only secondarily through the establishment of internal education and continuing education under the auspices of the firm. The high level of mobility is not limited to unskilled labour; it also applies to technicians, academics and even top management. This is the setting for the participation of Danish firms in the learning economy. It resembles the one found in high-tech regions such as Silicon Valley, and it has both positive and negative aspects.

It is a positive aspect that firms are able to recruit experienced employees from other firms. The relatively large flow of competent manpower between firms means that new ideas can spread relatively quickly through the economy. It also provides a foundation for interaction between firms, since workers to a great extent have relationships with their colleagues in other firms.

These advantages will be especially attainable for firms located in an 'industrial district' – a term we will discuss more thoroughly in the next chapter – that are specialized with regard to the firms' industry affiliation and technological basis. In this area, specialized regional labour markets will appear;

these will have workers with a high level of competence, and the exchange of knowledge through job changes between companies will be intense. In such a context, firms may also become more willing to invest resources in the education of their own employees, because they can count on a return on their investment indirectly in the form of new employees who have been educated in the other firms. Perhaps joint initiatives will be established in which firms that draw from the same areas of competence combine their resources in order to promote learning. In this context it is important to note that labour market policy is regionalized and implemented through tripartite bodies that involve representatives for regional government, trade unions and employers organisations respectively.

There are also negative aspects to this particularly Danish framework for the development of human resources. It is tempting for firms to act as 'free-riders', exploiting existing human resources without contributing at all to their development. The lack of interest in developing human resource management strategies in large and medium-sized Danish firms also points in this direction.

It is also a question of the degree to which a public effort can replace the efforts of the firms. In the DISKO project's analyses of the Danish system of continuing education, we have found that continuing education is particularly well suited to providing the labour force with well-established and stable qualifications, while it is less well suited to supporting technical and organizational change in firms (see the analysis in Chapter 12). Here a parallel may be drawn to R&D, where it has been shown that the economic effect of private R&D is markedly greater than that of R&D organized by the public sector.

In any case the Danish model demands intense, close collaboration between the working life and firms on the one hand and the public system of adult education on the other. Regional labour market boards have an important function in this connection. Innovative forms of collaboration between labour market policy, industrial policy and educational policy at regional level appear to be one possible response to the challenges facing the particularly Danish way of innovating.

THE STRUCTURAL WEAKNESS OF THE DANISH LABOUR MARKET

The Danish labour market seems to work quite well when compared to other countries. A high participation rate, low unemployment and a high level of mobility are traits that few other countries can compete with. And these results have been accomplished without widening the income gaps. In fact, after tax and subsidies income distribution became more equal in the 1990s than it was in the 1980s and the Danish economy remains the most egalitarian in the world in terms of income distribution (Regeringen 1999, pp. 328–9). On the plus side there are also low levels of long-term unemployment and youth unemployment, again viewed from an international perspective.

The positive picture nevertheless does have some serious blemishes; these have to do with the weak position of low-skilled workers, women and last but not least ethnic minorities. Unemployment for these groups is significantly above the national average (OECD 1997a, p. 30), and this problem may even worsen in the future. In the next chapter, we show how intensified competition may weaken the position of workers with little education and training. We shall also demonstrate how firms' in-house training investment accentuates this problem.

The groups mentioned above may be perceived positively as an unused potential in the learning economy. New organizational forms require that employees at all levels are able to participate actively in the processes of change, and this presupposes basic competence on the part of all employees. If these groups are not given the opportunity to attain such competencies, they will place a burden on the public support, and this will also increase the labour market's bottleneck problems. These problems may become even more dramatic as the new generations of young people entering the workforce decreases. Finally there is the danger that excluding large groups of people from the labour market will erode the Danish social model and the 'social capital' that forms the basis of the Danish innovation process. Especially, the lack of integration of foreigners in working life contributes to intolerance and puts strain on public welfare systems based on principles of collective solidarity.

In this connection it should be emphasized that this exclusion from the labour market is not just a problem in the private sector. Recent data indicate that even public institutions whose primary responsibility is personal service – home care and nursing – are among those responsible for a great deal of exclusion. This indicates that organizations in the public sector are no more aware than the private firms of the need for keeping up to date the qualifications of its least-educated employees.

Thus one of the most difficult challenges facing the Danish system is to make a major effort towards strengthening the position of unskilled workers on the job market while at the same time investing in a broad development of qualifications affecting the entire population. Recently, reforms that give the unskilled better access to training have been implemented, but at the same time the access of average employees to continuous training has been made more costly. Giving better access for workers without professional training is well motivated while increasing the costs for continuing training for the rest of the workforce is much less so, given the need for life-long learning for all categories of workers.

HOW CAN POLARIZATION AND MARGINALIZATION BE LIMITED?

An increase in the wage differential between the highest and lowest wages, for example through the reduction of minimum wage and a corresponding reduction of unemployment benefits, would most likely lead to a situation in which some workplaces would increase their demand for workers with fewer qualifications. This would provide more job opportunities for workers with the lowest competence levels. One disadvantage of this strategy is that it would make life easier for low-productivity activities. The Danish economy is already specialized in low-wage sectors and to reinforce this pattern might become a problem in the long run, as we saw in Chapter 5. Add to this the fact that it might be difficult for the majority of the Danish population to accept an increasing inequality in wages and working conditions. If this change were to have any visible effect, more than marginal changes in the wage structure would be needed. Temporary subsidies giving excluded workers an easier entrance into the labour market may be less damaging in these respects. Given the growing scale of the problem, such initiatives need to be considered in Denmark.

The other primary route toward solving these problems has, of course, to do with competence-building. Expansion of upper-secondary education would contribute by reducing the number of students that leave the school system without a professional education. As we pointed out above, this would require both economic resources and qualitative changes in the schools' mode of operation. Adult education and other competence-building schemes aimed at strengthening the position of unskilled workers on the labour market are the second primary factor in such a strategy. Again, a combination of more resources and curricula improvements would be necessary.

A number of points of criticism have been raised about vocational training and adult education courses. Workfare schemes for education have resulted in participants finding some of these courses irrelevant. Other complaints have to do with the fact that employers do not use the competencies that are acquired. As we shall argue in Chapter 12, these courses of education could be vastly improved, not least by strengthening the interaction with employers regarding the structure and content of courses. It is especially important to provide unskilled workers and their employers with incentives to enter into courses of study aimed at developing new competencies. This pertains for example to the provision for educational leave, in which the most generous support could be given to unskilled workers and special compensation could be provided to their employers.

A constant need to upgrade qualifications and competencies will be present for all categories of employees in the future, and it is to be expected that the upgrading of skills increasingly will become an integrated part of future collective labour market agreements. There is a particular need for employers and trade unions that organize unskilled labour to move in this direction. Trade unions that are very demanding in terms of salary and working conditions but neglect the skill upgrading of their members will erode their own position in the long run.

The fact that Denmark has proven less successful than other countries at integrating ethnic minorities (the 'new Danes') into the workforce has been interpreted as an expression of cultural intolerance, and there is certainly some truth in this. But, more basically, at least it partly reflects that the Danish mode of production and innovation is based so strongly on intense social interaction, and will continue to be so to an ever-increasing degree. On this basis, it is crucial to equip this portion of the population with effective access to the Danish language and culture while at the same time providing them with the other skills they need to gain admittance to the world of work.

For workers coming from other countries there may also be a need to give specific entrance subsidies and a lower entrance pay that make it possible for them to get a first footing in the labour market. If these schemes remain temporary and specific they may be implemented without undermining the Danish model of the labour market.

Finally, it is important to stress that the development of competence does not necessarily involve sitting at a school desk. For the groups that are particularly vulnerable in the learning economy, it is necessary to find forms of learning that place particular emphasis on experience-based learning and on communicating theoretical material with reference to practical problems.

THE FINANCIAL SYSTEM AND THE INNOVATION SYSTEM[2]

In the above analysis, we have shown that the Danish educational and labour market systems have their own logic, and how this helps to constitute in both negative and positive ways a particular Danish mode of production and innovation. This is not quite as clear when turning to the financial system. To a certain extent this is because financial systems have become more international in their mode of operation than education or the labour market.

One way of distinguishing between national financial systems is to examine to what extent they are market-based or credit-based. In market-based systems firms obtain a large portion of their finance through the sale of shares on the stock market, while bank allocation of credit plays a greater role in credit-based systems. The Danish system is primarily credit-based and in this respect resembles the German system, while the UK and the US are characterized by market-based systems. It is generally true that the credit-based systems' strength lies in channelling funds to established firms, while they are generally less helpful in supporting new firms. In high-tech regions – in particular Silicon Valley and the greater Boston area – a very active venture capital branch has been established in the US, while the attempts of most European countries to establish themselves in this area have been less successful.

This means that Denmark is also faced with the challenge of ensuring that venture capital is available to new firms, not least to firms whose central resource is knowledge. This is reflected in a number of recent public initiatives that aim at improving the financing possibilities for firms and making the financial system more sophisticated. For example:

- state guarantees to development companies;
- the innovation milieu programme;
- a new institute for responsible loan capital ('mezzanine capital');
- an information exchange market for small firms;
- authorized market-places;
- innovation funds.

At the same time there are spontaneous changes in the capital market going in the same direction: an increased number of subscription tenders, a lack of clear demarcations between sectors, and competition – also with regard to ownership shares. Combined with the initiatives that are under way or under consideration ('business angels' networks, loan guarantee markets, the official scheme for technology evaluation), the picture that emerges is one of an abundant supply, both with regard to the quantity and the character of the various forms of capital.

Competition policy has an essential and difficult task in relation to the financial sector in credit-based systems. The innovative ability of the entire economy depends on the efficiency of the banking system; it also demands that the banking system's market position is not too strong in relation to the customers and firms that depend on it. Competition is one consideration that may conflict with other considerations aimed at strengthening international positions in relation to foreign competitors as financial markets become more global. It is cause for concern that in the most recent 'competition evaluation statement', the financial sector appeared as one of the sectors in which there were signs of weakened competition (Danish Competition Authority 1999, p. 58).

THE FINANCING OF KNOWLEDGE-INTENSIVE START-UP FIRMS

While an abundance of venture capital exists, there are still firms with promising ideas that have problems getting funding. In particular, these firms have one or more of the following characteristics:

- they are primarily small/new firms;
- they are based on immaterial investments/innovations;
- they lack capital of their own;
- they are facing expansive growth that takes place at intervals.

In the 1990s there has been a general European tendency for financial institutions to make a relatively small contribution to the investments during the early phases of a start-up. Moreover this tendency has been reinforced in recent years as investments have moved away from technology-based firms. It should be noted, however, that very recently more attention has been focused on the involvement of European venture capital companies at earlier stages, not only because there is more competition on the market. The European organization of venture capital companies, EVCA, has also brought this problem into focus by the appointment of an 'early-stage group'; a European counterpart to the NASDAQ has also been established in order to improve the venture capital companies' opportunities for future sales. This counterpart was recently taken over by NASDAQ.

There are a number of reasons for this lack of commitment during the early stages of innovative firms. Firstly, it must be emphasized that the costs of entering into an innovation in its early phases are low and that there is a chance for a high rate of return on the investment. On the other hand, however, there is also great uncertainty connected with these investments. Thus it is realistic to operate with a high mortality rate.[3] Secondly, there are basically the same fixed expenses related to investment in a small, new firm as there are with investments in larger firms. In this connection fixed expenses also include expenses related to evaluating the potential of a possible investment. For this reason there is a greater potential for return on the investment (in absolute terms) connected with investments in larger companies. Investments in small new firms require a great degree of guidance and additional general competence on the part of the investors. In other words these are specialized investments, and most investors choose not to bother attaining the competencies needed.

For these reasons, the public sector may have a role to play with regard to the financing of the types of investments named above. The rationale for public intervention rests first and foremost on the small-scale argument. In Denmark it is difficult on a purely private basis to attain critical mass in investments so that risk is spread fairly among investors while at the same time investors, through specialization, increase their competence with regard to such investments – in other words, a learning effect takes place. There is therefore a dilemma between on the one hand attaining a learning effect through specialization and on the other hand shouldering the costs related to one's private economy with regard to building competence in the area of investment.

In principle, the aim of public intervention ought to be to reduce the costs of this learning process.

'BUSINESS ANGELS' IN THE DANISH ECONOMY

Private individuals who have the competence to invest capital in small innovative firms have been given increased attention in recent years in Denmark. Christensen (1998) points out that there is most likely untapped potential in this area if the 'market' could be induced to function better. The problem is that it is often difficult to establish contact between firms and investors. The accessible channels are usually very informal. The Ministry of Trade and Industry is currently considering initiatives to ease this problem.

Traditional methods of credit evaluation are often inadequate with regard to small knowledge-based firms. For this reason, there is a challenge in upgrading the ability of financial institutions to judge immaterial assets. It has been discussed whether firms without solid real capital or another form of collateral will in the future be treated unfairly with regard to the injection of capital. A number of investors do not acquire the necessary competence, even though they would like to provide venture capital. For this reason it is important to establish structures that give agents with investment competence the chance to use it, while investors with venture capital can bring this into play.

There are a number of difficult challenges in the development discussed above. It is not enough merely to stimulate the supply side. In many cases there is a lack of knowledge on the demand side as well. Many firms, particularly small ones, do not know enough about the forms and sources of potential capital. There is thus a need for more information about the increasingly sophisticated supply of various forms of capital. On this point, the greatest potential probably exists in initiatives in the area of capital exchange. Such an upgrade in business knowledge could occur either through direct information to the firms themselves or through the firms' advisors (financial institutions, accountants, executives and financial officers, Technological Information Centres and so on). In many cases, information could best be channelled locally or regionally.

GLOBALIZATION AND REGIONALIZATION AS A JOINT CHALLENGE

It is no longer unusual for Danish financial investors, including the pension funds of wage-earners, to invest in stocks with security on the other side of the globe. The most central prices on the financial markets – interest rates and currency exchange rates – are to an increasing degree determined by global events or more specifically by the development of the US economy. Historically, this aspect of globalization was largely the result of political decisions, but today it appears as an irreversible process; in other words it is difficult to see how a national regulation of the flow of finances in and out of the national economy could be recreated. But new regional state formations such as the EU may have the scale to do so.

At the same time globalization raises the question of whether national and regional supplies of capital to firms can continue to be assured. Can the credit-based organization survive in a more global regime? Does the growingly extrovert orientation of Danish financial investors mean that gaps will appear, particularly with regard to providing capital to small firms, including new knowledge-intensive services providers? Can one realistically count on the public sector to act increasingly on a national and regional level to fill these gaps? Or will the market itself be able to fill them? The last question has to do again with the conditions of competition in the financial sector.

The Danish education system and labour market, unlike financial markets, are still perceived as fundamentally national institutions. The normal situation is presumed to be one in which Danish institutions educate Danish citizens for jobs in the Danish labour market. This perspective is becoming challenged and it is hardly realistic in the long term. To an increasing degree we will be confronted with a reality in which it is necessary to accept students and workers from other countries while letting Danish students and workers move to universities and jobs in other countries.

Thus the idea of the systems of education and labour markets as nationally closed and closely related units will appear obsolete. It is thought-provoking that the most dynamic economies in the world are those that have been involved in the most extensive exchange of human resources. This is true not least for the US and the dynamic Asian economies of Korea, Taiwan and Singapore (OECD 1998c).

This does not mean that one should give up the cultural characteristics of the system of education and the labour market in Denmark and try to make them more similar to some international or European average. On the contrary, they can serve to attract foreign students and workers who are tired of authoritarian leadership and formality. Nor is the point to relinquish the ambition of a regulated labour market with strong organizations on both sides. Increased international collaboration might demand some adaptation in the way university education is organized, to make it less difficult to accept foreign students and to send Danish students abroad. But the unique emphasis on problem-oriented and project-organized principles of study needs to be retained. As mentioned earlier, much stronger investment in the language and cultural training for those who come to Denmark with a view to participating in the workforce is needed.

Such an international perspective is not irreconcilable with the realization that the Danish model for competence development may have its special strength in the organization of production at the local and regional level. A co-ordination of industrial policy, educational policy and labour market policy at the regional level, the aim of which is open experimentation and the exchange of experience with other Danish regions, but also with regions abroad, may prove to be a strong weapon in an arena of increasingly global competition.

SUMMARY

The Danish way of developing and utilizing the skills of people is unique. Overall we can say that it is in harmony with the current volatile international environment. The system of education fosters independent citizens who are willing and able to accept responsibility. This is crucial for firms' ability to delegate responsibility and create functional flexibility. The labour market promotes mobility between companies, and this is an important way of spreading knowledge while facilitating the development of networking relationships between those companies. There are weaknesses both in the educational system and in the labour market's way of functioning. But on the whole these are areas from which the Danish innovation system receives a great deal of the strength that enables it to compete internationally despite economic specialization in sectors that are, from an international perspective, characterised by not being science-based.

The financial system is beginning to offer a number of possible sources of capital to knowledge-based entrepreneurs. At the same time it might prove problematic for the innovation system that the financial agencies that should serve industrial development have too much market power in the Danish economy. In a credit-based financial system it is important that the financial institutions, too, experience an appropriate transformation pressure.

NOTES

1. The structural monitoring report published in May 1999 compares Denmark with other countries in various areas under the theme 'Denmark as an exemplary nation' (Regeringen 1999). In most of the areas the report paints a fairly accurate picture of Danish society. One must wonder, though, about the negative impression that is given of the labour market. The high substitution rate, and the length of eligibility for, unemployment benefits are emphasized as negative factors, while the high mobility of the Danish workforce is not even mentioned in connection with the discussion of the way in which the labour market functions. This is also an example of 'naive benchmarking', where there is no regard for the systemic interdependence of the crucial variables (Lundvall and Tomlinson 2001).

2. This chapter is based on Christensen et al. (1998), DISKO report no. 5, as well as on a specific written contribution from Jesper Lindgaard Christensen.
3. International studies indicate that three out of ten survive. One of these can typically be passed on without losses, one gives an expected return, and one is a potential 'golden egg'. A study carried out for the European commission shows that there is a negative correlation between European venture capitalists' yields and how early they enter into the company.

7. The learning economy

There is growing attention to the importance of knowledge for economic development internationally as well as in Denmark (Gibbons et al. 1994). In November 1994 the OECD organized its first international conference about the knowledge-based economy. It took place in Copenhagen, and the Danish Prime Minister Poul Nyrup Rasmussen gave the opening statement (see Foray and Lundvall 1996). In 1998 the National Council for Competence produced a report that aims to provide a perspective on the Danish economy in which knowledge and knowledge creation are at the very centre (Mandag Morgen 1998). There is still, however, a considerable gap between the interest being shown in the role of knowledge and learning and the analytical understanding of the area. The concept of the 'learning economy' and the analysis it leads to are attempts toward filling this gap (OECD 2000b).

To understand the role of the national innovation system, it is necessary to attain a better understanding of knowledge and learning as well as of the way in which knowledge and learning interact with economic development. By way of introduction we specify various types of knowledge and their respective importance to economic development. At the end of this chapter, we shall illustrate the proposed theses about the learning economy with data collected in connection with the DISKO project.

KNOWLEDGE AS INFORMATION

Modern information technology has resulted in the current situation, in which it is extremely cheap to send large amounts of information over great distances. For those with access to the necessary infrastructure, the information they have access to has become a virtually free commodity.

At the same time the very existence of modern information and communication technology provides strong incentives to convert all kinds of knowledge into information. When combined with the establishment of effective laws regarding intellectual property rights, such a conversion will make it possible also to sell that information; since the costs per unit for the reproduction of information are generally very low, it will be worthwhile to codify knowledge.

These developments mean that the ownership of knowledge will become a pivotal point. If pirates can easily copy compact discs, books and innovations, there is no 'carrot' involved in producing them.

In a world where all kinds of knowledge could be transformed into information that could easily be moved from one place to another, there would be no local or national innovation systems. The specific knowledge that was produced would be worthless and the systems would disintegrate. There would be no clear indication of the location of activities, and the location would primarily be a reflection of natural advantages such as proximity to raw materials and markets. Expert knowledge would decrease in value as that knowledge would become encoded into 'expert systems'. Competent managers would be replaced by 'management information systems'.

BOX 7.1   WE NEED TO KNOW MORE ABOUT HOW KNOWLEDGE IS PRODUCED

The Business Report of 1998 (Ministry of Trade and Industry 1998) refers to some essential characteristics of the 'learning economy', but there is a need for a more systematic approach in order to understand the limits of the globalization process described in the same report. The way in which knowledge is transformed between tacit and formalized forms affects the temporal and spatial possibilities for transferring knowledge and is thus of vital importance for the future role of the national innovation system. In this area, there is a need for basic research efforts.

It is also worth noting that the analytical approach and the recommendations are limited in their perspective and scope seen in relation to the knowledge creation that is taking place across the board in society. For example, very little if anything is being said about the labour market's way of functioning or about the form that the continuing education of workers has taken, despite the fact that these factors play a decisive role in the learning economy. And still in the report a 'well-functioning labour market' refers much less to competence-building than to price flexibility and efficient allocation of labour.

KNOWLEDGE AS TACIT COMPETENCE

We do not see any tendency toward a more equal income distribution or a downward movement of the income level of experts in the current economy.

On the contrary, there is a tendency toward polarization both regionally and on the labour market, and there are a number of strong indications that this polarization reflects an unequal distribution of competence. This is related to the fact that there are narrow limits to how far one can go in converting competence into pieces of information and codes. Tacit knowledge plays an important role in all parts of the economy.

Tacit knowledge is traditionally considered as immanent in practical activities such as cycling and swimming, in which the person carrying out the action cannot fully describe what he or she is doing. In the real world we find corresponding elements of tacit knowledge in all competence areas, also the most advanced theoretical ones.

The great scientist is not the one who has read the greatest number of scientific studies. She also possesses an experience-based intuition that enables her quickly to recognize and understand a complex situation, for example through recognizing patterns when confronted with very complex flows of information (Ziman 1979). The same is true for the business executive who must make a strategic decision – decisions will typically be made on the basis of experience from similar situations (Nonaka 1991; Nonaka and Takeuchi 1995). It is impossible to reduce these competencies to information. As we know, one does not become the world's best chef simply by having access to a cookbook containing the recipes of the world's best chef. Nor can one read one's way to a Nobel Prize or the ability to lead a large organization.

The general difficulty in formalizing and writing down what a particular competence involves is further heightened when the reality in which one operates is highly volatile. One reason why the computer chess programs have become so strong in their rating is that the game is played according to rules that have remained unchanged for centuries. The researcher, the doctor, the manager and the artisan will typically encounter new problems that cannot be solved just by repeating old routines. These professionals have an important advantage over expert programs, the limitations of which become particularly obvious when the skills demanded are flexibility and the ability to tackle new problems.

INFORMATION TECHNOLOGY AND TACIT SKILLS

It may appear paradoxical, but information technology may in fact have led to a situation in which tacit competence is more vital in the economy than ever. This could take place in two ways. First of all, the enormous wealth of information will lead to a situation in which there will be particular demand for competencies to select and use information; these competencies cannot be computerized or otherwise made automatic.

Secondly, the formalization of certain elements of the innovation process has increased enormously the speed of the processes of change and thus makes it less attractive to invest in expert systems. Analyses of the construction of expert systems show that these systems can be implemented only in relatively simple, repetitive processes. And even in these instances, a considerable loss of information is connected with their construction. What comes out of codifying expert knowledge is always different from the starting point (Hatchuel and Weil 1992).

'KNOW-WHO' AS A STRATEGIC NEW FORM OF KNOWLEDGE

The increasing amount of knowledge and the fact that specific activities – for example product development – demand more complex knowledge rooted in different disciplines and technologies means that the production and application of knowledge tends to become an increasingly collective process. For individuals as for organizations, it is important to know where to find and have access to various types of expertise. This means that 'know-who' (in contrast to 'know-why', 'know-what' and 'know-how' – see Lundvall and Johnson 1994) is becoming a critical competence in economic contexts.

'Know-who' – that is, knowing who has certain abilities and being able to mobilize those abilities – is also a type of knowledge that can neither be codified nor replaced by Internet search engines. These search engines might be able to provide a list of anonymous experts, but the ability to choose with whom to establish a working relationship, and to have a social contact that enables collaboration, can only be learnt through social interaction.

KNOWLEDGE AS AN INDIVIDUAL COMPETENCE

It is also important to localize the levels at which knowledge may exist. Is it something that only a particular individual possesses? Can organizations be the bearers of knowledge, and can knowledge be hidden even in regional structures?

Individuals will always possess abilities and skills that will to a varying degree be useful outside the organization in which they are employed. If the employee's competencies are central to the organization, in demand by other organizations and difficult to transfer to another information medium, the worker in question will be a 'key employee'. In this case the business will take great pains not to lose that employee to a competitor. The recent growth in the use of share options as remuneration of employees had as one objective to preserve this category of workers in the firm.

KNOWLEDGE AS AN ORGANIZATIONAL COMPETENCE

Alternatively to individual competencies we find competencies that are inherent in the organization's routines and joint problem-solving methods. As a rule, this type of competence is also unable to be completely transformed into information. Organization schemes and information systems are only pale shadows of what actually takes place within an organization. This usually becomes clear when one organization takes over or merges with another and when the management of an organization changes hands. Despite an abundance of documentation there will always be a number of surprises.

Attempts to document both individual and organizational knowledge can be more or less intense in different organizations. At the moment a number of international consulting firms are very concerned with 'knowledge-sharing' in the form of formal registering of activities and joint access to data banks and so on. Attempts are made to document every single activity and experience and then make that information available to the entire organization. The problem with such a strategy is that it uses a lot of scarce intellectual resources and that the documented experiences are constantly rendered obsolete as the organization's environment and the problems it faces change.

KNOWLEDGE AS A REGIONAL COMPETENCE

Alternatively knowledge may be anchored in a regional economy. Alfred Marshall, who introduced the term 'industrial district', first formulated this idea. The empirical background for his idea was that different regions in England had specialized in different industries and technologies. Marshall claimed that 'the secrets of business are in the air' and that they are passed down from generation to generation of business executives and workers.

A number of mechanisms can explain the strong regional specializations and the long periods of time these specializations tend to endure. The most crucial mechanism is the emergence of competencies in the individuals who make up the local workforce. These individuals are not necessarily loyal to a particular employer, but they do tend to remain in the region. The combination of a high degree of mobility among firms and a permanent connection to the region is particularly useful in promoting gradual transformation and learning throughout the business population. Silicon Valley has blossomed on the basis of such a combination.

Other elements can also contribute to a stable regional specialization. The system of education, the technological infrastructure and financial institutions all adapt to a certain degree to the specialized needs of the industry in question. The creation of new companies when new niches arise can take place on the basis of the learning that younger technicians experience; this in turn can contribute to the creation of continued transformation and change. And when the scale of production is expanded, markets for specialized suppliers are established.

LEARNING, COMPETENCE-BUILDING AND SOCIAL CAPITAL

Knowledge in the form of information is not always easy to acquire. For example there are codified mathematical formulae and theorems that can easily be sent from one end of the globe to the other by means of the Internet, but perhaps only a handful of researchers have any idea what to do with them (Dosi 1996). One aim of academic teaching is to communicate a specialist language and formal systems of interpretation that will enable the student to communicate within a scientific discipline. But there is often a great leap from the possession of elementary knowledge of the technical language of a particular subject to the ability to interpret information about recent scientific breakthroughs in that area.

Knowledge as the ability to do something (know-how), including the ability to solve an unstructured problem, can usually be attained only through practice and experience (Kolb 1984). Often the attainment of experience will take place in a form that resembles apprenticeship, where the young person imitates and later collaborates and communicates with the more experienced staff member. The efficiency of this type of learning can vary greatly. There are good teachers and those who are not so good, and there are conditions that are more or less conducive to learning. It is interesting to note that Nobel Prize winners when asked about crucial stages in their learning processes tend to refer to situations where they operated in apprenticeship-like relationships with other outstanding scholars.

This type of learning is socially rooted to a different degree than a process that simply aims to exchange information. A prerequisite for effective learning is a basic level of trust between master and apprentice. When it comes to interactive learning aiming at competence-building, the social context is crucial to the effectiveness of the learning process. Rigid hierarchical structures, corruption and a lack of transparency can block the effectiveness of the interaction that is crucial to the learning process. Thus social capital – the ability to work with and trust others – is crucial to the effectiveness of the learning processes and therefore for the learning economy as a whole (see Lundvall 1996 and Box 7.2).

BOX 7.2   SOCIAL CAPITAL AND ITS
          IMPORTANCE TO THE LEARNING
          ECONOMY

One usually assumes that the production and application of
knowledge are characterized by economies of scale. Once
knowledge has been produced, it can usually be used and
reused at low additional cost. For this reason one would suppose
that small countries would generally fare worse than larger countries in knowledge-based competition. This perspective underes-
timates the importance for competitiveness of socially-based
learning processes. Small countries have amassed a form of
social capital that enables citizens to cooperate and participate
actively in learning processes that promote growth and competitiveness more easily. Thus it is interesting that while the learning
economy is characterized by increased competition, it is also
characterized by an even more close collaboration between firms
and their customers and suppliers (Gjerding 1997, p. 65).

     In general the Danish innovation system is one dominated by
small organizations and easygoing people. It is a flexible system
in which it is relatively easy to do business, and it is not very
formal.* The key word is collaboration, both horizontally and vertically, internally within a business and externally in relation to
customers and suppliers. The primary purpose of collaboration is
incremental innovation in traditional product areas, and to an
increasing degree in knowledge-intensive services as well. The
fact that Denmark has managed to attain a high per capita
income through utilizing such a strategy demonstrates that it has
depended on some 'small-country advantages'. Closeness in
social relationships allows for rapid communication and allows
problems to be solved when they arise without much waste in
terms of formalities or social struggles.

     Social capital will be especially important in a society where,
as in Denmark, interactive learning and gradual innovation
provide the basis for economic prosperity. In a society without
mutual trust between individuals and groups, very little learning
would take place, and one might wind up in a situation resembling that in Russia: because of the disintegration of social capital, a significant amount of knowledge capital is disappearing as
well.

Note: *In the analysis of Jeurissen and van Luijk (1998)
Denmark comes out, together with the US, as the country in
which foreign business people find it easiest to establish business relationships.

THE LEARNING ECONOMY

In various contexts we have introduced an interpretation of what actually takes
place in the economy under the term the 'learning economy' (Lundvall and
Johnson 1994; Lundvall 1996; Lundvall and Borras 1999; Lundvall and
Archibugi 2001). The aim of this term is to establish a certain distance from
the term the 'knowledge-based economy'. The learning economy concept
signals that the most important change is not the more intensive use of knowledge in the economy, but rather that knowledge becomes obsolete more
rapidly than before; therefore it is imperative that workers constantly attain
new competencies. This can be illustrated by the reference in a recent discussion paper from the Danish Ministry for Education to a German source that
claimed that half of the knowledge of computer engineers has become obsolete within one year of the exam being passed, while it should take eight years
before 50 per cent of the professional training of the average wage-earner has
become obsolete (Ministry of Education 1997, p. 56).

A learning economy is one in which the ability to attain new competencies
is crucial to the performance of individuals, firms, regions and countries. The
background for this crucial importance of learning is that globalization, information technology and the deregulation of a number of markets leads to more
rapid transformation and change. For this reason individuals and companies
are increasingly confronted with problems that can be solved only through the
development of new competencies. The rapid rate of change is reinforced by
the fact that the intensified competition leads to a selection of organizations
and individuals that are capable of learning quickly, thus further accelerating
the rate of change.

The transition to a learning economy confronts individuals and companies
with new demands, and it also presents challenges to many of society's institutions and policy areas. This applies not least to knowledge-creating institutions, including the ones in the education system and in vocational training.
But it also challenges established practices in a number of seemingly more
loosely related policy areas such as social policy, competition policy and
cultural policy. For instance, ethics and morals in business life and in public
life in general become more important, because ethics tends to become a
national resource that must be maintained on a par with other scarce resources.

THE DOWNSIDE OF THE LEARNING ECONOMY: SOCIAL POLARIZATION

In the large OECD analysis of unemployment, the Jobs Study, carried out in 1992–94, one of the most striking general results was the relative weakening of the position of unskilled workers in the labour market that had occurred in every member country during the period 1985–95 (OECD 1994a, p. 23). In the US and the UK their relative earnings decreased, while in all OECD countries there was a growing exclusion of workers from the labour market and poorer job possibilities for those with the least amount of education.

Two possible explanations for this general tendency have been put forward: (1) growing imports of goods from countries with abundant access to unskilled labour and low wages, and (2) the introduction of new technology and especially information technology. In the DISKO project we have found a pattern that implies that the transition to a learning economy is the most important explanation. New technology, new competitors on the global market, and deregulation of markets have all contributed to increased demands for employees with skills to adapt and learn. To the extent that workers with less formal training and others with narrow and rigid skills have been unable to keep up with the rapid rate of change, they have been pushed out of the labour market.

This inherent tendency toward polarization makes the learning economy vulnerable and raises doubts about its sustainability. It is difficult to imagine a broad active participation in learning and adaptation processes in an economy where there is a clear divide between the A-team, B-team and C-team. For this reason it is important to respond to the growing transformation pressure with mechanisms aimed at counteracting the polarization that it brings about. Otherwise we risk undermining that very social capital that forms such a fundamental resource in the learning economy. This is of particular importance for an innovation mode like the Danish one, in which mutual cooperation and communication are keys to success.

THE DANISH ECONOMY IN THE 1990s AS AN ILLUSTRATION OF THE LEARNING ECONOMY[1]

One of the most important results of the DISKO project is an empirical illustration of the mechanisms discussed above. It appears that many Danish companies experienced an increase in competition during the period 1993–95.

Perhaps it is not so surprising that the majority of firms report they have experienced increasing competitive pressure over time. It is more interesting that the three categories perform very differently with regard to both innovative

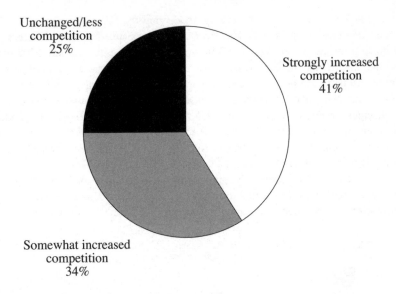

Unchanged/less
competition
25%

Strongly increased
competition
41%

Somewhat increased
competition
34%

Source: Lundvall and Kristensen (1997), p. 9.

Figure 7.1 *Share of firms that reported increased or unchanged competitive pressure during the years 1993–95*

Table 7.1 *The development in employment 1992–97 for three groups of firms arranged according to change in competitive pressure (index of the number of employees, 1992 = 100)*

	Nov. 1992	Nov. 1994	Nov. 1996	Nov. 1997
Strongly increased competition	68 440=100	102.5	100.1	102.1
Somewhat increased competition	46 141=100	103.3	102.1	103.1
Unchanged/less competition	19 071=100	103.8	104.3	103.5
Total	**133 652=100**	**103.1**	**101.6**	**102.7**

Source: Gjerding (1997).

behaviour and actual employment development. In Table 7.1 we summarize the development in employment for the three types of firms.[2] In the first column the total number of employees in all the firms surveyed belonging to the respective category is presented. The total number of employees covered (133 652) corresponds to almost 20 per cent of the total workforce in the sectors covered by the survey (for details see Table 13.1, p. 176).

Table 7.1 demonstrates the reality underlying the firms' survey responses about competition pressure. The firms that experienced strongly increased competition had no growth in employment over the entire period 1992–96, while the firms in the other two categories expanded employment by respectively 2 per cent and 4 per cent. But it is also interesting to note that the firms surviving strongly increased pressure experienced a stronger employment growth in 1996–97 than the ones who operated under less pressure in 1993–95. This may, as we shall see below, reflect the fact that the firms exposed to strongly increased competition are the ones forced to take initiatives in terms of new products and new forms of organization.

Firms exposed to increasing competitive pressure can respond in a number of ways. One possibility is that they have to close down. This alternative is by definition not included in the material we analyse here – we only include the

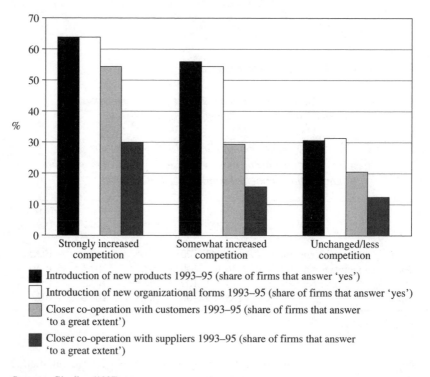

■ Introduction of new products 1993–95 (share of firms that answer 'yes')

☐ Introduction of new organizational forms 1993–95 (share of firms that answer 'yes')

▨ Closer co-operation with customers 1993–95 (share of firms that answer 'to a great extent')

■ Closer co-operation with suppliers 1993–95 (share of firms that answer 'to a great extent')

Source: Gjerding (1997).

Figure 7.2 Technical and organizational change in firms that reported increased or unchanged competitive pressure during the years 1993–95

firms that were surveyed and that exist and survive over the whole 1992–97 period. Another possibility is that they engage in technological and organizational change. In Figure 7.2 we have summarized the differences between the three types of firms with regard to organizational change, new product development and the implementation of new process technology respectively.

Figure 7.2 demonstrates that the firms that were particularly exposed to increased transformation pressure were most active with regard to both technological and organizational change. It may be of particular interest that the exposed firms reacted so strongly to competitive pressure by establishing closer cooperation with both customers and suppliers.

In our presentation of the learning economy, we stressed its inherent tendency to push out the portion of the workforce that has most difficulty keeping up with the rapid rate of change. To shed light on this hypothesis, we

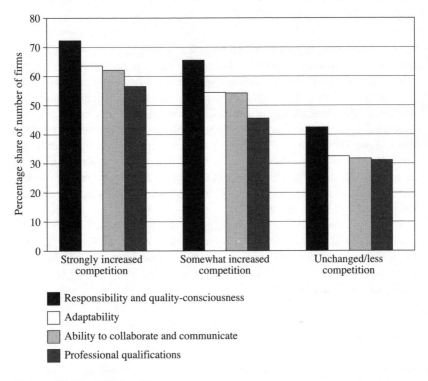

Source: Gjerding (1997), p. 67.

Figure 7.3   Share of firms that answer 'greater' to the question 'Has the firm altered its demands for qualifications in connection with hiring 1993–95?' and change in competitive pressure

Table 7.2   Employment of unskilled workers and all workers 1992–97 in
groups of firms experiencing varying degrees of increased
competition during the period 1993–95

		Nov. 1992	Nov. 1994	Nov. 1996	Nov. 1997
Strongly increased competition	All	68 440=100	102.5	100.1	102.1
	Unskilled	28 070=100	100.2	95.1	96.2
Somewhat increased competition	All	46 141=100	103.2	102.1	103.1
	Unskilled	18 426=100	99.9	97.2	97.5
Unchanged/decreased competition	All	19 071=100	103.8	104.3	103.5
	Unskilled	8 254=100	103.2	100.1	98.1
Total	All	133 652=100	103.1	101.6	102.7
	Unskilled	54 750=100	100.8	97.0	97.1

Source: Lundvall and Nielsen (1999).

have examined the degree to which there was a difference between the three
categories of firms with regard to changes in their requirements for employee
qualifications. By combining survey responses regarding competition with the
IDA labour market data, we can see what has actually happened to unskilled
workers in the three groups of firms. These data appear in Table 7.2, which
shows a decrease in the share of unskilled workers during the period 1992–97
(from about 41 per cent to 39 per cent). Most of the reduction (two-thirds of a
net loss of 1.588 jobs) took place in firms that had experienced a strong
increase in competition, while the rest took place in the intermediate group.
But the relative worsening of the position of unskilled workers was actually
rather similar in the three categories.

Again it is interesting to note that employment for unskilled workers grew
most strongly in the most exposed sectors from 1996 to 1997. The fact that
firms engaging in technical and organizational change may in the long run
create more and more stable jobs also for unskilled workers will be illuminated in more detail in Chapter 13.

SUMMARY

We have seen that many firms experienced a growing transformation pressure
during the period studied and that jobs were lost in this connection. We also
saw how this transformation pressure stimulated technical and organizational
change among the surviving firms as well as pushing toward more closely-knit
industrial networks for the exposed firms.

The demands for employee qualifications are increasing for general as well as specific qualifications. This is reflected in a changed composition of the labour force, with job losses for the unskilled workers. Most of the unskilled jobs that disappeared were in firms experiencing sharply increased competition; fewer job losses for unskilled workers occurred in firms that did not experience increased competition. But the data do not point to increased competition as the major factor behind the change in the composition of the workforce. The relative worsening of the position of unskilled workers was actually rather similar in the three categories. The data indicate that firms exposed to stronger competition in the longer run tend to create more jobs also for unskilled workers.

There is a connection between the dynamics we have concerned ourselves with in this chapter and economic internationalization; this, along with politically determined deregulation, exposes more and more firms to stronger transformation pressure. This in turn presents a challenge to the social cohesion that historically has been a key factor underlying the economic progress of small countries. Whether this cohesion can be re-established at levels other than the national – that is, at sub-national regional levels or at transnational regional levels (the EU) – is an open question.

In any case this analysis demonstrates the need to attune the transformation pressure to the ability of the economy to adapt to transformation and to innovate. The example of agricultural policy shows that extensive protection from transformation pressure leads not only to higher prices but can lead to negative effects on product quality and the environment. We have also been able to demonstrate that a certain degree of transformation pressure promotes technological and organizational improvements within firms. Conversely the data that have been presented suggest that too much pressure will result in lower levels of employment and not least in a polarization of the labour market that may undermine the development model that has characterized the Danish economy until now.

NOTES

1. The rest of this chapter is based on Lundvall and Nielsen (1999).
2. A description of the data sets used for Tables 7.1 and 7.2 is given in Chapter 13.

8. The learning organization

A recent OECD report emphasized that the average productivity growth for the entire economy can largely be explained by examining the activities of the individual firm.[1] In the majority of the countries studied, more than half of total productivity growth stemmed from changes at the level of the individual firm (OECD 1998a, p. 111). The PIKE (Productivity and International Competitiveness) project, which examined the reasons for the productivity decline in the Danish manufacturing sector during the mid 1980s, also concluded that the internal conditions in a firm were particularly effective in explaining this negative development. More specifically the blame could be placed on the lack of adaptation of qualifications and organizational forms in connection with a rapid introduction of new technology, particularly information technology (Gjerding et al. 1990). International analyses as well as the DISKO project indicate that there is a clear connection between firms' organizational development and their productivity levels.

The current focus among economists and in international organizations such as the OECD on how firms design and redesign their organizations represents a shift in perspective. The traditional assumption in standard economic analysis has been that firms by definition act in their best interest and that they are equally able to find out what is best practice. This assumption that firms act as well-informed, rational optimizing agents has conflicted with the growing effective demand for external advice from consultancy firms with regard to organizational changes (quality circles, just-in-time, lean production and so on).

In the 1996 survey of firms carried out by the DISKO project, organizational and technical changes were illuminated by responses from almost 2000 Danish firms in industry, construction, transport and various service sectors. This survey was followed up by two different sets of case studies: one of these focused particularly on organizational change and the other on the continuing education of employees in connection with these changes. Within these areas the project has built up a body of material that far exceeds that found in most other countries (for a comparison with three other national surveys see Coriat 2001). In the following text we shall look at a selection of the major results of the survey. (See also DISKO reports 1, 2, 3 and 8 as well as Voxted 1999a.)

METHODOLOGICAL PROBLEMS WHEN COMPARING FUNCTIONAL FLEXIBILITY INTERNATIONALLY

There are great difficulties in measuring the degree of organizational development, and particularly when making comparisons across national and sectoral
boundaries. One reason is that there is no clear scale that different organizational forms can be placed on that ranks them according to how 'advanced'
they are. Another reason is that a number of organizational techniques are
solutions to specific types of problems within organizations. That they are not
introduced in a particular organization or rarely occur in the firms in a particular country could thus be a sign of healthy conditions: the problem to be
solved does not appear. All studies, including those of DISKO, tend to show,
for example, that large organizations have a greater degree of functional flexibility (they use specific organizational techniques to a greater degree) than
small ones. To a certain extent this reflects the fact that small firms, because
they are small, do not need to implement job rotation or interdepartmental
work groups that include members who perform various functions within the
organization.

There are also examples indicating that certain traits are so ingrained in
daily practice that they are not referred to when one asks about them in a
survey. When Japanese firms were asked to what extent they used job rotation, surprisingly few positive responses were given; this was attributed to
the fact that job rotation is a part of everyday practices in almost all Japanese
firms and not seen as a specific management technique (OECD 1999a). This
latter aspect should be kept in mind when interpreting the relatively modest
placement achieved by Danish firms with regard to the delegation of responsibility to groups (see Figure 8.1) and the involvement of lower-level
employees (see Table 8.1). The international analyses we refer to below
should in general be interpreted with great caution. They represent the very
first fragile attempts to create data sets that can be compared across national
boundaries. Experience shows that a certain breaking-in period is necessary
before one can count on the reliability of the results, particularly when the
data in question are qualitative data collected by often very disparate survey
techniques.

HOW DO DANISH FIRMS FARE INTERNATIONALLY?

Figure 8.1 compares 11 different countries with regard to the degree of delegation of responsibility to individuals and groups respectively. As the figure
shows, Denmark's placement is close to average with regard to the delegation
to individuals but clearly below average with regard to delegation to groups.

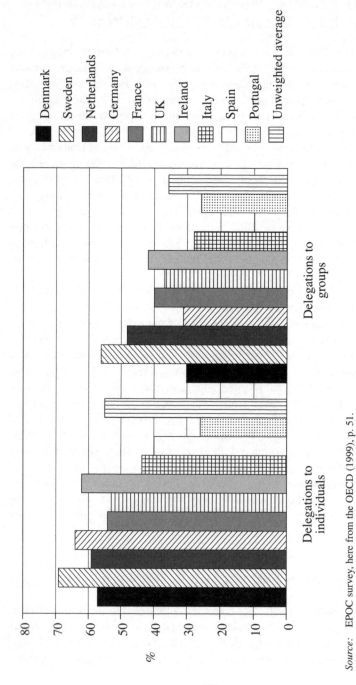

Source: EPOC survey, here from the OECD (1999), p. 51.

Figure 8.1   Indicators for delegation of responsibility to individuals and to groups (% of workplaces using this practice in 1996)

This could be an example of the respondents neglecting to refer to informal delegation because it is an everyday practice in Danish firms. As we shall see in a later section, the DISKO project has found that delegation takes place in the vast majority of Danish firms.

In connection with the start-up of the DISKO project a collaborative Nordic effort was established to carry out comparative analyses for the Nordic countries. Here the delegation of responsibility with respect to the planning of the daily work routine occurs more frequently in Denmark (62 per cent) than in Sweden (57 per cent), Finland (40 per cent) and Norway (20 per cent). If we look at another important element of the new form of organization, job rotation, Denmark has a low placement in relation to the other countries, especially when one takes into account the proportion of the workforce affected by job rotation.

The available indicators are characterized by a great deal of uncertainty regarding both the numbers and the interpretations. However it still seems as though Danish firms are considerably behind those of the countries we normally compare them to with regard to the implementation of new management techniques. To what extent this reflects and is counterbalanced by a particularly informal business culture and open communication is an open question that can only be answered in international studies that combine surveys with qualitative case studies.

One indicator that Danish firms have tended to lag behind their foreign competitors is data showing that they are catching up in areas where they have fallen behind. Table 8.1 shows that in three of four areas Danish firms are more active than firms in other countries with regard to the implementation of new organizational forms.

The very small number of changes involving the organization's lower-level employees demands a closer look. It is either a reaction among managers to the far-reaching *de facto* democratization or it could be that the involvement of these employees is such a natural thing that it is no longer seen as something that management needs to try and implement. The large numbers for Britain and France indicate that to a certain degree these changes are attempts to overcome barriers to communication rather than attempts to spread democracy further within firms. Finally it should be mentioned that a survey carried out by the same institution that collected the data for Table 8.1 regarding employee participation in decision-making processes reached the conclusion that there was greater participation in Denmark than in any other European countries (EPOC 1997, p. 32).

With these reservations as to the quality of the available data we must conclude that they indicate that while Danish firms got off to a slow start, they have been particularly active over the last few years with a view toward making up for lost time. Seen from this perspective, the LOK initiative, an

Table 8.1 *Share of workplaces with more than 50 employees that have*
implemented chosen management initiatives in the last three
years (%) (ten European countries presented by rank)

	Job rotation	Team-based work organization	Involvement of lower-level employees	Levelling of hierarchies
	Sweden (38)	**Denmark (40)**	Sweden (60)	Holland (47)
	Denmark (28)	Spain (34)	Great Britain (48)	Sweden (46)
	Spain (14)	Britain (33)	Holland (46)	Britain (45)
	Britain (13)	France (30)	France (44)	**Denmark (42)**
	Italy (13)	Sweden (29)	Spain (33)	Germany (30)
	Ireland (10)	Italy (28)	Ireland (32)	Ireland (23)
	Holland (9)	Ireland (27)	Italy (24)	France (21)
	Portugal (9)	Portugal (22)	Germany (19)	Italy (10)
	Germany (7)	Germany (20)	**Denmark (10)**	Portugal (3)
	France (6)	Holland (9)	Portugal (9)	Spain (-)
Unweighted average	15	27	33	29

Source: EPOC survey, here from OECD (1999a), p. 54.

inter-ministerial initiative that aims to support and facilitate the organizational changes of firms, must be said to be in line with the current needs of firms.[2] Another conclusion is that there is a great need for systematic research on organizational change and especially on developing data that make international comparisons more meaningful and reliable.

THE FUNCTIONAL FLEXIBILITY OF DANISH FIRMS

The data collected in connection with the DISKO firm survey enable us to highlight if a particular firm uses a particular type of organizational technique, if at all, and how widespread it is in the organization. In Table 8.2 we illuminate the dissemination of four different organizational techniques in both of these dimensions.

The most widespread organizational technique is the delegation of responsibility; this is also the one that involves the greatest percentage of the entire staff. A number of the other more specific, more demanding organizational techniques are also used by many firms, but as a rule they involve only a minority of the firm's employees.

Table 8.2   Dissemination of four organizational techniques promoting functional flexibility in Danish firms, 1996 (expressed in %)

N = 1882	Share that use the technique in question	Share in which more than half of the employees are involved
Delegation of responsibility	85.1	39.5
Integration of functions	57.0	13.2
Interdisciplinary work groups	49.6	9.2
Planned job rotation	36.0	6.6

Source: Gjerding (1997), DISKO survey question 6.

WHERE DO WE FIND FUNCTIONALLY FLEXIBLE FIRMS?

With regard to the use of specific organizational techniques there are important differences between small and large firms and among different sectors. In Table 8.3 we have presented the entire population of firms distributed according to size and five main sectors. We shall examine to what extent they use the techniques of the delegation of responsibility and the integration of functions respectively. When analysing the numbers one must remember that most of these sectors are anything but homogeneous. Business services includes both consulting engineers and cleaning firms; correspondingly the transport sector includes small haulage contractors as well as large advanced corporations.

If we look at the lower of the two rows of numbers in the table, we get an idea of how the group of firms in question deviates from the average of the 1862 firms surveyed. A picture emerges in which small manufacturing firms as well as large and small firms in the sectors of construction and transport respectively have done the least to implement organizational techniques that promote functional flexibility. Large manufacturing firms are in an intermediate position, while it is in the areas of trade and business services that we most often find firms that have implemented such techniques.

In the areas of manufacturing and construction, large firms are more apt to implement the various techniques than small ones. But this does not hold true for the other three sectors. Here one should note that we have examined the extent of the use of these techniques (their implementation must involve more than 50 per cent of the firm's workforce). If we had only examined the

Table 8.3 *Dissemination of two organizational techniques (delegation and integration of functions involving more than 50% of employees) in firms of varying size and with different sectoral affiliations given as (I=100 in the lower row indicates that the share is equal to the share for the entire population)*

	Manufacturing		Construction		Trade		Transport		Bus. Serv.		Entire Enco.	
	Del.	Int.	Del.	Int.	Del.	Int.	Del.	Int.	Del.	Int.	Del.	Int.
Firm with fewer than 50 employees	28.8%	9.3%	30.1%	6.8%	46.5%	16.6%	25.7%	11.8%	54.1%	17.4%	39.5%	13.2%
	73	70	76	52	118	126	65	89	137	132	100	100
Firm with more than 50 employees	40.0%	12.9%	41.2%	11.8%	43.9%	14.9%	26.7%	8.9%	50.0%	21.4%		
	101	98	104	89	111	113	68	67	127	162		

Source: Gerding et al. (1997), survey question 6.

appearance of the technique in question, the large firms would have dominated the picture to a greater extent.

Functional flexibility is a specific aspect of a firm's ability to react to changes in its surroundings and to strengthen its relative position in a turbulent environment. Another aspect is connected to the development of new products and services and to the cultivation of new markets. In connection with the analyses of the survey data, we have combined these two aspects with a view to defining those firms as 'dynamic' that combine functional flexibility with innovation. We have developed a scale measuring 0–14 to measure the 'degree of dynamics'. If we examine the different types of firms from this broader perspective, the picture changes slightly.

Now business services and manufacturing appear as the most advanced sectors. Trade and related areas take an intermediate position; construction and transport are the sectors that appear least 'dynamic'. The difference between small and large firms is considerable, with the exception of business services, where we find a big proportion of small dynamic firms. It also appears that there is a clear connection between being a branch of a bigger corporation and being functionally flexible. Independent firms have much less tendency to be dynamic than branches.

Thus a picture appears with this general trait: construction and transport are those sectors in which firms have developed the least dynamic organizational forms and innovative behaviour. Another general trait is that firms providing business services have largely adopted advanced organization forms and are active in terms of innovation. Small independent firms that operate as suppliers for large corporations have usually adopted only a modest amount of new organizational techniques.

ARE DYNAMIC FIRMS MORE EFFECTIVE THAN AVERAGE?

An OECD report (1999a) gives an overview of the studies examining the correlation between functional flexibility and economic results (OECD 1999a, pp. 9–10). The general conclusion is that functionally flexible firms tend to have both higher earnings and greater productivity than other firms. Furthermore, the relatively few studies that have been able to isolate the direction of causality indicate that the organizational form explains the high level of earnings rather than vice versa.

In the DISKO project we have found a clear correlation between the productivity levels and organizational forms. If we use the scale of the level of 'dynamism' within firms in terms of organization and innovation, as described above, we find a very clear correlation. As Table 8.4 indicates, the most

Table 8.4 The connection between the degree of organizational and technological change, and productivity (value-added in 1000s of kroner per full-time employee) in the areas of services (1993) and manufacturing (1994)

Index	0	1	2	3	4	5	6	7	8	9	10	11	12	13	14
Manufacturing	332	346	404	412	416	401	474	445	491	484	477	484	424	517	420
Service	440	402	341	390	412	465	461	472	473	475	547	592	585	649	696

Source: Lund and Gjerding (1996), p. 25.

dynamic firms have the greatest productivity. The connection is particularly marked for the service sector ($R^2 = 0.83$), but it also exists for the manufacturing firms ($R^2 = 0.51$).

While the correlation between the level of organizational development and productivity is pronounced among the participants in the DISKO study, this does not hold true for economic earnings. Those firms that had not implemented dynamic traits in their organizations in 1993 had a somewhat higher average rate of return (9.7 per cent) than those that combined functional flexibility with innovative behaviour (9.1 per cent). This brings us to the question about why firms introduce functional flexibility (Gjerding 1997, p. 122).[3]

WHY DO FIRMS INTRODUCE FUNCTIONAL FLEXIBILITY?

In principle there are two types of mechanism that can lead to a firm implementing organizational forms that provide greater functional flexibility. One occurs when the firm develops a pro-active strategy for organizational change and then gradually realizes it over time in order to enhance its performance. The other occurs when a firm reacts to a crisis situation, triggered for example by increased competition; this forces the firm to search for new ways of tackling problems. Our data indicate that the latter of these two forces tends to dominate the change that took place in Danish firms during the 1990s. Figure 8.2 divides the population of firms into three groups according to how they

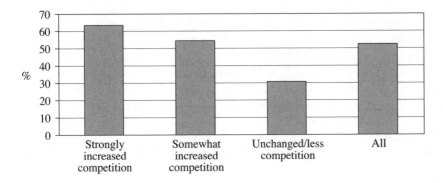

Source: Lundvall and Kristensen (1997), p. 10.

Figure 8.2   Share (%) of firms that answered 'yes' to the question: 'Has the firm implemented significant organizational changes in the period 1993–95?'

experienced changes in competitive pressure during the period 1993–95 and examines what percentage of the firms in the respective groups implemented significant organizational changes during that same period.

One clear tendency is that increased competition increases the probability that a firm introduces organizational change during the same period. In other words, many firms introduce new organizational forms or new products as a response to increased competition and to a lesser degree as a step in a more comprehensive rational strategy. This could also help to explain why earning ratios are not higher in the most dynamic firms – these will typically be found in sectors with intense and increasing competition, while static firms may be able to obtain good earnings with a minimum of organizational and technological change, because the competitive pressure they operate under remains modest.

A division of the data according to firm size and sector affiliation supports this perspective. It seems as if the sectors and size categories experiencing particularly sharp increases in competition are also those in which a large share of the firms that have introduced organizational changes are found. Table 8.5 gives an overview of organizational change and Table 8.6 illuminates changes in the competitive situation. Both tables refer to changes that took place in the period 1993–95.

With a single exception there is a one-to-one connection between the change in the competitive situation and the frequency of organizational change. This exception is made up of the small firms in transport and food services and similar sectors; despite an above-average increase in competitive pressure, they have carried out organizational changes to a significantly lower than average degree. This presumably reflects the fact that there are not as many options for organizational change in these sectors (there are limits to the number of ways that small shops and small haulage firms can be organized).

Table 8.5   *Share (%) of firms that have implemented at least one significant organizational change during the period 1993–95 divided by sector and firm size (I=100 in the second row of numbers means that the share is at the same level as the share for the entire population)*

	Manufacturing	Construction	Trade	Transport	Bus. serv.	Whole econ.
Fewer than 50 empl.	52.0% 99	28.5% 54	43.1% 82	28.3% 54	52.3% 100	52.3%
More than 50 empl.	75.2% 144	52.9% 101	64.9% 124	64.4% 123	66.7% 128	100

Source: Gjerding (1997), survey question 1.

Table 8.6   Share (%) of firms that report heavily increased competition in
the period 1993–95 divided by sector and firm size (I = 100 in
the second row of numbers means that the share is at the same
level as the share for the entire population)

	Manufacturing	Construction	Trade	Transport	Bus. serv.	Whole econ.
Fewer than	39.9%	23.3.%	35.2%	41.5%	39.5%	
50 empl.	100	58	88	104	99	40.0%
More than	49.4%	32.4%	48.2%	43.2%	45.3%	100
50 empl.	124	81	121	108	113	

Source: Gjerding (1997), survey questions 24 and 25.

FACTORS PROMOTING OR BLOCKING ORGANIZATIONAL CHANGE

There is much to suggest that the transition of even more Danish firms to organizational forms characterized by functional flexibility would help to promote innovation and productivity growth. With this background in mind it is of particular interest to analyse the particular factors that firms have experienced as stimulating or blocking in connection with organizational changes. This can provide firms and policy-makers with a better basis for choosing between various courses of action.[4]

In this connection it is of interest to differentiate between firms with respect to what extent they have progressed toward developing dynamic organization forms. Those firms that have not undertaken any steps towards organizational change will, of course, have limited experience with the barriers, while those at the forefront have a much more comprehensive experience to build their estimates upon. One can also imagine different sorts of barriers arising during different phases of the implementation of organizational change. Table 8.7 summarizes the responses divided according to 15 steps of a scale that spans the range from completely static firms (0 on the scale) to firms that have implemented a great number of organizational techniques and have also shown themselves to be innovative in terms of new products and markets (14 on the scale). For each group of firms, the factor most often referred to as positive or negative in connection with organizational changes is reported.

Table 8.7 shows first of all that those firms that have not developed flexible organizational forms have neither encountered significant barriers nor seen significant factors promoting innovation – see the low level of responses at levels 0–3. This supports the assumption that a portion of the population of

Table 8.7 Conditions emphasized as the most significant help or hindrance to firms at different levels of organizational development and innovative behaviour (index indicates degree of innovation, index = 0: completely static firm)

Index	Most significant help	Most significant hindrance
0	Employee qualifications (4.5%)	Employee qualifications (4.6%)
1	Employee qualifications (16.9%)	Employee qualifications (5.1%)
2	Employee qualifications (25.0%)	Employee qualifications (8.0%)
3	Employee attitudes (33.9%)	Employee attitudes (11.0%)
4	Middle management attitudes (37.0%)	Employee attitudes (12.3%)
5	Middle management attitudes (46.6%)	Employee attitudes (14.4%)
6	Middle management attitudes (48.2%)	Middle management qualifications (14.2%)
7	Middle management attitudes (54.6%)	Employee attitudes (16.2%)
8	Middle management attitudes (53.3%)	Middle management attitudes (24.1%)
9	Middle management attitudes (58.9%)	Middle management qualifications (28.4%)
10	Middle management attitudes (58.8%)	Employee attitudes (22.4%)
11	Middle management attitudes (58.6%)	Middle management qualifications (27.0%)
12	Middle management attitudes (61.1%)	Middle management qualifications (27.8%)
13	Employee attitudes (62.9%)	Middle management qualifications (38.6%)
14	Employee attitudes (68.8%)	Middle management attitudes (43.8%)
All organizations	Middle management attitudes (47.7%)	Middle management qualifications (18.9%)

Source: Lund and Gjerding (1996).

firms has not even considered developing new organizational forms. When these firms do indicate that a factor is particularly supportive or blocking, they refer to employee qualifications as the most important.

Firms that have made partial progress toward restructuring their organization will to a greater degree refer to middle management attitudes as a positive factor and to employee attitudes as the most significant hindrance (see levels 4–7).

Firms that have gone even further toward a dynamic organization form (levels 8–12) continue to emphasize middle management attitudes as a positive factor while indicating middle management qualifications as the most significant hindrance.

Finally, the most dynamic firms have a tendency to indicate employee attitudes as the most positive factor, and middle management attitudes and qualifications as the most significant hindrances.

The case studies carried out as an extension of the survey confirm a picture in which the attitudes and qualifications of employees and middle managers are of vital importance for the implementation of organizational changes. Middle managers will often play a decisive role also in connection with evaluating and carrying out the upgrading of employee qualifications necessitated by organizational change. The same is true for the implementation of courses designed to change attitudes. Middle managers are a key group in connection with organizational change; their contributions to the process can be both helpful and hindering the transition process. The fact that middle managers at the same time are the ones whose jobs are most often in danger in connection with these processes (see Chapter 13) makes their situation even more critical.

Shop stewards and workplace committees are mostly apportioned a positive role in connection with organizational changes – about a quarter of firms perceive them as helpful, while about one in 20 firms sees them as hindrances. This is also confirmed by case studies, which indicate that employee representatives increasingly tend to function in a similar role as middle managers when organizational change takes place. This makes it relevant to reconsider the future role of trade unions and of the opportunities for shop stewards to, at the same time, represent employee interests while contributing to organizational changes in the firm. If the participation in the process contributes to solutions involving better working conditions and more stable jobs the conflict of interest may be overcome.

One group that plays a key role in these transitions is, of course, the top management of the firm. We did not attempt to illuminate this in the survey, as it is problematic to ask management about its own efforts and successes. Our case studies showed, however, that top management often were quite hesitant about implementing needed organizational changes; thus most radical changes took place only after there had been a change in management. It must be kept in mind that firms that are a part of large corporations have been especially active in implementing organizational changes. A report by the Danish Management Centre has shown that top executives in Denmark are more often recruited from outside the firm than in other countries. Corporate executives in big corporations with several branches thus have the opportunity to ensure that an exchange of experiences about organizational developments takes place between firms by assuring a certain 'job circulation' at the executive level.

CAN DANISH FIRMS BE SAID TO BE LEARNING ORGANIZATIONS?

We can see how many Danish firms have been through a transformation in the direction of becoming learning organizations. But it does look as if this has been something of an imposed process. One understanding of the learning organization is one in which people are aware that what they are doing is learning and developing new skills. This underlies the concept of 'double-loop' learning, in which the individual is expected constantly to reflect upon what he or she has learned. It is also primarily in this way that individuals and organizations can 'learn to learn'. We may ask ourselves to what extent learning organizations – in this more demanding sense of the word – predominate in the private sector in Denmark. One way of finding out is to look at the portion of all organizations that (1) have implemented organizational changes during the period 1993–95, and (2) have indicated that the purpose of these organizational changes 'to a great degree' was to improve the ability to develop and improve the knowledge and know-how of the firm.

The combination of these two criteria indicates that about 14 per cent of all Danish firms are 'learning organizations' in the sense that they are clearly aware of the importance of learning and knowledge creation for their futures. It is of course interesting to examine more closely in which particular sectors we find these learning organizations. Table 8.8 indicates that learning organizations are most often either large manufacturing firms or smaller firms in the area of business services. They are rare in construction and among the population of smaller trade and transport firms.

The aim of the criterion used above is to evaluate the awareness of the importance of learning. Another criterion that is more closely related to actual behaviour could be to focus on what percentage of the entire workforce takes part in courses specifically designed to create new competencies. With our point of departure in Pedler, Burgoyne and Boydell's (1991, p. 1) definition of a 'learning company' as 'an organization in which skills are learned by all members and automatically enter into an organizational context', we have

Table 8.8 *Share (%) of firms that implemented at least one significant organizational change during the period 1993–95 and report that to a great degree it was to promote the development of knowledge in the firm, divided by sector and firm size. (I=100 in the lower row means that the share is at the level of the share for the entire population)*

	Manufacturing	Construction	Trade	Transport	Bus. serv.	Whole econ.
Fewer than 50 empl.	13.8% 96	10.1.% 70	9.5% 66	8.1% 56	19.6% 136	14.4%
More than 50 empl.	22.6% 157	11.8% 82	16.7% 116	15.5% 108	14.3% 99	100

Source: Gjerding (1997), survey question 2.

listed four criteria that an organization must meet in order to be considered 'learning':

• The firm has implemented organizational changes and technological improvements during the period 1993–95.
• A delegation of responsibility has taken place that includes more than 50 per cent of employees.
• More than 50 per cent of employees have participated in internal or external continuing education.
• The firm reports that long-term educational planning has great or some importance in ensuring that employees have the desired qualifications.

Only 138 of the 1802 firms, or 7.7 per cent, answered yes to all four questions in the study and can be characterized as learning organizations on the basis of the criteria outlined above. This emphasizes the fact that, while a large number of firms have implemented organizational changes, these changes may conceal an internal polarization in firms rather than indicating a development toward an inclusive strategy for increasing the qualifications of the majority of the workers – that is, a personnel strategy in which all or the majority of the members of the workforce develop their qualifications (Kern and Schumann 1984; Nielsen 1995). The vast majority of firms that implement organizational change and initiate the improvement of their employees' qualifications limit their activities to particular areas of the organization. This is a problem we shall return to in Chapter 13, in which among other things we analyse in detail the tendency toward polarization that characterizes the Danish labour market.

SUMMARY

Both OECD analyses and DISKO data show a connection between productivity and organizational and technical change. Particularly in service fields we find a pronounced correlation between the degree of organizational and technological change on the one hand and the level of productivity on the other. In a later chapter (Chapter 13) we shall demonstrate that the firms that have made most progress toward organizational and technical change – those organizations we characterize as 'dynamic firms' – also create a greater than average number of jobs and more stable workplaces.

On this basis it is interesting to see the status of Danish firms relative to the outside world. In this area, unfortunately, we find that the data are particularly unreliable and difficult to interpret. They indicate that Danish firms are lagging behind in a number of areas, but they also indicate that Danish firms are making progress toward catching up. If one sets up the 'learning organization' as the ideal, only about 7 to 15 per cent of the Danish firms meet these criteria. Such organizational forms are particularly unevenly spread over the various sectors. They are found particularly in large manufacturing firms and in small firms providing business services, while appearing seldom in the areas of construction and transport.

Thus there is still ample room for initiatives that will stimulate technical and organizational change at firm level. One important result of the analyses carried out in this chapter is that the attitudes and qualifications of middle management are a key factor. The case studies show that shop stewards and top executives are two other important groups in the transition process. Education and courses that aim to strengthen these groups' readiness to accept and implement change are thus important steps towards promoting transformation and change. This readiness to accept change reflects both attitudes and competence as we shall see in Chapter 12, which deals with continuing education. A significant number of new initiatives could consist of increased exchange of experience between firms that are at different steps in the process of organizational transformation. In this area industrial federations and labour market organizations have an important role to play.

NOTES

1. This chapter is based on DISKO reports 1, 2 and 3 as well as specific written contributions from Reinhard Lund and Allan Næs Gjerding.
2. As we shall see below, Danish firms distinguish themselves through a significant dissemination of the implementation of various types of organizational techniques. The question is thus to what degree the LOK programme can simultaneously meet the needs both of the most advanced firms and of those that have not even begun to implement organizational change.

The latter in particular might demand efforts that lie beyond the initiatives of the current LOK programme.

3. For an analysis of how the correlation between organizational form and performance appears for various types of firms divided according to Pavitt's taxonomy (Pavitt 1984), see Kristensen (1997) as well as Lund (1998).

4. Since the survey questionnaire was filled out by management in the firms, top management will not appear either as a help or a hindrance in this part of the analysis. We will return to the role of top management later in our presentation, where we will base our conclusions on case studies.

9. Knowledge intensity and knowledge flows in the Danish innovation system[1]

One portion of the knowledge that firms use comes through internal development – investment in research and development, the development of competence through courses or through learning by doing. Another portion that carries great weight in Danish firms is embodied in the products and tools that the firm purchases from outside sources. It is this side of the development of firms' competence in particular that we shall examine more closely in this chapter.

Thus we begin by examining the knowledge intensity of different parts of the Danish economy; thereafter we shall examine how firms belonging to different sectors, including the service sectors, act as producers and purchasers of knowledge. We shall use several different types of knowledge indicators as the basis for this analysis. In Chapter 10 we move forward and analyse the interactive learning and direct exchange of knowledge that takes place between firms in connection with product development.

DENMARK'S RELATIVE POSITION IN TERMS OF KNOWLEDGE INTENSITY

Increasingly we find the understanding that the current phase of economic development is characterized by 'knowledge-based competition' and it is argued that the knowledge foundation for production, distribution and consumption is becoming increasingly important for economic development (Foray and Lundvall 1996b; OECD 1996). In this light Denmark's position relative to countries at comparable levels of economic development is of particular interest. It is especially worrying when analyses (Mandag Morgen 1996) claim that Denmark receives mediocre placement internationally with regard to the knowledge content in production measured on the basis of indicators such as: the general education level of the population; the number of researchers in the labour force; the intensity of patenting, research and development; and the number of innovative firms.

Using these common indicators as standards of measurement we find that

Denmark is not among the group of countries characterized by the most intensive research and development effort; its level is, however, comparable to such countries as the Netherlands, Finland and Norway (it is paradoxical that these countries together with Denmark are among those that perform best in terms of economic growth according to recent OECD study of the 'the new economy', OECD 2000a; 2001b). With regard to patent intensity Denmark ranks higher than Belgium, Italy and Norway but considerably lower than such comparable countries as the Netherlands and Sweden. The third knowledge indicator is the average level of education, measured as the average number of years of education after comprehensive schooling. This number has been constantly rising in Denmark; in 1992 it reached the level of 2.8 years. This development is also expressed in an employment pattern in which the proportion of the workforce that had completed vocational education overtook the number of employees without vocational education in the mid-1980s. But measured on a purely quantitative basis the Danish educational level is not impressively high in an international context. Belgium and France rank lower than Denmark with respect to the number of average years of education for the entire population, but the Danes are at an equivalent or slightly lower level than such countries as Finland, the Netherlands, Sweden and Norway. Germany has a significantly higher level than Denmark (Drejer 1998).

But the above description is only a part of the truth about knowledge generation and, more importantly, knowledge application in the Danish innovation system.

'DIRECT' VERSUS 'INDIRECT' KNOWLEDGE

The OECD (Papaconstantinou et al. 1996) carried out an analysis in 1996 of what they called 'embodied technology diffusion', that is, the spread of technology through goods and services. 'Embodied' refers to the fact that the technology is an integral part of the goods and services. The analysis included the G7 countries (the US, Japan, the UK, Germany, France, Italy and Canada) as well as Australia, the Netherlands and Denmark and covered the 1970s and 1980s. The analysis was based on the assumption that the research and development activities of a firm within a given industry benefit not only the firm and the industry in question, but also the purchasers of its goods and services.[2] The technology or knowledge that is embodied in a product from a particular firm or industry is thus the sum of the firm's or industry's own knowledge-generating activities and the knowledge-generating activities that are embodied in the production input that comes from other firms and industries. The main principle underlying this line of thought is illustrated in Figure 9.1.

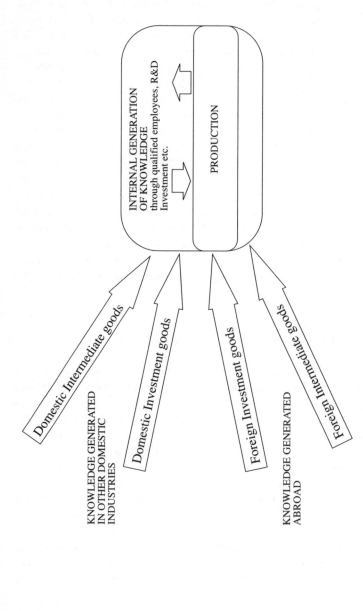

Source: Drejer (1998), p. 84.

Figure 9.1   Internally developed versus acquired knowledge (contained in a product)

OECD analyses demonstrate that research-based innovations are developed primarily in a cluster of high-tech manufacturing sectors, while a cluster of service sectors appears as the primary recipient of technologically sophisticated machinery and equipment. When both direct and indirect technology (research and development) is involved, the traditional distinction between high-, middle- and low-tech sectors becomes much less clear. Furthermore the overall technology intensity of small countries rises considerably when acquired (indirect) technology is taken into account.

KNOWLEDGE-INTENSIVE AND KNOWLEDGE-EXTENSIVE SECTORS

The OECD analysis can be further elaborated by considering a number of other knowledge indicators, leading us to the following overview of which are the most knowledge-intensive sectors in Denmark.

The knowledge indicators are the same as the ones discussed in the introduction to this chapter, although in this instance we chose to use the proportion of personnel with technical and scientific educations as an educational indicator instead of the average length of education. In Table 9.1, however, indirect knowledge intensity is included in the ranking. Every one of the sectors mentioned is also the most knowledge-intensive, based on direct knowledge intensity. The inclusion of indirect knowledge brings with it only minor shifts in ranking. Thus in connection with knowledge-intensive sectors, the outcome is not much affected by the inclusion of indirect knowledge as it is by a combination of different knowledge indicators. It is worth noting that the introduction of the education measure means that business services are included in the group of most knowledge-intensive sectors. In general, the

Table 9.1 Sectors with the highest total knowledge intensity in Denmark, 1991

	Tech-Sci./ employees	R&D expenses/ production	Patents/ production
1	Telecom materials	Pharmaceuticals	Instrument manuf.
2	Business services	Instrument manuf.	Chemical
3	Instrument manuf.	Telecom materials	Telecom materials
4	Other electronics	Machine manuf.	Other electronics
5	Pharmaceuticals	Other electronics	Pharmaceuticals

Source: Drejer (1998).

Table 9.2   *The share of indirect knowledge in sectors with low knowledge*
            intensity, Denmark 1991*

	Indirect Tech-Sci/Total Tech-Sci	Indirect R&D/Total R&D
Textiles and clothing	80%	74%
Construction	57%	93%
Trade	57%	53%
Other services	70%	85%
Food	71%	61%

Note: *Patents are not included, as the majority of the low-intensity sectors either do not take out patents or do so only to a very limited extent.

Source: Drejer (1998).

traditional measures of innovation (R&D and patents) have underestimated the role played by knowledge-intensive business service firms in the collective production of knowledge.

When we consider the area of the economy with low knowledge intensity, indirect knowledge plays a much greater role. Table 9.2 shows that sectors with the lowest levels of knowledge intensity – that is, other services, construction and within the manufacturing industry the textile and clothing industry and foodstuffs – depend to a great extent on the transfer of knowledge from more knowledge-intensive sectors. Regardless of which knowledge measure is used, the knowledge that comes from suppliers makes up 60 to 90 per cent of the knowledge content of the production carried out by construction-sector firms. This extreme degree of outsourcing of all kinds of knowledge-demanding activities could help to explain why firms in this sector appear to be so extremely 'static' in terms of technology and organization in the various DISKO analyses.

SOURCES OF KNOWLEDGE DISSEMINATION IN DENMARK

There is no simple connection between the sectors with the highest level of knowledge intensity and the sectors that are the largest sources of knowledge dissemination in the Danish innovation system.

Based both on delivery size and the number of recipient sectors, machinery production and business services are the largest sources of knowledge

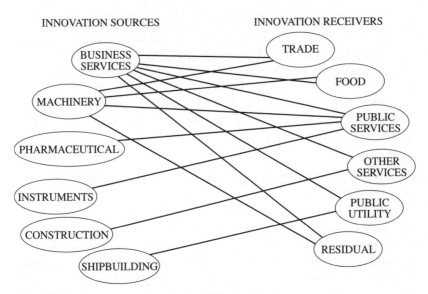

INNOVATION SOURCES INNOVATION RECEIVERS

OTHER INDUSTRIES OUTSIDE THE CENTRAL FLOWS:

Agricultural machinery	Other transport
Rubber/plastic	Electronics
Chemical raw materials	Textiles
Iron and metal	Other chemical
Stone, clay, glass	Telecomm

Source: Drejer (1998).

Figure 9.2 Knowledge flows in Denmark in 1991 (based on R&D expenses)

dissemination in Denmark (calculated on the basis of the value of the individual indicators). In contrast, the pharmaceutical industry, despite its high level of internal knowledge production, plays only a marginal role as a source of knowledge dissemination. It appears to be a very isolated industry with very limited linkages to the rest of the domestic private sector. Figure 9.2 shows the pattern for product-embodied knowledge flows in Denmark in 1991, illustrated on the basis of research and development expenses (only so-called 'significant' flows, those which exceed a fixed minimum limit, are included in the diagram).

Foodstuffs is the only industry in manufacturing that appears as a heavily weighted recipient of the input of knowledge contained in goods and services, while the other recipients are a broad range of service-related industries in the areas of trade, other services and public service. Foodstuffs, an area that continues to play an essential role in the Danish economy from the point of view of both production and export, has a low knowledge level from the outset. But the food industry is a significant recipient of production input from sectors with high knowledge intensity, that is, it is a branch that applies inputs with a high content of 'embodied' knowledge.

While the role of the machinery industry as a general source of knowledge in the Danish economy is rooted in tradition and supported by Pavitt's taxonomy, in which it is classified as the classical case of a specialized supplier (see Pavitt 1984), it is worth devoting more attention to the other general supplier of knowledge, business services.

THE INCREASING IMPORTANCE OF BUSINESS SERVICES

Over the last few years there has been an increased focus on the role of the service sector in the economy. The traditional focus of economic analyses – and the political initiatives that have resulted from them – has been on manufacturing as the crucial value-creating sector; the importance of services, in particular knowledge-intensive services, is now becoming more obvious. Tomlinson (2001) has analysed the importance of the consumption of knowledge-intensive business services for productivity and for the extent of production in different countries, including the UK and Japan. Growth in the service sector is partially a result of the fact that manufacturing firms outsource activities that are not directly central to their core production: in other words growth in the service sector may be overrated, particularly when compared with growth in the manufacturing sector. This reflects the way in which the national accounts are calculated: here branch accounts hide the movement between sectors.

But it is also a question of the gains in productivity that takes place through the transfer of knowledge from the knowledge-intensive services firms to manufacturing firms. Tomlinson assumes, just as in the DISKO results above, that the goods and services that are transferred from one branch to another contain knowledge; in this case it is assumed that this knowledge is proportional to the price of the transaction. Based on this analysis Tomlinson concludes that production input from communication and business services has had a significant positive effect on the growth of value-added and productivity in the receiving sectors, particularly in Japan.

Tomlinson also supports the view of a knowledge transfer in the opposite direction: the knowledge-intensive service industries receive knowledge from the manufacturing industries (Tomlinson 1999). Here, however, other types of mechanisms are at work; these mechanisms are related to learning and to tacit knowledge, since it is the flow of knowledge 'embodied' in the workforce that is in focus. Based on data from a UK labour market survey,[3]

Tomlinson illustrates that the increase in employment in the knowledge-intensive service professions is to a great degree due to the fact that 'knowledge employees', that is, employees who are not directly involved in production or administration, have been transferred from the manufacturing industries to the knowledge-intensive service industries. The transfer of production workers from manufacturing to the knowledge-intensive service professions is much more limited.

These results indicate that knowledge in the form of employee competence tends to remain in knowledge-intensive service professions and that knowledge transfer from the knowledge-intensive service professions to the manufacturing sector occurs primarily through the sale of goods and services. They also indicate that the manufacturing industry is an important source of the expansion within the service industries. And the employment-based results help to emphasize the general problems with the knowledge indicators that have been used up to this point: the indicators that have been used to analyse knowledge intensity and knowledge flow reflect only the formal development of knowledge either in the form of R&D expenses or in the form of formal education. This is especially problematic in relation to the concept of the 'learning economy', in which the focus is on the continual acquisition of new competencies as the old become obsolete. Employment data, combined with 'life histories' that show employees' acquisition of experience and continual updating of their qualifications, are indicators that could help to estimate the measures of such intangible qualifications. But our knowledge of this aspect of competence-building in the economic sphere is still very limited.

KNOWLEDGE, RELATIONSHIPS AND DYNAMICS

The dissemination of knowledge and technology is of vital importance for the overall dynamics of the Danish innovation system. For this reason, innovation policy cannot just aim toward increasing the level of knowledge and innovation activity in the most dynamic and knowledge-intensive industries related to, for example, information technology and biotechnology. It is important to realize that the more integrated the system is, that is, the more relationships there are both between firms and between industries, the greater the opportunities for effective dissemination and development of knowledge. Finally, it is vitally important that the firms that need to use knowledge developed elsewhere have the capability to do so. The ability to absorb knowledge is at least as important as the ability to produce new knowledge.

Therefore, any effective policy that is oriented toward the economy's knowledge foundation must contain at least three different elements. First of all, it must aim to improve the level of knowledge in those sectors that are important sources of knowledge, that is, primarily machinery manufacturing and business services. Secondly, it will be necessary to promote relations and interaction among firms and industries sectors. Thirdly, the development of competence and 'absorptive capacity' in the large user sectors must be promoted. In most cases the different aspects of such a strategy are closely related. Relations between producers and users of knowledge will work well only if the recipients are able to absorb and apply the acquired knowledge; their capacity for absorption will depend on their internal knowledge. In order to gain access to external knowledge, a solid internal knowledge foundation must exist.

The opportunities for promoting knowledge dissemination among firms, also those belonging to different sectors, is not only dependent on access to knowledge. A conscious effort to strengthen essential connections in the economy can facilitate the process. The new orientation of Danish industrial policy towards 'resource areas' has been an important step in connection with promoting – and indeed making visible – relations between firms, both within and among sectors. The same is true for Dutch industrial policy with its emphasis on cluster formation. Because these concepts distance themselves from the traditional sector view of the economy and look at a group of sectors that is interconnected by common framework conditions and mutual relations, they are an important contribution to a revised understanding in which the economy is perceived as a network of relations and not just as a collection of firms or sectors that exist independently of one another.

SUMMARY

This chapter has shown that a significant amount of the knowledge that is put into circulation internally within a firm is embodied in tools and semi-manufactured articles procured from other firms; this is particularly true for some of the firms that do not make extensive use of internal R&D. It has also shown that different firms are operating at different stages in the production and application of new knowledge in the Danish economy. According to the criteria used here only a small portion of Danish employment (about eight per cent) is in knowledge-intensive firms, while the rest to a large degree depends on receiving knowledge developed externally.

Among the knowledge-intensive firms there are several types that play key roles in the knowledge dissemination that takes place from one sector to another. This is particularly true for the machinery industry, which has played this role since the beginning of industrialization. What is new is that elements of business services now seem to be taking on a similar role in relation to the entire economy. In the previous chapter we saw that small firms in the area of business services, particularly, appear especially active both in terms of technical innovation and organizational change. Recent econometric analyses show that input from this sector helps to promote productivity growth in the recipient sectors. Thus there is good reason to direct a larger part of the attention of innovation policy toward knowledge-intensive firms in the area of business services.

NOTES

1. This chapter is based on DISKO report 4 (Drejer 1998) as well as a specific written contribution from Ina Drejer.
2. Technically the method is based on the use of input–output tables, since supplies of semi-manufactured articles and objects of investment are viewed as 'carriers' of knowledge between sectors and countries. Technology is expressed here for instance by research and development expenses.
3. The data cover the period 1980–92.

10. Inter-firm collaboration

In Chapter 8 we saw how firms react to situations of increased competition by developing greater functional flexibility in their internal organization.[1] The purpose of these organizational changes is to increase transformation ability and to ensure that signals from external partners are quickly converted into action. Another way of increasing the capacity for transformation and change is to forge closer ties to these partners. Well-established networking relationships make it easier to sort through and use the growing flow of external information and to use that knowledge in product development. In this chapter, we shall examine more closely the collaboration between firms in the development of new products.

We base our analysis on comprehensive telephone interviews with a representative cross-section original sample of 1022 manufacturing firms. In these interviews, which were carried out in two steps, we determined which types of Danish and foreign partners firms collaborate with in connection with the development of new products. The first part of the study involved a total of 531 firms that have collaborated on product development in the last two years. The second part of the study, in which we focused on the firm's most important development project, included 297 firms, 256 of which were also asked about their entire line of product development projects (a total of 3254 product developments).

The survey should be seen on the basis of the theoretical understanding of the innovation process that was referred to in Chapter 3. This view takes into account that the innovation process is complex, with interaction between research, design, production and marketing. It also takes into account that it is characterized by interactive learning – and hence collaboration – taking place between different agents at all levels of the economy (Lundvall 1992).

Furthermore, it has been argued that the current stage of technological and economical development more than ever before necessitates such collaboration. Conditions such as higher development costs, greater risks, increased complexity, demands for more rapid product development and increased competition create a need for the sharing of risks and costs, and requires more knowledge than the individual firm has available in-house. The increased demand for speedy development processes means that partners must be involved at earlier stages in the development process, which in itself brings increased collaboration. Along with the increased need for collaboration, the development in information technology has facilitated certain types of collaboration across great distances.

It has long been known that firms often draw on their surroundings when they develop new products. It has been, and continues to be, a common assumption that firms, and small firms in particular, through an increased degree of collaboration would be able to develop more and better products. But detailed knowledge about the extent and pattern of firms' collaboration in the area of product development has been scarce. The aim of this chapter is to provide such knowledge on the basis of data from the Danish manufacturing. More precisely the aim is to analyse formal and informal collaboration on large and small product developments for both large and small firms in all industries of manufacturing.

FIRMS OFTEN COLLABORATE

The main result of the study is that collaboration is a necessary element of product development for firms. Almost all firms that have product development experience have also had the experience of developing one or more of their products in collaboration (97 per cent of the firms that carried out product development had at some occasion collaborated with external parties in connection of developing a new product).

The types of collaboration partners appear in Figure 10.1. The butterfly-formed figure should be read from left to right. Production inputs come from the left (suppliers), while the finished product is sold to the right (to customers). Danish partners are listed downwards and foreign partners upwards. If large wings appear over the horizontal line, this indicates a great deal of collaboration with foreign partners.

The most pronounced result is that collaboration takes place with suppliers of materials and components with the same frequency as with private customers, which is interesting in the light of earlier results indicating the customer as the most important source of product developments. And if one looks at the most important project (not shown in the figure), suppliers appear more often than customers. But when customers participate in product development, they are still the most important type of partner.

Figure 10.1 shows that the public sector plays an insignificant role as collaboration partner in product development for the firms. This raises the question of whether this reflects an as yet unexploited opportunity for industrial policy. Public procurement has proven to be a quite efficient instrument in promoting innovation in areas such as energy saving and environmental protection (Westling 1996; 1997).

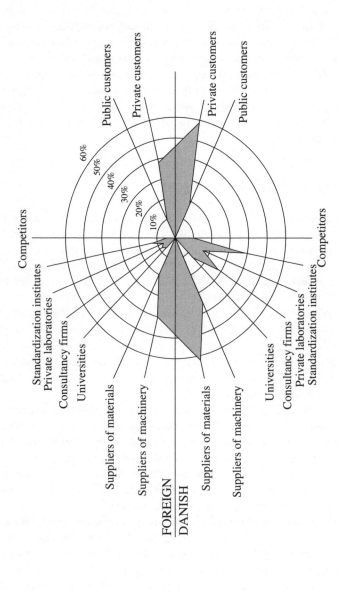

Source: Madsen (1999).

Figure 10.1 Frequency of collaboration with different types of domestic and foreign partners (N = 531)

Finally, Figure 10.1 shows that universities and research institutes do not play any important part in the product development of Danish firms. They are seldom involved in collaboration at the product development stage and no great importance is attributed to them even when they are involved in a project.

If we differentiate between Danish and foreign collaboration partners it appears that foreign partners are of some importance. Collaboration with them occurs less often than with Danish partners, but when it occurs it is assigned great importance by the firm.

An important question is why collaboration takes place. Our results show that it takes place among other reasons because the firm has collaborated with the same partner before and that the resource aimed to get access to is primarily technical knowledge.

Another way of illustrating Danish firms' experiences in the areas of collaboration and product development is to establish a comparative perspective (Christensen, Rogaczewska and Vinding 1998). Thus one can demonstrate three central areas in which Danish firms' collaboration experiences with respect to product development differ from that of other countries:

- Danish firms collaborate more frequently with regard to product development over a two-year period than Norwegian, Spanish and Austrian firms.
- Firms in the other countries have a greater degree of collaboration with universities and research institutes.
- Danish firms collaborate more often with suppliers of materials and components and private customers than firms in the other three countries.

In the next chapter we shall examine more closely the possible problems involved in the low degree of collaboration between firms and knowledge institutions such as universities and research institutes. Part of the explanation is of course the Danish production and export specialization which, as demonstrated in earlier chapters, is dominated by product areas that are not science-based. On the other hand, it looks as if Danish firms are in the lead internationally with regard to collaboration with suppliers and customers on product development. To a certain extent this can also be explained by the Danish industrial structure with its preponderance of small and medium-sized firms. Other possible explanations could have to do with a cohesiveness in social relations that has its roots in a national 'village culture' (Maskell 1998b).

GREAT VARIATION BETWEEN SECTORS

At industry level the most interesting result is that product innovation and inter-firm cooperation is frequent also in so-called low-tech product areas. The firms that develop the greatest number of new products are in furniture and other industries; the food, drink and tobacco industry; the textile and clothing industry; and the chemical industry – in other words, primarily in low-tech sectors. This illustrates the fact that dynamic technical and market behaviour cannot be wholly attributed to high technology and science-based production. But it also reflects the fact that the study, based on our definition of product development, leaves it up to the firms themselves to interpret when they have developed a new product.

With regard to collaboration patterns within industries, it is a general characteristic that collaboration takes place with both suppliers and customers in product development. It cannot be concluded, however, that a broad-spectrum collaboration base is necessary for product development. For certain types of partners, such as universities and research institutes, only two sectors collaborate with them to a high degree. Not surprisingly these are the chemical and electronics industries.

To illustrate these branch-related differences, in the Figures 10.2a and 10.2b we have chosen two extreme positions of collaboration patterns with regard to product innovation at industry level. The textile and clothing industry clearly has contacts with the broadest spectrum of partners. It has a broad wingspan and a long tail in Figure 10.2a. At the other extreme we see that the stone, clay and glass industry (Figure 10.2b) has small wings. The wings are suppliers and customers and the tail represents Danish institutes of certification. The fact that the wings are so large with regard to product development can generally be attributed to the fact that firms in the textile and clothing industry often have a greater number of products being developed and for this reason report a greater number of partners.

It is striking how little the stone, ceramic and glass industry collaborates with customers to develop new products. Whether this can be explained exclusively by technological conditions or whether the forward connection, for example to the construction industry, which we must suppose is an important customer, is too weak a relationship cannot be determined from these numbers, but it certainly warrants further investigation.[2]

THE PRODUCT DEVELOPMENT EFFORTS OF SMALL FIRMS MUST NOT BE UNDERESTIMATED

There is a tendency to underrate the importance of product innovation for small firms (those with between 10 and 49 employees), but our study shows

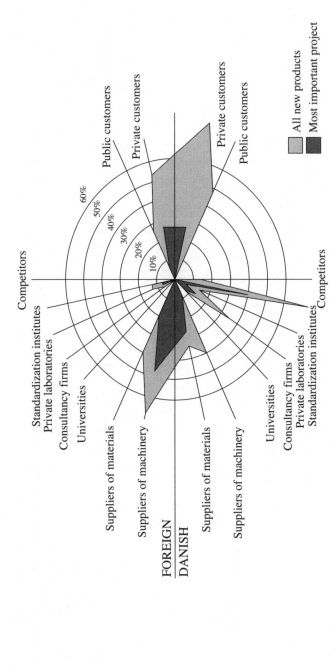

Source: Madsen (1999).

Figure 10.2a   Collaboration partners for the textile and clothing industry for one or more product developments and on the most important project

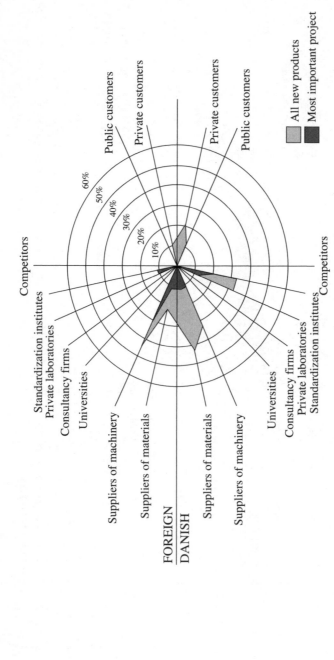

Source: Madsen (1999).

Figure 10.2b *Collaboration partners for the stone, ceramic and glass industry for one or more product developments and on the most important project*

the vital importance of these small firms for product development in Denmark. This is supported here in that:

- Small firms that develop new products have a relatively greater number of product developments per employee than large firms.
- In particular, firms with 20–49 employees seem to be crucial for product development activity in Denmark.
- Somewhat surprisingly, the most important development project of small firms greatly resembles that of large firms (equally long gestation periods and an equal number of man-years).

There are, however, also some important points where the larger firms stand out:

- Large firms make further developments of product innovation to a greater extent.
- Large firms more often report that they have experienced greater than expected market success for their most important project.

In other words, although the measures of innovation projects in some areas are surprisingly uniform for large and small firms, the product development of large firms will more often end up with economic success. And there are indications that this is because they are dealing with products where further development is possible; the larger firms also have the resources to follow up on these.

Christensen and Kristensen (1997) inform us that the larger the firm, the more experience it will have with collaboration in research and development. Conversely one might imagine that smaller firms are relatively more dependent on product development collaboration than they are on collaboration with regard to research and development. But it appears that:

- Small firms collaborate neither more nor less, but just as often as other firms.
- Small firms do not indicate other motives for collaboration than large firms do.
- There is nothing to indicate that small firms neglect collaboration on product development simply because they are small.

More pronounced differences between small and large firms appear when one looks at the types of collaboration partners. Knowledge institutions and foreign partners are used less by the small firms, a fact that is also demonstrated in

Christensen and Kristensen (1994). In addition, small firms have fewer partners on their most important project than larger firms do.

Viewed comparatively, the smallest firms (those with between 10 and 19
employees) seem to be responsible for a larger portion of product development
and related collaboration than is the case in Norwegian, Spanish and Austrian
firms.

THE TYPOLOGY OF COLLABORATION PATTERNS

With the aid of a so-called latent structure analysis (for more detail see
Madsen 1999) one can identify four different typical potential contacts for all
the product developments that 548 firms have made in the last two years (17
firms that carried out product development without collaboration during the
period are included here):

- 'Infrequent collaborators': 28 per cent of the firms collaborate infre-
  quently during the course of product development.
- 'Supplier collaborators': 11 per cent of the firms carry out product
  developments particularly in collaboration with suppliers.
- 'Frequent collaborators': 17 per cent of the firms clearly have the broadest spectrum of collaboration partners.
- 'Customer–supplier collaborators': 45 per cent of the firms surveyed.
  These typically collaborate with Danish suppliers of materials and
  components and with customers.

An analysis where these groups have been matched with industrial structure
indicates that none of the various sectors dominates in any of the groups. In
general, we are dealing with organization strategies for product development
activity that supersede specific industrial characteristics. Two sectors,
however, have a preponderance of firms with a pattern corresponding to one
of the groups above. The contact pattern in the electronics industry corresponds to the one of 'frequent collaborators', while the portfolio of the
'supplier-customer collaborators' corresponds to the contact pattern of the
machine industry.

It is characteristic for the 'infrequent collaborators' that their product development is also infrequent. This group includes the 17 firms that develop products without collaboration; the other firms in the group also seldom
collaborate during the course of new product developments.

This type of analysis also supports the conclusion that the product development activities of the small firms should not be underestimated: 39 per cent
of the frequent collaborators have fewer than 50 employees.

SUMMARY

In general there is nothing to indicate that Danish firms collaborate with each other too seldom, and there does not seem to be a need to establish new network development programmes that aim at promoting collaboration on product development.

Given more turbulent surroundings (see Chapter 7) the need will arise for firms to continuously re-evaluate their network position more frequently than before. New technical opportunities and new market opportunities may impose a need to detach oneself from old partners and forge ties to new ones. Particularly in the most turbulent technological areas, but in general in the entire economy, a need will arise for more frequent partnership changes.

On the other hand, there is some indication that Danish firms do not involve knowledge institutions in their development of new products as much as one could wish from a perspective emphasizing knowledge-intense product development. We will examine this problem more closely in the next chapter. Here, it suffices to say that there may be grounds for considering particular measures aimed at small firms. A more developed interaction between small firms and knowledge institutions could contribute to eliminating the survey results indicating that small firms pursue further product development to a lesser degree and experience less market success than large firms.

To the extent that one believes that collaboration should be promoted politically, one can take as one's point of departure the division of firms into the four groups we constructed through latent structure analysis. The experience of 'frequent collaborators' is helpful when it comes to handling the problems inherent in collaboration and which they clearly have learnt to live with, since they continue collaborating frequently and with a number of partners. Their experiences could be communicated to 'supplier collaborators' and 'supplier–customer collaborators'. The fourth type – 'infrequent collaborators' – needs to be approached separately since they have very limited experience with collaboration on product development.

Another dimension has to do with the weighing of the choice between national and international orientation with regard to network positioning. On the one hand it is usually easier to communicate with domestic partners, but on the other hand international collaboration might be particularly helpful in giving attention to new technical and market opportunities. Small firms that are used to operating in their home market normally encounter barriers to their entry into international collaborations. In this area various types of information services from embassies and other authorities would be able to play a role, but the upgrading of the workforce in smaller firms so that it includes people possessing linguistic and cultural knowledge is also particularly important.

The public sector makes up a very large portion of aggregate Danish demand. Still it is very seldom that the firms surveyed mention the public sector as playing any role at all as a collaborative customer in the innovation process. Areas in which the public sector is of particular importance as a customer, for example large public construction projects, do not appear to belong to the most innovative in the economy. Conversely special studies show that there has been positive experience with an innovation-oriented collaboration between medico-electronic firms and doctors in the public health care system. The development of measures to ensure that public demand promotes rather than hinders change and innovation is an important task; perhaps there is a particular need to implement such measures with respect to less knowledge-intensive areas. New rules and procedures of public procurement connected to enterprises in the area of construction is one example.

There is generally a need for competent purchasers in the public sector who are not only price-conscious but also have a sense of the existing development potential. Particularly in the areas of environment and energy, there are good international examples of the way in which conscious collective demand can promote desirable technical developments (Westling 1996; 1997).

NOTES

1. This chapter is based on DISKO report no. 6 (Madsen 1999) as well as specific written contributions from Anker Lund Vinding and Poul Thøis Madsen.
2. One should be aware that the two industry accounts are based on a small number of observations (nine and 15 firms respectively).

11. Collaboration between firms and knowledge institutions

In this chapter[1] we will examine more closely the collaboration between firms and knowledge institutions in Denmark.[2] The concept of knowledge institutions includes both those involved in technological consulting (private consulting firms as well as the certified technological service institutes, in Danish abbreviated 'GTS institutes') and research (that is, universities and sector-specific applied research institutes). Our focus is still on competence creation within the individual firm either through the purchase of knowledge or through network collaboration. The presentation here is built in part on the same survey data as referred to in the previous chapter. This means that this portion of the analysis focuses on collaboration in connection with product development in manufacturing firms. But these data are supplemented with personal interviews with key persons in firms and knowledge institutions and with other data and sources available to the DISKO project.

One important result that appears in the international comparison with Norway and Austria is that national collaboration patterns have retained their characteristics to a great degree; this also holds true for the Danish innovation system. One characteristic of the Danish pattern is that collaboration with other firms is more widespread than in the other two countries. The level of collaboration of Danish manufacturing firms with the technological consultancy network is at the same level as that found in the other countries, while the collaboration with universities and sector research institutes is significantly less developed.

These Danish deviations from an average of other countries cannot, however, be used directly to inspire policy recommendations. The basic hypothesis for analyses of national innovation systems is that they differ from each other also in the institutional dimension. Among other things, the division of labour between the central agents in the innovation system is specific to the country in which they are found. There is no single 'best practice' independent of context, and it is not necessarily expedient to move the national pattern toward an international average.

In order to evaluate the functional adequacy of knowledge institutions it is necessary to look at them in a broader perspective. In Chapter 3 we distinguished between 'the innovation system in the narrow sense' and 'the innovation system in the broad sense'. We may say that the interplay between firms and knowledge institutions corresponds to 'the innovation system in a restricted sense'. In order to assess the role of Danish knowledge institutions we must see them in the context of the Danish innovation system 'in a broad sense'.

THE DANISH INNOVATION SYSTEM IN A BROAD SENSE

In the first part of this book, we demonstrated a specifically Danish innovation mode; this had particularities with regard to the organization of firms, patterns of specialization, and the labour market. This particularly Danish innovation mode thus includes:

- A preponderance of small firms and very few large firms according to international standards.
- A specialization in products with little direct R&D content.
- Many small and medium-sized firms without employees with academic training.

These distinctive features must be seen in connection with the fact that firms in all sectors, including low-tech firms, are innovative with regard to products, processes and organization. But the innovations that are carried out usually take the form of local adaptations of new knowledge produced abroad. Innovations are very seldom technically radical, and only a few Danish firms introduce products that are new to the global market.

The mode in which innovation is pursued in Denmark often reflects a practical, experience-based interaction between skilled labour, technicians, engineers, designers and marketing experts. Firms achieve competence through the recruitment of personnel with a broad base of experience in a flexible labour market; competence is also acquired through intense collaboration with other firms, especially customers and suppliers in Denmark and elsewhere.

This picture does not cover the entire Danish economy. There are two areas in particular where other modes of innovation predominate. One of these is the food industry, which is based on standardized products and scale economies (particularly large slaughterhouses and dairy factories). The other area is the pharmaceutical industry, where Denmark has established itself at the forefront with regard to both research and innovation. The production of foodstuffs is based on intense marketing of goods characterized by uniformity and stable quality rather than on variation and gradual innovation. The innovation methods of the Danish pharmaceutical industry, on the other hand, are extremely strongly rooted in scientific research. Patenting will often reflect (and directly cite) research results that have been produced in both private and public research laboratories.

It is in this broader context that we must evaluate whether the particular Danish pattern of collaboration between firms and knowledge institutions is satisfactory or not. One could argue that it is natural that Danish universities have oriented themselves more toward the public than the private sector, because the private sector has only a limited need for scientific information in the innovation process. In those areas of the Danish business community that require continuous collaboration with research institutions, for example pharmaceuticals and parts of the electronics industry, there will normally not be any major problems with establishing collaborative efforts with researchers at universities and research institutes. In this instance the problems experienced by business interests will more likely involve the capability of the teaching institutions to deliver a sufficient number of educated personnel needed by these research-intensive firms.

With this background in mind it could be concluded that there is no reason at all for concern when connections between the universities and the business sector appear weak and selective in Denmark. But the question is whether the Danish innovation mode will remain sustainable in the light of broader changes, for example globalization and the growing importance of science-based innovation discussed in the introduction. To answer this question we must return to the question about what particular types of knowledge will be needed by firms in the future. Different types of knowledge will require different types of relationships between firms and knowledge institutions.

THE DIFFUSION OF INFORMATION AND THE DEVELOPMENT OF KNOWLEDGE ARE TWO DIFFERENT PROCESSES

In Chapter 7 we divided knowledge into two types: information and tacit knowledge. Implicitly most reflections on the character of knowledge have regarded it as information, that is, as a form of knowledge about the world that can be formulated explicitly and communicated via information technology. In recent years it has been increasingly realized that much of the most essential knowledge, economically speaking, is implicit and built into the routine practices of everyday life.[3] At the same time, there has been a tendency toward an explosive increase in the general availability of information.

Generally then, the amount of information available is no longer a limiting factor for firms. What is crucial is rather their ability to seek, find, choose and process information and to accumulate experience and skills in connection with this processing. This situation has far-reaching implications for the methods that are relevant for the communication of knowledge. There are two very different functions that must be carried out. One has to do with firms' use of information, while the other to a great extent is connected to the production, communication and use of unstructured, tacit knowledge.

On the one hand different types of information services need to be developed in which scientific and technical information is made available, for example through the creation of databases and information search systems. The know-how that is found in the technological consultancy system and in universities and sector research institutes could be used to support search processes in areas where the specific information is very complex and difficult to locate. In this context, the establishment of special network functions connected to knowledge institutions would represent a useful kind of investment. The network centre established in connection with Aalborg University with a subsidy from the EU has been quite successful in reaching many different groups of users in the region. This example also shows that this goal does not require any radical changes in the basic functioning of the knowledge institutions. It is, however, essential that these services are made visible and that potential users are introduced to them in such a way that they can evaluate the usefulness of the services in practical use.

On the other hand, it must be expected that in the future this task will eventually cease to be a simple transfer of concrete knowledge or information. Technological consultancy firms in particular will have to adapt themselves to this shift in the way the communication of knowledge takes place. It is namely primarily by entering into forms of practice that one can learn the hidden or tacit dimensions of knowledge. For this reason, it is probable that future knowledge communicators will need to take on the role not only of transferring information but also of assisting firms in its use and ensuring that the knowledge thus acquired is stored in the firm. Perhaps 'transfer' is a poor term for what will take place in this connection, as it will more often be production of new knowledge that will take place in collaboration between the firm and the knowledge institution.

This last type of knowledge production and transfer will demand quite close relations between the supply and demand sides. The gradual creation of people-based collaboration patterns and relationships based on mutual trust will be necessary for an effective process. In general, this type of knowledge-generative collaboration will turn out to be particularly dependent on people both in firms and knowledge institutions. Policy schemes aimed at promoting personnel exchange between the different communities will thus be crucial to supporting this type of interaction.

THE DIVISION OF LABOUR BETWEEN FIRMS, TECHNOLOGY CONSULTANTS AND UNIVERSITIES

As Table 11.1 shows, there is a clear tendency for Danish firms to collaborate less with universities and research institutions than firms in other countries do.

The international context thus shows that Danish firms collaborate directly with Danish research institutes only to a very limited extent in connection with product development. This corresponds to the results of other international comparisons. For example, the OECD report on the Danish research and innovation system remarked that there were noticeably weak commercial ties between firms and research institutions in Denmark (OECD 1995, p. 138).

This has also been a predominating theme in the debate on industrial policy, and currently a number of ideas are flourishing about how Danish universities can be integrated with and made useful to the business community. The question remains, however, to what extent the relatively low frequency of Danish firm collaboration with research institutions should be perceived as a sign of weakness. To a certain extent it may reflect, as already mentioned, a Danish innovation mode that differs from that found in other countries.

To this we must add that in Denmark, a highly developed technological consultancy system exists – including the GTS institutes, engineering firms and management consultancy firms – that function to a certain extent as bridge-builders between research and firms. It would be problematic to evaluate the interplay between firms and research institutions without considering the role played by the consultancy system. Ideally, a strategy of research and innovation policy ought to consider all three components of 'the innovation system in a restricted sense' (firms, the technological consultancy system and research institutions).

Table 11.1   Collaboration with research institutions according to firm size: share in % that reported collaboration in connection with product development*

| | | No. of employees | | | |
		10–19	20–99	100+	All
Denmark	Universities and sector research inst.	9	16	31	17
Norway	Universities	17	23	34	28
	Research institutes	32	41	56	48
Austria	Universities	9	22	48	33
	Contract research organizations	18	20	29	24

Source: Christensen et al. (1999).

Thus one important function of the GTS institutes and other consultants is to translate both old and more recent scientific knowledge into a form that enables a larger population of user firms to adopt it and use it in practice.[4] They operate under conditions resembling those in the private sector, thus facilitating mutual communication. In this way they differ from universities and research institutions, which neither can nor ought to be transformed into profit-oriented private firms. On this basis, it appears more expedient to strengthen the scientific competencies of the consultancy system than to strengthen the commercial aspects of the academic system.[5]

As we pointed out in the first part of the book, however, there are a number of research areas where the boundaries between basic research, applied research and commercial use are becoming more difficult to define. This is especially true for biotechnology and pharmaceutical-related activities. In these areas a stronger basis for interaction would also help to promote basic research. This is true because often the private sector takes the lead with regard to the development and use of expensive advanced instrumentation in these areas.

There is also a general tendency for more scientific and formalized knowledge to become more important to competitiveness within more traditional product areas. Here it would be an advantage if firms could enter into more interaction directly with research institutions when working on problem-solving. The kind of scientific knowledge needed in such areas is often a mix of 'old science' results and engineering competence and the mechanisms needed to link up with universities is different than when it comes to high-technology areas referred to above.

In recent years industrial policy schemes have been developed to ensure public support for new forms of collaboration (such as centre contracts, innovation milieus, the mobility programme and the business researcher scheme) aimed at overcoming possible barriers between the three worlds. The various DISKO analyses indicate that in this context as well, people make up the most fundamental element of the innovation system. This is true not only for the types of competencies that exist in the workforce but also for the interaction that takes place between the different parts of the system. This claim is supported by the data shown in Table 11.2 about the correlation between presence of academically trained employees in the workforce and the frequency of connections between firms and universities.

In Table 11.2 we compare firms with and without employees with graduate and postgraduate degrees (long academic educations, abbreviated LAE). It appears that firms without employees with academic educational background strengthened ties to the institutions of knowledge during the period 1993–95 to a much lesser degree than firms with highly educated employees. These data were produced by linking the responses from the DISKO firm survey to

Table 11.2 *Share of firms that have strengthened their collaborative ties to knowledge institutions according to firm size and presence of highly educated employees (LAE) (of firms that report strengthened collaboration in the period 1993–95)*

	<50 employees			≥50 employees		
	With LAE	W/O LAE	All <50	With LAE	W/O LAE	All ≥50
Strengthened collaboration	17	9	11	29	21	26
Did not strengthen collaboration	83	91	89	71	79	74
Total	100	100	100	100	100	100
N	196	787	983	405	197	602
% row	20	80	100	67	33	100

Notes: Anm.: with LAE <50: missing=5; With LAE >50: missing=3; w/o LAE <50: missing=14; w/o LAE >50: missing=3.

Source: Christensen et al. 1999.

the IDA labour market data. (IDA is the Danish individual labour market data base and registers the career path of every single individual and every single firm in Denmark).

Table 11.2 shows that larger firms strengthened collaborative efforts with knowledge institutions during the period to a greater degree than smaller firms (26 per cent of firms with at least 50 employees versus 11 per cent of the small firms strengthened collaboration with knowledge institutions). However, the table also shows that it makes a difference for both categories of firm whether the firm does or does not have highly educated employees on staff. For small firms the probability of strengthening ties to a knowledge institution is nearly twice as great if there are highly educated employees in the firm (17 per cent versus 9 per cent).

On the whole, it is worth noting that as many as one out of three of the larger firms (those with at least 50 employees) do not have one single employee with a long academic education. Among the small firms only one out of five has employees with long academic educations. This is one of the reasons why 'icebreaker schemes' – schemes giving firms in the private sector subsidies for hiring their first academic – should continue to be considered. The rationalization for such schemes has, until now, been primarily based on labour market considerations, but there are also reasons related to innovation policy to support such schemes. They can help especially small firms to develop their approach to innovation in such a way that the firms achieve stronger ties to formal and academic knowledge and, as well, to knowledge institutions.

Another means for strengthening the interaction between researchers, consultants and the business community are programmes to promote mobility between these three communities. There is a need to consider new measures that would provide stronger incentives than those than have been used to date. Experience from other countries, not least from Stanford University, which has experienced highly favourable effects due to such mobility, indicates that the barriers are so great that very strong special initiatives are needed to start the process. One possibility might be to allow a certain local experimentation with central support in order to determine which measures are most effective.

On the other hand, there is probably cause to treat with a certain degree of scepticism some of the suggestions for university reform that are circulating at the moment. Often a clear analysis is lacking of the problem that these reforms are expected to solve and of the connection between means and end results. The pattern we have uncovered in the DISKO project, not least with regard to the organization of knowledge-intensive firms, is one in which extensive dele-gation of competence is a key element. Some of the suggestions which focus rather one-sidedly on creating 'visible' and 'strong' leadership that is exter-nally recruited appear on this basis, as though they have their roots in a special sub-species of modern public sector management logic that ignores the significance of the fact that we find ourselves in a rapidly changing learning economy.

Transformation and change are needed, but these must necessarily rest on the broad participation of researchers, teachers and students. The command economy functions particularly badly with regard to organizing knowledge production – this may be the most important reason for the breakdown of centrally planned economies. The key problem, at the university, as elsewhere, is to establish incentives that make it attractive to experiment and to learn from those experiments as well as to create a common culture in which the production of new ideas is positively valued. Nor are authoritarian forms of leadership necessarily conducive to the primary function of the university: the education of highly qualified, creative (and democratically educated) graduates.

Recently there has been a great deal of focus on the issue that universities should patent the results of their research to an increasing degree. It is also apparent that the patenting of university research is growing dramatically within some very specific knowledge areas in the US, for example biotechnology and pharmaceuticals. At the same time, one must consciously consider the fact that increased patenting conflicts with another fundamental function of the university, which is to ensure the production and dissemination of readily available knowledge. Seen in relation to the picture we have drawn of the Danish innovation system, there are grounds to prefer solutions in this area which attempt to limit patenting activities to separate institutions that operate on the fringes of the universities' core areas, for example research parks and similar arrangements.

Much of the debate on how to organize universities have thus been based on rather narrow and specific high-technology experiences. This is especially problematic for a country where the mode of innovation is incremental and located in so-called low-tech areas, and specifically it neglects the fact that economic performance cannot be derived directly from the use of advanced technology. In order to convert new theoretical technical insight into innovation and to survive increasing competitive pressure it is also necessary for firms to possess up-to-date knowledge of organization, leadership, culture, languages, financing, marketing and so forth. In Chapter 8 we showed, for example, that the organizational form within which firms choose to operate has great significance for their productivity. Therefore it is important that the debate about research and education policy does not just focus on the necessity of strengthening the research-related and educational activities of areas of science and technology but takes a broader perspective, with a view to the fact that innovation and change require the presence of, and a combination of, a number of different competencies at all levels.

On this point there appears to be a systematic delay in the general discussion and the policies that are carried out. Agriculture is a sector that still enjoys strong political support. Attention to the manufacturing sector, particularly high-tech manufacturing, is increasing. The fact that knowledge production and interactive learning processes are increasingly dominating the actual economic dynamics is still a fact that is mainly referred to at festive occasions. And only recently have we seen examples of policy action taking this fully into account. One positive policy response is the recent establishment of the LOK initiative aiming at promoting management, organization and competence-building in firms in collaboration with university research (Nyholm et al. 2001).

The universities are currently creating 'development contracts' that will specify what challenges they intend to meet in the future with regard to research, teaching and collaboration with external users of knowledge. The idea of development contracts is fundamentally sound because it provides an opportunity to reflect on the activities taking place within the organization and to prioritize among them. It is much preferable to naive benchmarking where top-down criteria are used to identify so-called centres of excellence. If these development plans could be built up in a bottom-up process with broad participation of researchers and students they might become important instruments of change that will at the same time open universities up to external users.

THE INTERNATIONALIZATION OF KNOWLEDGE PRODUCTION MUST BE CONSIDERED IN ANY NATIONAL STRATEGY

In connection with steps aimed at strengthening the interplay between Danish firms and Danish knowledge institutions, it is important to take into account the internationalization that is occurring in these contacts. Both for the firms and for the knowledge institutions, a narrowing of perspective to a national level could become a barrier for renewal and learning. Quantitative and qualitative analyses in the DISKO project show that the knowledge used in Danish firms is only to a very limited degree developed within the country's borders. The majority of knowledge comes from other countries. As Table 11.3 shows, Danish firms already collaborate to a certain extent with foreign knowledge institutions. There is every possible reason to expect that increasing specialization will strengthen this tendency in the future.

The table shows that, on average, four out of ten of the firms that have collaborated with knowledge institutions and consultants have been involved in an international collaboration. It also appears that even small firms have

Table 11.3   *Product-innovating manufacturing firms' collaboration with*
Danish and foreign technological consultants and research
institutions according to firm size – share in % reporting
collaboration in connection with product development
(N = 548)

| | Number of employees | | | |
	10–19	20–49	50+	All
Technological service				
Danish institutes (a)	18	29	36	28
Foreign institutes (b)	6	8	20	11
Degree of internationalization (b/a)	**33.3**	**27.5**	**55.5**	**39.3**
Private technical consulting				
Danish firms (a)	10	16	24	17
Foreign firms (b)	4	3	10	6
Degree of internationalization (b/a)	**40.0**	**18.8**	**41.7**	**35.3**
Universities and sector research institutes				
Danish institutions (a)	8	10	25	14
Foreign institutions (b)	1	4	10	6
Degree of internationalization (b/a)	**12.5**	**40.0**	**40.0**	**42.9**

Source: Madsen (1999), p. 78.

established this type of contact, particularly with regard to technical consulting. This direct connection to foreign knowledge producers is essential for ensuring the rapid exchange of knowledge within areas where technical developments take place at great speed.

This international collaboration does not preclude the fact that in certain areas of knowledge a strengthening of regional and national ties may facilitate learning processes in Danish firms. But initiatives aimed at promoting a development in this direction must be designed in such a way that they do not weaken the incentives of firms to search for relevant information and competence internationally.

An interesting proposal recently initiated by the Danish Agency for Trade and Industry and carried out under the auspices of the Danish Board of Technology concerns the possibilities for creating a Danish technology foresight, that is, a continuous search for new developmental tendencies in technology. It is obvious that a small country such as Denmark does not need the same type of technology foresight that we find in large countries at the technological forefront in the development of key technologies. One can, however, imagine a particularly Danish version that could support the continuous balancing of the advantages between internationalization and regionalization of Danish knowledge production.

RESEARCH INSTITUTIONS AS AN INTEGRATED PART OF THE 'LEARNING REGION'

As knowledge production becomes more international, there is much that indicates the increasing importance of the regional interaction between firms and research institutions. This interplay between the international and the regional sphere of collaboration confronts research institutions with complex management and coordination problems. They must simultaneously appear as essential agents in learning regions and participate in globally organized knowledge production.

The location of firms is a compound and complex problem. Proximity to research institutions must be weighed against economic conditions, human factors, environmental factors, the availability of qualified labour, transportation conditions, the location of customers and vendors, corporate affiliations and so on. The regional differences in the collaboration pattern that the DISKO material has brought to light in this book support other Danish and foreign studies showing that firms' collaboration with universities and sector research institutes largely reflects a process of industry-specific clustering and agglomeration effects. The examples we gave in Chapter 5 were the Copenhagen metropolitan area's particular specialization in biotechnology and pharmaceuticals and Northern Jutland's high-tech specialization in telecommunications technology (particularly mobile phones). For both of these examples it is true that close contact and geographical proximity to research institutions is absolutely crucial.

In recent years a renewed understanding has arisen of the fact that the production and use of knowledge are to a great extent anchored locally (regionally). Seen in this light, research institutions play a crucial role not just for the national innovation system but also to a high degree for the possibilities of developing and transforming regional innovation systems. From a perspective of regional development one of the roles of the universities (not, however, the most important one) is the production of advanced new technical knowledge which can be put to use in new technically advanced products and production processes, perhaps via mediation through the technological consultancy network.

It is important, in this context, for national research and higher education policy to strike a balance that concerns the geographic distribution of resources. On the one hand, viable research units should be established so that the scarce resources allocated to research and education are not spread too thin. On the other hand, it is not acceptable if the geographical division of knowledge production is too unevenly distributed. Porter's analyses of national innovation systems showed that the most dynamic industrial development took place in countries and sectors where a few national competitors faced off against one another (Porter 1990). We believe that a corresponding mechanism exists in the area of research and that therefore national monopolies within specific research areas should be avoided. Further it has been shown that an important factor behind regional uneven development in Europe is unequal access to knowledge and knowledge institutions (Fagerberg and Verspagen 1996).

NEW CHALLENGES FACING THE CONSULTANCY SYSTEM

The analyses we have carried out indicate that the technical consultancy system functions satisfactorily in Denmark. As indicated in Table 11.3, both small and large innovative firms use it. It is used not only by high-tech firms but also, though to a lesser degree, by firms from more traditional sectors. There is a tendency for those who have used the services of technological consultants to do so again; this in itself indicates that the users are satisfied with the services they have received. The 14 certified technological service institutes (GTS institutes) have made progress not only on the Danish market. They now export about 25 per cent of their total turnover, while their basic public subsidy is now down to 12 to 13 per cent, the rest being financed by market transactions (Christensen et al. 1999).

Private consulting, too, seems to function satisfactorily. The total sales of services more than doubled during the period 1994–98. Certain difficulties for the user firms remain; these are connected to the ability to survey the market and to determine what services are needed. In particular, firms without academic employees are less satisfied with the implementation of initiatives suggested by consultants. But on the whole, customers seem satisfied with the quality of the services they receive (Industry and Trade Development Council 1999).

On this basis, there is no need to propose extensive reforms for this sector. However, in our discussions with experts we have discovered some areas where the system will encounter new challenges in the future. A number of these points of criticism are also found in the Industry and Trade Development Council's analysis of the private consultancy system (Industry and Trade Development Council 1999).

We have already mentioned the fact that technological consultants to an even greater degree need to serve as a connecting link between the research and business communities. This requires that they establish research-related activities to a greater degree than has been previously possible. For private consultants there will be an increased need for specialized research educations in the area of knowledge production and the knowledge economy; these should be established in cooperation with institutions of higher learning. This situation could also make topical a re-evaluation of the size and utilization of the basic grants to the GTS institutes.

At the same time, we have also discovered another challenge, one that pulls in the opposite direction: that consultants should become even more deeply involved in the practices of the firm. We have thus argued in favour of the future need for closer participation in firm problem-solving and follow-ups aimed at rooting the newly produced knowledge in the recipient organization. Thus there is a need for a new type of 'knowledge management' to ensure that professional consultation and advice leaves a permanent mark on the organization. An important factor is to contribute to the training of employees in client firms in connection with the working out of technical and organizational solutions. More and more consultants and institutes have already begun cultivating a market in the area of continuing education, and offer assistance with the dissemination of knowledge. This aspect of consultancy activities will increase in importance in the future.

Another related challenge has to do with the focus of the advice to be given. In the next chapter we shall show that firms are simultaneously seeking specialized workers and workers who are able to work in an interdisciplinary way and have broader, rather than more narrowly specialized, professional qualifications. We can draw a parallel to the consultancy area, since a number of the firms we visited expressed their disappointment in the consultants' lack of ability to see the firm's concrete problem in the context of the whole firm and as part of a larger picture. According to the Industry and Trade Development Council's analysis of management consultants, this ability to see the users' situation as part of the big picture is a competence that is in growing demand (Industry and Trade Development Council 1999, p. 94).

This does not mean that advice about anything and everything without any basis in specialized knowledge could replace the current type of consultancy. A gradual integration of new expertise that is more oriented toward the big picture and a conscious education of those experts who want to expand their analytical perspectives are two elements in a strategy that aims to counteract the problems that exist in an extreme specialization and 'technification' of the problems of firms.

SUMMARY

One of the major points of this chapter is that when evaluating the effectiveness of knowledge institutions with respect to the innovation system, we must look at their mutual divisions of labour and not analyse them separately from one another. Another point is that the lack of connection between firms and universities is related also to the demand side. To the extent that firms do not have any academic employees, they will of course have difficulty communicating in a meaningful way with universities and other research institutions.

On this basis, there is reason to place great emphasis on the human dimension and on how experts are distributed between the private and public sectors as well as between different types of firms. A large portion of Danish firms has done well until now in international competition without a strong formal knowledge base. General tendencies are at work having to do with globalization and increasing demands on quality from big firms to their suppliers; these tendencies raise doubt about the long-term sustainability of a model where firms operate primarily on the basis of experience-based knowledge. This also means that the location of public knowledge institutions as well as private consulting services will play an increasing role in relation to regional development potential.

A particularly significant new challenge for the consulting system, perhaps the most important in the learning economy, lies in helping client firms to become better at learning and at communicating, selling and using knowledge. Concretely this involves the particular task of the consulting system to communicate competencies to do with managing and developing human resources and with knowledge management.

NOTES

1. This chapter is based on DISKO report no. 8 (Christensen, Gregersen and Rogaczewska 1999).
2. In the Ministry of Research and Information Technology publication (1995, p. 57), which was concerned with the Danish institutional framework for research consultancy, a specific need was indicated for further analysis of the interplay between research and the business community.
3. In several other DISKO reports the practical importance of 'tacit' knowledge is indicated. Polanyi's analyses are examples of theoretical analyses of this form of knowledge (Polanyi 1958; 1966).
4. Other fundamental functions and their relative importance in the various institutions are presented by Christensen et al. (1996).
5. The Institution Council that coordinates the GTS-system, in a report published in November 1998, has similarly indicated the need for strengthening research activities within the GTS institutes.

12. Qualification requirements and organizational change: new challenges for continuing education and vocational training

One of the areas in which the Danish innovation system and its system for the development of human resources stand out dramatically is the publicly financed investment in the areas of adult and continuing education.[1] Denmark uses more than one per cent of its GNP on this type of activity, while the OECD average is about one-third of one per cent (see OECD 1997a, pp. 183ff). This national specificity has focused attention on this sector both in connection with OECD analyses and in the national public debate. In the following discussion we shall concentrate on the qualitative aspects of the system of continuing education. But before we examine this area more closely, we need to make a few comments on the extent and financing of the system.

First of all this is an area where there is good reason to put Denmark forward as a model to be studied by the rest of Europe. Other European countries, for example France, are now on their way toward introducing elements of the Danish system; in general the learning economy and a consistent investment in 'lifelong learning' demands a greater public responsibility for adult and continuing education than has previously been assumed in the other OECD countries. Only if one is ideologically biased and views public activities as being by definition less effective than private ones is there grounds for such unilaterally negative opinion as was voiced in the policy section of the OECD's country analysis of 1997 (OECD 1997b, pp. 120–22).

Secondly, the Danish economy has a number of systemic features that dictate a greater portion of public financing in this area in Denmark than in other countries. Some of these are discussed in the OECD publication in question (small firms, small differences in income and the high risk of marginalizing unskilled labour in a situation in which the number of new workers entering the labour force is decreasing). Other characteristics that are not registered in the OECD report have been at the centre of attention in previous chapters. Specialization in low-tech sectors places particularly great demands on general qualifications and the ability to innovate; therefore the need for the continual updating and improving of qualifications will be of particular significance for the Danish economy. High levels of mobility weaken the incentives of private firms to invest in the education of their own workforce.[2]

For these reasons we do not find it wise to implement political recommendations aimed at a rapid decrease of public efforts in this area. There is nothing to indicate that private investments will automatically replace public funds. Conversely, though, limiting the use of continuing education courses as a kind of 'holding-pen' for employees when firms experience periods of downturn should be considered. Also, activation programmes of the workfare type where unemployed and social clients are forced into training of dubious quality should be limited.

The 'holding-pen' function is not as negative as it first sounds. It contributes to a flexible use of the time of employees without affecting the security the employee feels when hired. The disadvantage is that firms are not motivated enough to make long-term plans for their utilization of the skills of their employees, and as indicated previously, Danish firms tend to show limited interest in planning their human resource development, also when compared with foreign firms. In any case it is important that this 'holding-pen' function is organized in such a way that it does not undermine the legitimacy of the entire system of continuing education; we mentioned earlier that the courses offered are often perceived as irrelevant, by both employees and managers.[3]

One way of ensuring relevance could be the gradual phasing in of partial firm financing, especially with regard to courses aiming at the creation of 'firm-specific' competencies. But more crucial than the angle of public financing is an analysis of the curricular and organizational changes that are needed in the area of adult education in order to ensure that this sector internally has a good ability to cope with new challenges.

Of the results in the DISKO survey, we call attention in this chapter to three conditions that in a crucial way have changed the demands made on the system of continuing education. First of all there is a direct correlation between organizational, product-related and technological change on the one hand and skill demands on the other. In general, requirements for the skill level of the Danish workforce have become more stringent, and this change is most pronounced in firms that are most heavily involved in processes of technical and organisational change. Secondly, organizational change in particular requires employees to have new types of qualifications. The DISKO survey shows that in the hiring of new employees, the qualities most in demand are 'responsibility', 'adaptability' and the 'ability to collaborate and communicate'; that is, general professional skills and attitudes are seen as more important than specific technical qualifications. Thirdly, the DISKO study shows that even among the most 'dynamic' firms, the investment in skills tend to increase the polarization in the labour market. As a rule only a small portion of the organization's employees have their competencies continually updated through continuing education.

THE CHANGING QUALIFICATIONS STRUCTURE

One of the results of the DISKO study was that organizational changes are often connected with new demands for several types of qualifications, just as those changes demand that existing qualifications are upgraded to a higher competence level. The DISKO study also shows that innovation leads to requirements for qualifications that are more firm-specific.

In a number of cases, all or part of the workforce already possess the necessary qualifications and thus innovations do not pose a problem with regard to the qualification structure. But in other cases the qualification structure is inadequate, and for this reason it is necessary to give the organization the qualifications it needs through the hiring of new employees and/or the continuing education and training of the existing staff.

To this we must add, our case studies show that when changes take place, employees risk acquiring qualifications that are either inadequate or downright irrelevant. For example, we found cases where management believed that a lack of attitudinal qualifications was the real barrier to change and therefore initiated courses for its employees in this area. The problem was, however, actually related to employees' lack of specific technical qualifications to deal with the changes taking place. While qualification does take place in this situation, the efforts are either in the wrong area or in the best case insufficient, and the qualification structure as such remains inadequate despite the further education that has taken place. This type of misguided qualification takes place especially in firms that have no strategy for training their employees.

As we have seen, there is a general movement toward more flexible organizational forms, and this will affect the qualifications that will be required in the future, thus also providing new challenges to the system of continuing education. In what follows we will see how organizational changes also change job content and qualification requirements in the Danish innovation system.

TYPES OF QUALIFICATIONS

Qualification types may be divided into four categories:

- Qualifications related to work speed, demonstrating the ability to maintain a job-specific demand for work tempo.

- Specific technical or professional qualifications, such as knowledge of materials, the ability to use machines and tools, customer service, the understanding of processes and so forth.
- General professional qualifications including qualifications regarding methods, organizational overview and the ability to act within an organizational framework; mathematical abilities; communication, including language skills; computer and IT skills and so forth.
- Attitude-related qualifications, demonstrating the individual's attitude towards work assignments, management and colleagues. These may also be called 'soft' or 'personal' skills.

When the DISKO study asked about changes in the nature of the work, the particular demands singled out by the respondents in the firms that have implemented organizational change are increased independence of the worker and collaboration with colleagues and management (see Table 12.1).

Throughout the study, the answer patterns differ markedly between the firms that have introduced new organizational forms and those that have not. General demands for more independence, collaboration with external partners and an improved ability to work with management have increased significantly in firms that have carried out organizational changes relative to the firms that have not done so. This also holds true, however, for the demands

Table 12.1   *Changes in the nature of the work for employees during the period 1993–95 for firms that have carried out organizational changes (number outside parentheses), compared to firms that have not (number in parentheses) % of number of firms (total number of firms = 1933)*

	More	Less	Unchanged
a. Job independence	72.6 (37.1)	4.2 (2.7)	21.2 (56.3)
b. Emphasis on professional qualifications	56.4 (36.3)	7.5 (5.3)	33.3 (53.8)
c. Specialization	33.9 (26.2)	20.8 (7.8)	39.3 (58.4)
d. Routine work	5.6 (8.2)	41.8 (15.5)	45.0 (67.1)
e. Customer contact	51.6 (29.3)	5.1 (3.1)	37.2 (59.9)
f. Supplier contact	34.9 (18.0)	7.1 (4.3)	46.4 (62.0)
g. Contact with other firms	24.7 (14.0)	5.5 (4.3)	56.8 (68.9)
h. Cooperation with colleagues	59.1 (27.1)	5.8 (4.5)	31.8 (63.3)
i. Cooperation with management	64.9 (28.6)	5.9 (4.2)	26.1 (62.2)

Source: Nielsen (1999).

for specific technical or professional qualifications. Among the firms that have implemented organizational changes, nearly 60 per cent also had increased their professional qualifications requirements, compared to just under 40 per cent of the firms that had not implemented organizational changes.

The increased demands for skills occur in connection with organizational changes for all types of qualifications, with the exception of speed-related qualifications. Routine work is diminishing in the change-oriented firms and a large share of these firms indicate a lower degree of demand for specialization than previously. This indicates that speed-related qualifications are not as highly prioritized in firms that have carried out technological or organizational innovations.

COMPETENCE LEVELS

Innovation does not necessarily bring with it a need for completely new types of qualifications. Increased demands will often involve the raising of existing qualifications to a higher 'level of competence'.

One way of illustrating the connection between levels of competence and innovation is by looking at the differences between employees' education levels in firms that have not implemented changes and those that have carried out technological and organizational innovations. Employees are divided into the following four categories:

- Employees with graduate or postgraduate degrees
- Employees with a baccalaureate or equivalent degree
- Skilled labour
- Unskilled labour.

As the numbers in Table 12.2 indicate, firms that implement technical and organizational changes tend to have a more highly educated workforce than those that do not implement such changes. This is reflected in the presence of all three educational categories and it is most pronounced for individuals with baccalaureate or graduate degrees. The proportion of unskilled workers, on the other hand, is greatest in firms that did not carry out changes.

Firms that have carried out organizational and technological changes have more than twice as many employees with graduate and postgraduate degrees than firms that have not carried out changes. This educational category makes up only a small percentage of the total workforce, and this group is also concentrated in a few sectors, particularly business services.

With this in mind, the differences relating to employees with a baccalaureate

*Table 12.2   Distribution of employees, 1990 and 1994, in firms that had not
and firms that had carried out organizational change*

	Firms that did not carry out changes		Firms that carried out changes	
Personnel category	1990	1994	1990	1994
Employees with graduate or postgrad.				
degrees	1.2	1.6	2.9	3.4
Employees with baccalaureate degrees	5.7	6.2	11.5	12.8
Skilled labour	45.0	46.5	41.9	43.5
Unskilled	48.2	45.6	43.8	40.3
Total	100%	100%	100%	100%

Source: Nielsen (1999).

or equivalent degree is actually more interesting. There is a over-representation
of employees with these degrees in innovative firms in almost all sectors, and
this employee category comprises a significant volume of total employment.

The group of skilled labourers is over-represented in the innovative firms
only in the service industries.

The numbers also reflect a labour market development toward a higher
level of general qualifications. This is true regardless of whether or not the
firm has carried out innovations – the education level of the workforce is
improving. There is also a slight tendency for the level of qualifications to
increase more strongly in firms where organizational and technical changes
are implemented; those with baccalaureate or equivalent degrees have tended
to increase their share at the expense of unskilled workers. But the difference
in this respect is more limited than could be expected.

The DISKO study shows that this development is not only attributable to
the abolition of some job functions and the creation of new ones requiring
different formal qualifications, although this has been the explanation for
many years. The DISKO study shows that a growing number of skilled
labourers wind up in job functions that were originally carried out by
unskilled labour. In 1990, 20.5 per cent of unskilled jobs were carried out by
skilled workers; by 1994 the number had risen to 24.6 per cent. There is a
process going on where workers with little formal education in jobs
normally not requiring much education are squeezed out by better-trained
workers.

There are a number of possible reasons for this. In some cases working
conditions could be better; there may also be wage-related arguments. It
could also be that there is high unemployment among certain groups of

skilled workers, causing them to seek employment in other areas. But the reason that employers are increasingly choosing skilled workers to perform unskilled job functions must be, all other things being equal, that the skilled workers possess some advantages over unskilled workers. In case studies we found a number of examples to illustrate that when organizational changes took place the demands for general qualifications increased, and this may be part of the background of the replacement of unskilled with skilled labour in unskilled jobs (Voxted 1999a, p. 52). (An alternative hypothesis compatible with the patterns observed would be that employers without much reflection always select those with more formal training.)

Both the development toward a higher level of basic education among employees and the fact that unskilled job functions are increasingly being performed by skilled workers indicate the need for competence levels to be raised, at least for some types of qualifications and job functions.

GENERAL VERSUS SPECIFIC QUALIFICATIONS

Another element of the qualification structure is the generality of the use of qualifications. The DISKO study indicates contrary tendencies with regard to the shifts in qualification requirements in this dimension; this duality is also found in other studies. The fact that the workforce as a whole is continually increasing its basic educational level indicates a growing demand for general qualifications.

But at the same time, the continuing education that firms are demanding is becoming more and more specific. This is particularly true for those firms that have carried out organizational and technological changes.

There is only a small difference between non-innovative firms' demand for standard courses providing general qualifications versus courses tailored specifically to the firms' needs, while the difference is pronounced for the firms that have carried out technological and organizational changes. The most innovation-oriented firms have a much greater demand for courses tailored to their needs than for standard courses.

Another finding of the DISKO study that indicates that continuing education in the most development-oriented firms aims to provide employees with specific qualifications is that these firms themselves organize individual courses to a greater extent.

The concrete qualifications that are demanded are primarily related to technology. In the DISKO study, the area in which the most development-oriented firms provide the greatest amount of continuing education is 'new technology', and here the greatest use is made of internal courses and continuing education from private providers.

Table 12.3   *Elements with great or some significance for management*
efforts to ensure that employees develop their skills

	Firms that have not carried out organizational and technological changes	Firms that have carried out organizational and technological changes
a. The completion of tasks	84.2	93.5
b. The allocation of time for sparring with management/colleagues	58.4	85.2
c. Planned job rotation	18.8	38.8
d. The organization of teams	38.9	72.1
e. Incentives to work across departments and groups	35.1	74.8
f. Standard courses and educations (e.g. AMU* centres and business colleges)	38.9	48.1
g. Courses tailored to the needs of the individual firm	40.8	67.5
h. Long-term educational planning	31.5	63.6
i. Other measures	4.9	10.6

Note: *Translator's note: 'AMU' is the Danish abbreviation for 'Labor Market Education'.

Source: Gjerding (1997), DISKO survey.

THE CHANGING NATURE OF THE QUALIFICATIONS STRUCTURE

Thus in relation to earlier analyses, the results of the DISKO study present a more complex picture of the qualification structure that is beginning to take shape in the most innovative portions of the Danish business community.

On the one hand, there is a demand for general professional and attitudinal qualifications at an increasingly high competence level, with emphasis on the individual's ability to apply these qualifications to his or her own work situation.

On the other hand, increasing importance is placed on continuing education providing specific, often technical, qualifications; the purpose of these is partly to integrate new employees and partly to allow employees to improve their specific technical skills. Increased specialization and an ever more rapid technological and product-related development has been the result of increasing competitive pressure in the most development-oriented sectors. These changes have led to demands for the workforce to be able to cope with work processes and technologies that are often unique to the firm in question. As a consequence, firms demand more specific training typically aimed at small groups of employees (Voxted 1999b).

Both the quantitative and qualitative data in the DISKO study show that the need for this double qualification structure appears for all personnel categories. Of course, there are differences in the specific qualifications within the various categories, just as there are differences in how these qualifications are established among personnel categories. The precise technical professional qualifications required of engineers are different from the demands placed on skilled workers. But the overriding pattern is similar. In the example of the engineer and the skilled worker this is illustrated by the fact that technical professional demands are becoming more specific for both groups.

THE COMPLEX CHALLENGE FACING THE SYSTEM OF CONTINUING EDUCATION

The great challenge to the system of continuing education, seen as a factor in the national innovation system, is that of qualifying the workforce regardless of personnel category for the conflicting needs required by changes to the qualification structure. The acceleration of technical and organizational change will in general increase the importance of adult education and 'lifelong learning' for economic and social development. This is especially true for the Danish innovation system, which has built up many of its positions of strength through experience-based learning and incremental innovation rather than through scientific research and radical innovations.

The first part of the challenge is to be able to fulfil the expectations of the business community in terms of upgrading of specific employee qualifications. The DISKO study shows that firms that have carried out organizational and technological changes use continuing education provided in-house or procured from the private sector to a much greater extent. And it can also be shown that the public system of continuing education comprising the following three components: AMU centres ('AMU' is the Danish abbreviation for Labour Market Education), the schools for vocational training and, finally, the schools responsible for adult education at high school level (VUC), are not used to a corresponding degree by the innovative firms. The data indicate that the public system of continuing education has difficulty adapting to the demands for updated specific technical qualifications placed on them by firms involved in technical and organizational changes.

One possible conclusion of the DISKO study could be that changes are needed in the system of continuing education that aim at providing more specific qualifications. It is not obvious, however, that this ambition should be taken very far – there will always be a gap between the most sophisticated technical problems to be solved in the most dynamic parts of the private sector and the kind of problem-solving capacity that can be built into the public training system. Also the rate of change in the specific skill requirements may now have become so high that it is more important to give the students the capability to learn new skills all through their working life. This would be compatible with the fact that the public system of continuing education has another essential function related to technical and organizational change. Another of the DISKO study's conclusions is that the innovative firms, in particular, demand workers with general qualifications and with social skills.

For this demand to be met, it will be necessary for the workforce to possess a minimum of general qualifications. What seems to be happening is that this is reflected in informal upgrading of the skill requirements for unskilled jobs. Firms increasingly recruit individuals with technical or continuing education, even for job functions that are formally defined as unskilled. This exposes unskilled workers to increasing competition and reduces the options available to the large group of unskilled workers employed in the private sector. They will need continuing education if they are to meet the demands placed on them in connection with innovation. This problem is illustrated by Table 12.4, which compares unskilled workers in the DISKO study firms based on unemployment rates and job changes during the period 1990–94 with regard to worker participation in AMU courses.

The group with the greatest participation in formal continuing education is constituted by those who have changed jobs once or more, while those employed by the same firm throughout the entire period participated less in these courses. Thus stable employment is no guarantee that an unskilled worker will receive an upgrade of his or her formal, and thus to a great degree general, qualifications.

Table 12.4   *Share of unskilled workers that participated in AMU courses, 1994 (%)*

Unskilled workers with under 15% unemployment, employed by the same firm 1990–94	Unskilled workers with over 15% unemployment, employed by the same firm 1990–94	Unskilled workers with under 15% unemployment, employed at two or more firms 1990–94	Unskilled workers with over 15% unemployment, employed at two or more firms 1990–94
9.6	10.2	12.5	9.7

Source: Nielsen (1999).

The fact that AMU education increases mobility and improves employment opportunities for unskilled workers has also been the conclusion of studies carried out by the Danish National Institute of Social Research.

The challenge to the public system of continuing education is thus not only to meet the immediate needs of the business community and adapt their study programmes to them. On the contrary, it seems more important than ever to give priority to the upgrading of general qualifications, where the focus should shift not least to attitudinal professional qualifications.

This requires different pedagogical methods than those that currently characterize the system, and tendencies are beginning to develop in this direction. First of all, a number of studies and reports unanimously indicate a generally more positive attitude toward and understanding of the continual need for upgrading qualifications as a natural element in the business community (Mandag Morgen 1999; IFKA 1998).

Secondly there is currently a pedagogical discussion about the principle of alternating educational methods, that is, the interplay between formal education and the learning that takes place in the workplace. New courses have been established that intend to change people's attitudes to change processes under the auspices of AMU and Open Education. There is also a growing demand for courses organized by adult education centres, not least from the process industry and for the qualifying education to become a process operator.

There is thus a double challenge implicit in qualifying people to handle change. This challenge can be tackled through close collaboration among all basic and continuing education systems with a basis in the strengths and core competencies of each system. By 'all systems' we mean that the collaboration cannot simply be limited to technical schools and AMU centres but must also include the learning that takes place internally in the individual firm and, last but not least, the private educational sector.

In this context we would like to emphasize that the most important task for the publicly funded portion of the continuing education system should continue to be to ensure the general qualifications of the entire workforce. At the same time it will become more and more difficult in the learning economy to differentiate between firm-specific and general qualifications. A great number of the general and personal qualifications that are in greatest demand (responsibility and the ability to work with others) will to a great degree continue to be acquired in the workplace, while the very specific qualifications will be acquired in the public system.

It is of the utmost importance to review and reform the institutional framework around the public system of continuing education, so that it stimulates change and gives stronger incentives to the testing of new ideas. Conservative management of this part of the innovation system would eventually undermine the innovative ability of the entire Danish economy.

SUMMARY

The Danish public effort in the area of adult and continuing education is internationally unique. It aids realization of the ideals of 'lifelong learning' that international organizations are increasingly beginning to propagate. It is also an integral part of a specifically Danish system for the development and utilization of human resources, a system that during the next phase will have a major impact upon how the entire Danish system of innovation and competence-building will perform in both economic and social terms.

The entire system for human resource development, including the private providers of courses and the knowledge creation that takes place in firms on a daily basis, is at the moment facing three new challenges. Firstly, there is a need to improve the general qualifications of the entire workforce, particularly for those adults who are most vulnerable from the outset. Secondly, there is a need to ensure that certain basic professional qualifications connected to the firms' more routine activities are maintained. Finally, there is a need for a special effort responding to the demands made in the most change-orientated firms. The DISKO project has shown that a particular effort is needed to strengthen the qualifications of the weak groups and to involve the qualification needs of the dynamic firms in the development of educational programmes.

The efforts that are currently made to simplify the structure of adult and continuing education should not lead to attempts to hide the complexity of the tasks facing the system as a whole. A common and unified organizational framework must not get in the way of attempts to take into account the varied needs of radically different target groups and goals. Small traditional construction firms have completely different requirements of the system of continuous education than big firms producing engineering products, and both categories of firms will go through rapid change in the near future. A great deal of room for experimentation, not least at regional level, is a prerequisite for the necessary renewal and adaptation to take place in this area, which is and certainly will remain a key element in the Danish innovation system.

NOTES

1. This chapter is based on DISKO report no. 3 (Voxted 1998) and Voxted's report 'Can courses change attitudes?' (Voxted 1999a) as well as a specific written contribution from Søren Voxted.
2. Some of the arguments in the OECD report, by the way, appear to be rather dubious. For example it is claimed that there are no clear conclusions with respect to the correlation between technical development and increased demands for qualifications. By now there are

both macroanalyses (Abramovitz and David 1996) and microanalyses (Lauritzen et al. 1996) that show strong correlations between the use of information technology and an increase in qualification demands.

3. Of course, this also holds true for the activation programmes that are now being carried out with increasing intensity. A certain flexibility in the implementation of these programmes is preferable to a situation in which course activities get the reputation, among those who most need to develop new competencies, of being meaningless punitive measures.

13. Labour market dynamics, innovation and organizational change

One very crucial way for firms to acquire new competencies is to hire qualified personnel.[1] In this chapter, we shall analyse how firms with different profiles with regard to technical innovation and organizational change behave in relation to the labour market. We shall thus examine differences in patterns with regard to job creation, hiring, firing and new qualification requirements. The analysis refers to a special DISKO subset of the labour force comprising all persons who were employed during the period of 1990–94 at a total of 1610 workplaces for which we have information from the DISKO survey about technical and organizational innovation. In some instances it has been possible to update so that the period covered is 1992–97.

Among other things the DISKO survey shows that despite great variation between sectors there is an overriding tendency for firms to move toward a larger degree of functional flexibility through such initiatives as the delegation of responsibility, and planned job rotation (Gjerding 1997). What consequences will these changes have for the entire labour market? By comparing the organizationally most advanced firms with the average regarding their conduct in the labour market (for example quantitative flexibility and labour market exclusion), one can form a picture of how changes in firms' behaviour may give rise to new labour market tendencies in the future.

Our main interest in this analysis is thus how different types of firms fare in terms of job creation and employment stability. We shall also, specifically, ask whether the introduction of functional flexibility at the firm level places unskilled workers in a more vulnerable position.

DELIMITING DISKO's LABOUR MARKET SUBSET

In continuation of the survey that was used as the basis for our presentation of the learning organization in Chapter 8 we have, with the help of the Danish labour market's statistical database IDA, constructed a special 'DISKO labour market'. This subset comprises all of those who were employed during the period 1990–94 at 1610 workplaces in different areas of manufacturing and services. These workplaces were chosen in the following way. They had to be

Table 13.1   *Employment development in the DISKO labour market subset*
compared to the development of the entire private labour
market

	Nov. 1990	Nov. 1991	Nov. 1992	Nov. 1993	Nov. 1994
DISKO					
1610 workplaces					
Number of employees	142 745	143 290	141 413	138 019	145 469
Index 1990 = 100	100	100.4	99.1	96.7	101.9
IDA					
57 461 workplaces					
Number of employees	803 048	805 446	796 496	781 618	827 928
Index 1990 = 100	100	100.3	99.2	97.3	103.1

Source: Nielsen (1999), IDA-data combined with DISKO survey.

parts of those firms that responded to the 1996 survey on organizational
change. If one of the firms responding to the survey included more than one
workplace, the largest workplace was chosen. Finally, we included only workplaces and firms that existed during the entire period 1990–94 (or 1990–97).
This left us with 1610 workplaces, corresponding to 85 per cent of all of the
possible survey firms.[2]

In Table 13.1 the employment development of the DISKO labour market
subset is compared to the development for the entire private labour market.
Employment development is largely parallel in the two aggregates. The
slightly less favourable employment growth during 1990–94 in the DISKO
subset reflects, among other things, the over-representation of large workplaces in the DISKO material. While the average size of an IDA workplace is
approximately 15 employees, the corresponding number for a DISKO workplace is around 90 employees. This reflects that in the construction of the
population of firms for the survey, we included all firms with more than 100
employees, while we excluded service sector firms with fewer than ten
employees and manufacturing firms with fewer than 20. On the other hand
this selection procedure means that a very large portion of the entire employment in the private labour market is included in the DISKO subset (17.6 per
cent).

The purpose of constructing such a subset is to link the qualitative information collected by the survey to the actual conduct and performance of the
firms in terms of employment and qualifications development. This is perhaps
the most innovative element in the entire DISKO project. In a recent OECD
overview of research on organizational change the issue is raised about the

connection between changes in firms' organizational forms and the labour market's way of functioning (OECD 1999). The answer is largely that almost nothing is known about this issue. For this reason, the data presented below represents new knowledge – also relative to international research.

In the following presentation we shall analyse the differences in behaviour among various types of firms and compare them with the behaviour of the entire population. One division is according to the industry affiliation of the firms and another the degree to which they have developed a strategy for human resource development. Finally we compare 'static' with 'dynamic' firms. The 'static firms' are characterized by a low degree of introducing new organizational forms and a low degree of activity in the development of products and markets. The 'dynamic firms' are those that combine organizational change with product and market development activity.

PRODUCT INNOVATION AND EMPLOYMENT DEVELOPMENT IN THE DISKO LABOUR MARKET

In connection with analyses of technology and employment it has been demonstrated that product innovations normally have a positive effect on employment. The DISKO labour market subset can be divided into two parts. One refers to the firms that have introduced new products (approximately 93 000 employees in approximately 800 firms) and the other to firms that have not introduced new products or services (approximately 42 000 employees in approximately 725 firms). In Table 13.2 we compare employment trends 1992–97 for these two aggregates.

Table 13.2 demonstrates that firms that introduce new products and processes tend to create more jobs than those that do not do so. There is a marked difference in employment creation between firms that reported product innovations for the period 1993–95 and those that did not report such innovations. It is also interesting to note that the difference tends to grow with time.

Table 13.2 Employment 1992–97 in firms with and without product and service innovations 1993–95 (index 1992 = 100)

	Nov. 1992	Nov. 1994	Nov. 1996	Nov. 1997
P/S Innovative	92 764 = 100	103.6	103.1	105.5
Non P/S Innovative	42 368 = 100	102.5	98.6	97.1

Source: IDA data combined with DISKO survey.

*Table 13.3   Index for employment development, divided into product/service
                innovation and branch subset*

	Nov. 1992	Nov. 1994	Nov. 1996	Nov. 1997
Metal products				
P/S innov.	38 409 = 100	105.5	103.2	103.6
Not P/S innov.	11 116 = 100	102.0	100.3	94.2
Construction				
P/S-innov.	1 554 = 100	105.7	125.8	118.2
Not P/S innov.	4 230 = 100	114.1	116.1	109.4
Business services				
P/S-innov.	3 657 = 100	106.9	123.2	126.1
Not P/S innov.	1 711 = 100	90.6	105.2	109.4

Source: IDA data combined with DISKO survey.

We find a similar pattern in the sector-level. This is apparent from Table
13.3, in which we have selected three industry subsets for closer analysis.
The first column shows the distribution of employment between innovative
and non-innovative firms at the starting point. More than three-quarters
of the employees in the metal industries were employed by firms that
had implemented at least one innovation. This holds true for more than
half of the employees in business services. On the other hand less than one-
quarter of the employees in construction are affiliated with innovative
firms.

In all the three sectors firms with product and/or service innovations had
the most favourable employment development. Construction shows a peculiar pattern in which the innovative firms experienced poorer employment
development in the short run (from 1992 to 1994). But also in this sector,
job creation turns out to be strongest in the innovative firms in the longer
run.

These results are important, because they illustrate that the dynamic
processes taking place may be different in nature in different parts of the economy. Aggregated analyses will often hide correlations that go in different
directions in the various sectors and thus cancel each other out in the collective picture. The results are of course also interesting in themselves. They indicate that the development of new products and services tend to create more
jobs in the innovating firms.

HUMAN RESOURCE MANAGEMENT AND CHANGES IN MANAGEMENT STRUCTURE

Based on the survey data we categorized firms according to how far they had gone in terms of developing 'human resource management' (HRM) (Gjerding 1997, p. 84ff). In order to measure the degree of HRM we used the occurence in the firm of the following elements:

- delegation of responsibility;
- quality circles;
- quality- and result-based salary;
- integration of functions;
- cross-disciplinary work groups;
- planned job rotation;
- employee sharing of the goals and visions of the firm.

On this basis we divided the population of firms into three groups with respectively low, intermediate and high levels of HRM. The following analysis (see Table 13.4) examines the development of firms with different degrees of HRM in terms of the employment of executive personnel (here defined as top managers/company presidents and executive officers) and middle management. It is not unusual in the literature – usually with reference to case studies – to indicate that the employment of middle managers tends to be squeezed in connection with the implementation of new organizational forms. The assumption being that the breakdown of hierarchies involves the establishment of more direct communication between top management and employees. As far as we know, systematic quantitative analyses of this phenomenon have not been carried out until now.

The first column shows that at the outset there is a certain preponderance of top executives in the most HRM-orientated firms, while the opposite is true for the firms in the two other HRM categories. In firms with a high HRM level, employment grew for top managers gradually over the period, while middle managers' employment levels declined sharply – especially at the end of the period. In the two other HRM categories middle managers have the more favourable employment development.

Thus the dynamics of the DISKO subset supports the assumption that more direct communication is established between management and employees in the organizationally most advanced firms. This is apparent in that the proportions between top management and middle management changed to the advantage of top management in firms with a high level of HRM. More detailed analyses of the material support this view.

Table 13.4 Index of employment development for top and middle management in firms with high, intermediate and low levels of HRM

	Nov. 1990	Nov. 1991	Nov. 1992	Nov. 1993	Nov. 1994
High HRM					
Top management	5 254 = 100	100.2	102.9	103.3	103.9
Middle management	4 869 = 100	113.6	114.0	98.9	99.1
Intermediate HRM					
Top management	2 651 = 100	102.2	99.9	92.0	86.1
Middle management	2 954 = 100	105.3	108.5	99.5	101.0
Low HRM					
Top management	401 = 100	101.0	111.0	101.2	94.3
Middle management	535 = 100	109.9	120.9	103.2	102.2
Entire DISKO subset	142 745 = 100	100.4	99.1	96.7	101.9

Source: Nielsen 1999, IDA data combined with DISKO survey.

EMPLOYMENT DEVELOPMENT IN STATIC AND DYNAMIC FIRMS

On the basis of the survey data we developed a classification of firms in which we combined their degree of organizational development with their activity in terms of the development of products and markets. In this way, we could differentiate between firms that did not meet either demand (we characterize these as 'static' firms), those who met one of the two demands ('flexible' and 'innovative' firms, respectively) and finally those that met both demands (these we characterize as 'dynamic'). In the following discussion, in order to maintain a certain degree of clarity, we shall concentrate on comparing the two extremes – that is, the static and dynamic firms – with each other and with the average of all the firms in the survey.

Table 13.5   Employment in dynamic and static firms, 1992–97

	Nov. 1992	Nov. 1994	Nov. 1996	Nov. 1997
Dynamic firms	70 227 = 100	103.5	103.5	106.6
Static firms	24 983 = 100	99.7	96.0	93.4
Entire DISKO subset	137 445 = 100	103.0	101.4	102.5

Source: Nielsen 1999, IDA data combined with DISKO survey.

To begin with we shall examine the ability of the two types of firms to create jobs during the period 1992–97 (Table 13.5). The firms that combine the introduction of new forms of organization with the introduction of new products 1993–95 create more jobs than those that do neither. Between 1992 and 1997 there was a total gain of about 3400 jobs in the subset of DISKO firms. There was a gain of about 4600 jobs in the dynamic firms and a loss of 1650 in the static firms in this period. Again it is worth noting that the divergence between the employment trends is modest to begin with but that it keeps growing as time goes by. This might reflect the fact that radical change in technology and organization has a positive impact on performance only after a period of organizational learning. The data show that not only are the dynamic firms more productive (see Table 8.4), they were also much more successful at creating jobs than the static firms – at least this is true in the Denmark of the 1990s.

JOB DYNAMICS IN DYNAMIC AND STATIC FIRMS

In the previous section, we could see that employment grows more rapidly in dynamic than static firms. It is of interest to discover the different labour

Table 13.6   Jobs created and jobs lost at firm level in dynamic and static firms (% of employees)

	1993–94 (upswing)				1992–93 (downturn)			
	Creation	Loss	Turnover	Net	Creation	Loss	Turnover	Net
Dynamic firms	9.0	2.7	11.7	6.3	3.5	5.9	9.4	−2.4
Static firms	9.1	6.1	15.2	3.0	5.8	9.8	15.6	−4.0
All firms	9.6	4.2	13.8	5.4	4.6	7.0	11.6	−2.4

Source: Nielsen (1999), IDA data combined with DISKO survey.

market dynamics underlying these net movements. Would a development in which more firms introduced more advanced organizational forms and became more active in terms of innovation increase or decrease the already considerable inter-workplace mobility of the Danish workforce?

In order to illuminate this question, Table 13.6 provides the numbers for the share of newly created and lost jobs in dynamic and static firms respectively. The table shows that the dynamic firms had lower than average job turnover, while turnover in the static firms was above the average. The most pronounced difference in turnover between the two types of firm has to do with the fact that significantly fewer jobs were lost in the dynamic firms during periods of both economic upswing and economic downturn. One possible underlying explanation for these differences could be that the dynamic firms build up a larger core workforce and that they retain a larger portion of their workforce when hard times come so as not to lose the knowledge capital represented by the core workforce. In any case, it seems that a movement toward more dynamic organizational forms might be able to slow down the high rates of turnover that characterize the Danish labour market.

The high job turnover does not necessarily imply large flows of personnel between firms. One firm could, for example, get rid of job X and create job Y, letting A, who was employed in job X, move to job Y. Conversely, personnel turnover can take place without any creation or loss of jobs. If A leaves job X, for example, to take early retirement, management might recruit B from the labour market to take over job X. In order to shed light on personnel turnover or workplace mobility one must directly examine rates of hiring and firing, resignation and retirement.

Table 13.7 shows first of all that the movement of manpower in and out of firms is significantly higher than the creation and loss of jobs. One reason is that some of the personnel turnover takes place when an employee with a history in the firm leaves a specific job that is then taken over by a person hired in from outside. Also in this respect, the dynamic firms have significantly lower

Table 13.7 Hiring and leaving of personnel at firm level in dynamic and static firms (% of employees)

	1993–94 (upswing)				1992–93 (downturn)			
	Hiring	Leaving	Hiring/Creation	Leaving/Loss	Hiring	Leaving	Hiring/Creation	Leaving/Loss
Dynamic firms	21.1	16.4	2.34	6.07	14.8	17.0	4.23	2.88
Static firms	24.4	22.5	2.68	3.69	19.7	23.3	3.40	2.38
All firms	23.0	19.1	2.40	4.55	17.1	19.4	3.72	2.77

Source: Nielsen (1999), IDA data combined with DISKO survey.

turnover than the static firms. Both during periods of upswing and downturn they are less likely to fire employees. They are, however, also more cautious about hiring new employees during both periods.

In Table 13.7 we have also related 'hiring' with 'job creation', and 'leaving' with 'job loss'. The purpose of calculating these two ratios is to illuminate to what degree differences exist between the two types of firm with regard to their behaviour during the phases of an economic cycle. If one first examines the entire population, we find a significant difference between the two years studied, especially with regard to the relationship between leaving and job loss. For every job function that is abolished during the upswing (1994), nearly five (4.55) employees leave a firm. During the economic downturn (1993) the corresponding number is just under three (2.77). This means that mobility out of firms is strongly reduced during periods of downturn. This could be connected to the fact that firms want to hang onto their key employees but also to the fact that employees are less likely by their own will to leave a firm during a period when the opportunities of finding jobs elsewhere are diminishing.

If we examine how the dynamic and static firms behave in this respect we find that the general pattern is strengthened for the dynamic firms, while it is less clearly expressed in the static firms. While more than six (6.07) employees leave the dynamic firms every time a job function is abolished during an upswing, the corresponding number for the downturn period is under three (2.88). The difference between these two ratios is significantly smaller for the static firms (3.69 versus 2.38). This indicates that the dynamic firms have a larger portion of core manpower and, when the downturn comes, they are more oriented toward keeping employees in whose competencies they have invested.

Another way of illustrating this problem is to examine personnel turnover, that is, the sum of 'hiring and firing' rates for different personnel categories divided according to the employees' educational backgrounds. This is done in Table 13.8 for 1993–94. (The hiring rate is calculated on the basis of 1994 employment, while the leaving rate is calculated on the basis of 1993 employment.) Table 13.8 shows that personnel turnover (hiring + leaving rate) is greatest in the static firms for all educational categories and conversely that it is below the average in the dynamic firms for all categories. If we compare job turnover between educational categories, we find high numbers for unskilled workers but, more surprisingly, also relatively high numbers for academics. These high numbers for academics particularly reflect the fact that the static firms have high hiring and leaving rates for this group.

Thus we can substantiate the hypothesis that the dynamic firms are more likely than the average of all firms to retain the workers they have. This is true for all educational categories, but it is particularly true for the academics. It is

Table 13.8   Personnel turnover ('hiring and firing' rates) for different educational groups in dynamic and static firms 1993–94 (% of employees)

	Postgrad.	Bacc.	Skilled	Unskilled
Dynamic firms	32.9	31.3	33.4	44.2
Static firms	45.7	39.8	40.5	54.7
All firms	38.6	35.2	36.8	49.8

Source: Nielsen (1999), IDA data combined with DISKO survey.

in this category that we find the greatest deviation from the average with regard to job turnover.

The existing data also make it possible to divide the workforce into a core workforce and a more loosely attached workforce. Our criterion for belonging to the core is full-time continuous employment in the firm for more than one year and a maximum degree of unemployment of 15 per cent during the calendar year in question. The use of this criterion means that the 'more loosely attached' employees make up about one-third of the DISKO subset for the year 1994. As expected, Table 13.9 shows that the core workforce makes up a larger percentage in the dynamic firms than it does in the average for all firms.

Thus it is characteristic, throughout, that the dynamic firms – that is, the firms that have implemented extensive organizational and technical changes – have less pronounced swings in their employment numbers and that they have a larger core workforce. To the extent that we see a development in this direction in the Danish population of firms – and the DISKO survey data seem to point in this direction – we should expect a certain decrease in the very high Danish labour market mobility, in particular through a reduction of lay-offs during periods of economic downturn. This would in itself function as a stabilizing factor in relation to the cyclical development in the entire economy. During periods of upswing a significant portion of the workforce would continue to seek and find new and better jobs with other firms.

Table 13.9   Share of core workforce in dynamic and static firms, 1994

	Dynamic	Static	All firms
Share of core workforce	66.8%	60.7%	64.3%

Source: Nielsen (1999), IDA data combined with DISKO survey.

Table 13.10 The index of employment development for highly educated and for unskilled labour in dynamic and static firms, 1990–94

	Nov. 1990	Nov. 1991	Nov. 1992	Nov. 1993	Nov. 1994
Graduate/postgraduate degrees					
Dynamic firms	2 363 = 100	105.3	110.0	114.1	125.9
Static firms	329 = 100	94.8	107.3	115.5	121.3
Unskilled					
Dynamic firms	30 753 = 100	98.0	93.5	88.4	94.2
Static firms	11 949 = 100	96.7	96.1	89.8	92.1

Source: Nielsen (1999), IDA data combined with DISKO survey.

QUALIFICATION DEVELOPMENT IN DYNAMIC AND STATIC FIRMS RESPECTIVELY

The DISKO data also allow us to illustrate how the demand for employees with various educational levels develops in dynamic and static firms respectively. Table 13.10 shows that the growth in demand for highly educated employees takes place both in static and dynamic firms. There is a corresponding reduction in the number of unskilled workers in both static and dynamic firms. Neither is there any obvious tendency for dynamic firms to shift their qualification structure in the direction of highly educated personnel to a greater degree than the static firms. The dynamic firms are characterized by more intense growth in demand for highly educated personnel, but there is also a slight decrease in their demand for unskilled labour. On this basis we cannot conclude that a transition to more developed organizational forms would in itself make the position of unskilled workers on the labour market more precarious. The level of demand for formal qualifications seems to be growing to the same degree in the static firms.

Earlier in this book we demonstrated that increased competitive pressure helps to promote the development of more advanced organizational forms but also that it has a negative effect on total employment. On this basis it is interesting to compare how the employment development of unskilled workers is affected by increasing competitive pressure in dynamic and static firms respectively. This is illustrated in Table 13.11, which shows that the dynamic firms in the longer run (between 1992 and 1997) were able to compensate for the negative impact on employment of much stronger competition. It also shows that massive job losses (25 per cent over five years) for unskilled workers took

Table 13.11   Employment of unskilled workers in dynamic and static firms, 1992–97

	Nov. 1992	Nov. 1994	Nov. 1996	Nov. 1997
Strongly increased competition				
Dynamic firms	16 500 = 100	100.3	96.9	102.1
Static firms	4 218 = 100	92.3	81.9	75.0
Somewhat increased or milder competition				
Dynamic firms	11 262 = 100	101.5	98.5	102.0
Static firms	5 862 = 100	99.3	97.0	93.5

Source: Nielsen (1999).

place in those firms exposed to much stronger competition that neither used new forms of organization nor introduced new products. Again, it seems as if a transition to more highly developed organizational forms does not in itself make the unskilled workers more vulnerable. They are, however, vulnerable to strongly increased competition on their product markets. Unskilled workers that work in firms and industries strongly exposed to competition where the opportunities or ability to engage in change are limited are the ones most strongly at risk for losing their jobs. Policies aiming at promoting competition need to be combined with policies enhancing the capability to innovate and introduce organizational change.

Table 13.12　Share of the core workforce in dynamic and static firms for employees with different educations, 1994

	Grad./postgrad. degree	Bacc. or equivalent degree	Skilled labour	Unskilled labour
Dynamic firms	77.8%	77.3%	69.9%	59.4%
Static firms	65.9%	71.7%	66.6%	52.8%
All firms	75.9%	75.9%	68.7%	55.9%

Source:　Nielsen (1999).

Another way of characterizing the labour market situation for different employment categories is to examine the portion that belong to the core workforce. In Table 13.12 we illustrate this for skilled labour and unskilled labour in dynamic and static firms respectively. Table 13.12 shows, as expected, that the share of those with graduate and postgraduate degrees in the core workforce is larger than the corresponding share of unskilled workers. Skilled labourers are in an intermediate position. It is also interesting to note that the differences between the two types of firms are most pronounced for the two groups at the educational extremes. In other words a transition to more highly developed organizational forms would involve a more stable connection to the employer for those with graduate and postgraduate degrees and for unskilled workers respectively.

At the end of the previous section we found that the size of the core workforce grew both absolutely and relatively in the period studied for the DISKO workplaces. This does not preclude a situation in which employees who belong to the peripheral part of the workforce will become more vulnerable than before. To illustrate this problem we can examine more closely the status of the more loosely connected employees the year after they were registered as loosely connected. This is illustrated in Table 13.13, which shows that the situation of the loosely connected employees has worsened somewhat over time.

Table 13.13   *The situation of the more loosely connected employees the*
year after their registration as such, 1990–93 (%)

	1990	1991	1992	1993
Connected to original firm	72.2	73.3	71.0	68.1
Connected to new firm	13.7	12.9	13.4	18.9
Unemployed	8.3	8.6	9.6	6.3
Out of the workforce	5.9	5.3	5.9	6.7

Source: Nielsen (1999).

At the end of the period, a smaller share of these employees remains connected
to the firm and a larger share winds up outside the labour market. To this we
must add that the dynamic firms appear to have the greatest difficulty in rein-
tegrating unskilled workers after lay-offs. The risk that an unskilled worker
who is laid off by a dynamic firm will remain unemployed is greater than if that
worker is laid off by a static firm. So, while the dynamic firms, on average, tend
to create more stable jobs, those employees who get into a peripheral position
may tend to become more vulnerable to exclusion especially in this category of
firms. Perhaps one important consequence of moving toward new forms of
organization is a selection process where some vulnerable groups get excluded.

SUMMARY

This chapter has presented new material that enables us to begin to examine
the connections between organizational changes and innovative behaviour at
firm level on the one hand and the entire labour market's way of functioning
on the other.

   Our analyses show that product innovation helps to promote employment
growth in the individual firm especially in the medium to long term. Thus
there are good reasons to stimulate the firm's development of new products,
also seen from the point of view of employment.

   Another interesting result of this chapter is that we can show, in black and
white, how middle management jobs tend to be squeezed as firms develop
more advanced organizational forms. This is important in the light of our
analysis in Chapter 8 where it was showed that this same group of middle
managers plays a key role in successfully carrying out the process of organizational change. On this basis, it is even more crucial to focus on the competence development of this group both in the public system of continuing
education and in the firms' own personnel planning.

In general, the picture of an increasingly polarized labour market is confirmed with a weakening of the job opportunities for unskilled workers. The demand for unskilled labour is falling and demand grows for more highly educated workers. At the same time it is particularly interesting to ascertain that this polarization does not seem to spring from the development toward more dynamic organizations.

The labour market conduct of dynamic organizations (those that have combined technical and organizational changes) differ from the static (those that carried out neither technical nor organizational changes) at a number of points.

The dynamic firms have a larger core workforce than the static firms. A gradual dissemination of this type of business behaviour might thus mean that firms will hold on to their workers to a greater degree, particularly during bad times. All other things being equal, this will mean a more stable labour market with fewer swings in unemployment and stronger incentives for firms to invest in the competence of their employees. And, actually, this stabilization also holds true for the unskilled workers. There is nothing in the material to indicate that the relative position of unskilled workers on the labour market will worsen in this respect as firms make the transition from static to dynamic. This gives employees strong grounds to take active part in processes aiming at new products and new forms of organization.

It is perhaps even more important that the dynamic firms create more jobs. This means not only that they are more productive, as we showed in Chapter 8; they are also characterized by more rapid employment growth. This gives policy-makers further grounds to take steps to promote technological and organizational changes within firms. Especially in the long run, increased competition may stimulate such changes but in sectors where the capacity and the opportunities to engage in change are limited, a strongly intensified competition will result in massive job losses. To identify sectors getting into this kind of situation and to develop programmes that strengthen the capacity of firms to implement technical and organizational change is a major task for industrial and innovation policy.

NOTES

1. This chapter is based on DISKO report no. 7 (Nielsen 1999) as well as a specific written contribution by Peter Nielsen.
2. In some of the tables it has been possible to update the data and here we cover the period 1992–97. Here the total number of employees in 1990 is reduced somewhat – from 142 475 to 138 974 – reflecting that some DISKO workplaces that were closed down between 1994 and 1997 are not included in these tables.

14. Lessons to be learnt

In this final chapter we will characterize the Danish system of innovation and competence-building and consider what lessons can be drawn for innovation policy and knowledge management in other countries and for Europe. Before entering this analysis it is important to summarize some of the characteristics of the broader framework in which innovation and competence-building take place. The Danish society at large has its own unique features and neglecting those makes it difficult to understand the way innovation is pursued in Denmark.

It should be recognized that some of the most important features have roots far back in history. It should also be realized that the Danish system of innovation and competence-building is not in any way the outcome of a planned political effort. In most instances its strengths, as well as its weaknesses, reflect unintended consequences of pragmatic policy, the impact of unique personalities and small historical events. One way to illustrate this is to start with two individuals who each in his way shaped the Danish innovation system (see Box 14.1).

BOX 14.1   GRUNDTVIG AND ØRSTED: THEIR
          IMPACT ON THE INNOVATION
          SYSTEM

N.F.S. Grundtvig (1783–1872) – a great social inventor

In the second half of the nineteenth century Danish society went through a dramatic transformation. The traditional export markets for vegetable products were crumbling. Production had to be changed toward animal products. This dramatic transformation was to a high degree self-organized in collaboration between small independent farmers. It found its ideological support in the ideas of the popular priest Grundtvig. Grundtvig initiated the 'folkhøjskole' (a school open to adults and aiming at general education but without exams or gradings – organized locally but with support from the state). The main objective was

---

to educate farmers and to give them self-confidence. One major indirect outcome was the formation of strong democratic and decentralized producer co-operatives in dairy and meat production – the dominating export goods at the time.

This peculiar period of Danish history is important in order to understand some of the current characteristics of the Danish innovation and competence-building system. It is reflected in the industrial structure as well as in the mode of innovation. The fact that the most important export products – dairy and meat products – remained under the control of farmer co-operatives explains why the basis for establishing big export-oriented firms in the core manufacturing sectors was much weaker in Denmark than in for instance Sweden. The high regard for decentralized general education and for learning in general, established in this period, is reflected in the mode of innovation and in the organization of continuous education where the major role of the state is to support local initiatives.

H.C. Ørsted (1777–1851) – a Copenhagen scientist

There is a proverb in Denmark that Jutland, the big rural peninsula where Grundtvig spent most of his life, is 'far from Copenhagen'. In the first half of the nineteenth century, Copenhagen was still a small city with a small highly interactive intellectual elite. Among the elite the mathematician and physicist Ørsted, after academic struggles, became the founder of the Polytechnical University in Copenhagen and he remained its Director from 1829 to 1851. He succeeded in giving this institution a highly academic profile with a strong emphasis on natural science. Practical engineering disciplines were not appreciated (Wagner 1998).

When the Danish firms interact less with universities than firms do in other countries there are two factors at play. One is, certainly, that Danish firms are small and operate in low-technology areas. But the other factor may be that the technical university was founded by a natural scientist. This last interpretation is compatible with the fact that the single strong science-based sector in Denmark – pharmaceuticals – actually seems to have stronger roots in science than firms in this sector have in other countries.

It may be argued that the peculiar mix found in the Danish

innovation and competence-building system of a predominately experience-based production and a small high-technology sector reflects the influence of both Grundtvig and Ørsted. Grundtvig has put his mark on education policy while Ørsted's ideas dominate science and technology policy.

DANISH SOCIETY AT LARGE

Denmark is a small country dominated by small-scale production. The public sector is big but efficient and quite service-minded. Public sector activities are often organized in close contact with local civil society. There is little popular respect for the 'elite' in society. Some, like the Danish Norwegian author Sandemose, have said that it goes too far and results in an intolerance to anybody who does not behave as an average citizen. (He coined the so-called Jante law – do not ever believe that you are something special!)

In Denmark almost everybody belongs to a trade union or similar interest organization and many belong to grass-roots movements. Citizens are active in local affairs related to schools or child care institutions. At the same time, Danish society is characterized by a high degree of individualism as opposed to being dependent on the classical family. Traditional family commitments to small children, the disabled and old people have been taken over by the state. Young people and women are more independent of adult male wage-earners than in most other countries.

As pointed out in the beginning of the book, Denmark combines a high degree of social equality with a high level of income per capita (Andersen et al. 2001, pp. 1–8). It reflects the high participation rate – most citizens contribute to production through wage work. The high level of participation of Danish women makes life more demanding for both men and women. Danish men are more active in housework than they are in most other European countries. All in all, life in Danish society may be too hectic for families with small children and, especially for old people, it may be too lonely. But the society has many qualities and it might be quite well prepared to cope successfully with the new stage of the learning economy.

One important downside of this constellation of factors is the difficulty of integrating people with a different ethnic background into working life and social life. The combination of a production mode that is very demanding in terms of communication skills, and a high minimum wage makes, it difficult for foreigners to enter into the labour market. The social support system makes it too easy to leave weak learners in a position where they are excluded from work. And in Denmark, without access to work, people remain on the outskirts of society as such. To find ways to maintain social cohesion and equality, while opening the labour market for those with a different ethnic background, is the single most important challenge for Danish politics.

CHARACTERIZING THE DANISH SYSTEM IN TERMS OF INNOVATION

Denmark is Specialized in Low-Technology Products and in Sectors Characterized by Small Firm Size

It is a fact that Danish export and production is strongly specialized in low-technology products. We find a low-technology specialization in several other small high-income countries but Denmark also stands out as extreme among those (together with Finland). There are some high-technology islands in the Danish economy, and in particular the sector producing pharmaceuticals (dominated by NOVO) is extreme in its strong connection to science. This has resulted in misinterpretations of Danish innovation as being more strongly science-based than in other countries (OECD 2000a, p. 44).

Denmark is especially successful in the production and export of 'low'- and 'low-medium'-technology goods. These include food products, furniture and clothing. In addition, it has successful niche products in telecommunications (mobile communications) and in process regulation (Danfoss). Within all these fields firms are quite successful in absorbing and using technology from abroad, including information technology. Incremental product development characterizes both the high-technology and the low-technology firms.

The Mode of Innovation is Highly Interactive but not Science-Based

Within firms there is a growing emphasis on interaction across departments, between colleagues and between management and workers. Danish manufacturing firms interact with customers and suppliers more frequently than firms in other countries. The growth in the interaction is taking place in relation to both Danish and foreign parties.

On the other hand, the interaction with universities is less developed in Denmark than abroad. To a certain degree this reflects a rather well-functioning system of technological institutes that communicate new technological insights to the firms. But it is also true that the university system historically has been strongly geared toward the needs of the public sector regarding both education and research. Research policy in Denmark has been designed in collaboration with a handful of experts working in the most strongly science-based firms who, referring to their own experience, have seen few problems in the interaction between industry and universities.

The Use of Human Resources is Biased in Favour of the Public Sector

Historically most of the academically trained workforce has been employed in the public sector. This has gradually been changing through the last 1990s, where especially business services have absorbed a growing proportion of the candidates. But a large proportion of private firms still have no academics in their workforce. We can show that firms belonging to this group collaborate much less with universities than those that have engineers and other employees with academic training in their staff. Most of the innovation activities in the first group are either experience-based and incremental, or come from suppliers, including knowledge-intensive business services.

IMPLICATIONS FOR INNOVATION POLICY

There are good reasons to continue to invest in cutting-edge scientific competencies. This is especially true when these competencies are connected to rapidly growing markets (mobile communications) and dynamic technologies with great potential (pharmaceuticals and biotechnology). In a number of areas there is room for the start-up of small knowledge-intensive firms, and in these areas we find the justification for new instruments such as 'centre contracts' and 'development contracts'. New initiative on the financing of knowledge-intensive entrepreneurs, for example by giving 'business angels' a more active and attractive role, is another element (Christensen et al. 1998). Greater attention should be paid to facilitating the start-up of small knowledge-intensive service and software firms.

But it is even more important to upgrade the knowledge foundation of the rest of the economy. The method of innovation in more traditional sectors is normally experience-based and makes only limited use of scientific knowledge. This in part reflects technical conditions, but it also reflects a historically conditioned imbalance in the use of highly educated labour in the Danish economy. Only a relatively small portion of those with graduate and postgraduate degrees are employed in the private sector, and the majority of them are attached to a small number of large firms or to small knowledge-intensive service firms. In future there will be a greater demand for the accessibility of formal knowledge in all areas of manufacturing and services, and the Danish industrial structure is particularly vulnerable in this area. A systematic long-term effort to promote the use of highly educated workers in 'low-tech' firms would provide these firms with more direct access to various types of knowledge institutions.

Actually, the slow-down of the so-called new economy sectors – including firms operating in E-commerce, software and Internet solutions – may have a long-term positive impact on the economy as a whole. During the extreme upswing of these sectors it has been difficult for 'normal' firms to recruit IT expertise. The tranfer of some of these employees to firms using rather than producing the new technologies may in the longer term create a big potential for new products and for productivity growth. This is true not only for the Danish economy but also for Europe as a whole. Here the exaggerated cautiousness and strictness of European financial and monetary policy may become a major barrier for realizing such a potential.

Our analyses show that, in Denmark, there are particular problems and opportunities connected to certain sectors. The construction sector is one extreme case. It carries out few technical and organizational changes (Chapter 8) and in the short run those firms that do implement changes seem to perform worse than average (Chapter 13). This reflects inherent historical characteristics as well as the framework within which these firms operate. A combined strategy that promotes reform of the sector-specific system of education, the principles for the division of labour in the construction process, the procedures for bidding on contracts and the competition conditions in supply industries is required in this sector. Another focus should be on business services and personal services that make up the fastest-growing sectors. It is important that competition in these sectors is monitored, since monopolistic conditions in this area tend to undermine the competitiveness in client firms belonging to sectors that are directly exposed to competition.

As shown in Chapter 9, there are various indications that business services increasingly will play a key role in the development and growth of the entire economy. The production of knowledge and information makes up a large share of the production and distribution that takes place in this sector. In manufacturing the most advanced firms increasingly sell knowledge and competence rather than physical products. It is vitally important that policies concerning the labour market, education and industry take these new tendencies seriously. Public access to knowledge needs to be balanced against the protection of intellectual property rights.

CHARACTERIZING THE SYSTEM IN TERMS OF KNOWLEDGE MANAGEMENT

One reason why it is difficult to change the pattern of specialization in the direction of science-based and high-technology products is that the Danish pattern of human resource development tends to support the established mode of innovation in a systemic way. The Danish human resource development system (the school system, vocational training and the efforts made by firms to develop the skills of their employees) is quite unique. And, in certain respects, it matches quite well the Danish incremental approach to innovation in low- and medium-technology sectors. Therefore, an upgrading and a stronger emphasis on formal knowledge (as contrasted with practical experience-based knowledge) in the production system must be combined with changes in knowledge management.

The Danish Education System Fosters Independent and Responsible Workers with Weak Formal Competencies

Young people are expected to be independent and responsible in Denmark. International studies show that they spend little time on homework but a lot of time on small jobs to earn their own income. When finished with high school they take a year off and work or go abroad before entering higher education. They rate quite weakly (the extent and causes are still under debate among educationalists) in international tests on skills in reading and mathematics, at least in the earlier school years. But they seem to be extremely well prepared for working in a turbulent economy where there is a need to delegate responsibility to the lower levels in the organization. They are also used to communicating directly and freely with those in authority (teachers and employers).

The Danish Labour Market gives Weak Incentives to Firms for Investing in Training their Personnel

The Danish labour market is characterized by high mobility between firms (as high or higher as in the US) but a more limited geographical mobility. Danish firms invest less in training their own personnel than firms in other countries. On the other hand, the public sector has built a unique and quite comprehensive and ambitious system for continuous education. This means that Danish workers on average get more time for training within a year than workers in other countries. Firms contribute through a wage tax to the financing of the public training, and tripartite bodies representing labour, industry and the public sector at the regional level organize an important part of it. This specific division of labour between the private and the public sectors reflects among other things the fact that there are many small firms in the Danish economy that could not take on the responsibility for training their employees on their own. But it has also resulted in bigger firms using fewer resources on internal training and developing explicit human resource development strategies to a lesser degree than their foreign counterparts.

The Danish Labour Market is Flexible and Efficient but it is also Characterized by Polarization to the Disadvantage of Unskilled and Foreign Workers in Terms of Job Opportunities

There are a number of unique features of the labour market that need to be taken into account when considering the working of the overall innovation system. The substitution rate of unemployment support is higher and support is less restricted in time than in most other OECD countries, and this fact explains many of the peculiarities. It is one factor behind the high participation rates and it also explains the fact that workers in Denmark feel more secure in their jobs than their colleagues in other European countries with stronger legal protection from firing and with less mobility. High mobility reflects to a certain degree that employers meet almost no legal restrictions when it comes to firing personnel. But it also reflects that workers at all skill levels are less afraid of getting lost between jobs when looking for new job opportunities. OECD and labour market economists have emphasized the negative impact on job incentives of the prevailing wage and tax structure. But an 'irrational' willingness to work seems in many cases to overcome this negative incentive. Among women, for instance, 20–30 per cent work for a wage in spite of the fact that, in economic terms, they could be as well or better off staying at home. The Danish labour market is performing well also in terms of low and falling rates of structural, long-term and youth unemployment.

There is one area where it does not fare as well, however. Unskilled workers and workers with a different ethnic background are much worse off than the rest of the labour force in terms of job opportunities and employment. Here Denmark is performing worse than most other OECD countries. DISKO data also show that the training initiatives inside firms tend to reinforce the polarization. The chance for unskilled workers to get training in-house is much less than for other categories of employees.

IMPLICATIONS FOR KNOWLEDGE MANAGEMENT

In the learning economy, qualifications quickly become obsolete while it becomes even more important to have up-to-date qualifications. For this reason it is essential that elements of continuous education and learning are built into the normal course of life for all categories of people on the labour market. Daily work should be arranged so that the individual is given opportunities to develop his or her abilities further. This requires that firms take the form of learning organizations and that management allows employees space and time in their daily routines for reflection about learning. From time to time the need will arise for the individual to enter also into more formal courses of study. An important task for labour market organizations is to develop frameworks for employment contracts that make this a regular activity.

To an increasing degree general, personal and social qualifications are required besides specific technical abilities. This indicates a need in education at all levels for practical and problem-oriented forms of study aimed toward developing competence in the areas of problem-solving, communication and interdisciplinary collaboration. At the same time, the basic differentiation between general and firm-specific qualifications is becoming less clear, indicating the need for a more flexible division of labour between public institutions of education and firms. There must also be increased opportunities for employees with higher education to update their knowledge as it becomes out of date. This points toward new challenges for institutions of higher learning, which will increasingly become responsible for continuing education.

In all OECD countries there is a tendency for the relative position of unskilled workers on the labour market to get weakened. This is also true in Denmark. The risk that those belonging to this group will be pushed out of the labour market and onto public means-based benefits is particularly great. This problem is worsened by the tendency of firms to provide continuing education primarily to those who already have an education. In order to counteract these tendencies toward polarization, there is a need for special efforts aimed at upgrading the qualifications of unskilled workers and reducing the number of young people who do not complete any education beyond required levels. This will also require new pedagogical methods combining practical and theoretical elements in a new way.

New types of contracts and selective leave for further education, giving the strongest incentives and easiest access to those with the least education, should be considered. Another group that is particularly vulnerable in the learning economy is ethnic minorities (immigrants and refugees). The growing emphasis on internal communication in firms means that the public sector will have to step up its teaching of language and culture to members of this group if they are to have realistic opportunities on the Danish labour market.

The Danish model for competence development outlined above gives particular advantages for regions characterized by a specialized business community (industrial districts). In such regions high mobility could be compensated for by the fact that several of the firms in the area have similar needs for competence creation among their employees. Regional education programmes can to a certain extent be arranged according to the industrial specialization. This indicates the potential for further decentralization and regional coordination of labour market, educational and industrial policy. One must, however, also take into account the vulnerability of regions that such a strategy of regional specialization could bring with it.

Education and labour market policy are areas where radical effects due to economic globalization can be expected. In the future, these policy areas must be arranged so that, while maintaining national institutional characteristics, they also have to become more open to the rest of the world. In the future we can expect growing numbers of students and workers to come to Denmark from other parts of the world and, vice versa, increasing numbers of Danes to be educated and find jobs abroad. These areas are to a certain extent regarded as being at the core of the Danish cultural heritage and therefore it will be particularly difficult for interest groups and public authorities to think and act globally with regard to them.

BOX 14.2   SIX LESSONS FROM THE DISKO STUDY

Lesson no 1: On the compatibility of equality and growth

The Danish economy is the most egalitarian in the world in terms of income distribution and it is among those with the highest GNP per capita. The growth success of the US has gone hand in hand with increasing inequality. The experience of Denmark illustrates that there is no necessary connection between strong growth and growing inequality.

Lesson no 2: On the compatibility of flexibility and security in the labour market

In international organizations such as the OECD there has been a general message to increase flexibility in labour markets. Trade unions have opposed this and pointed to the need for more secure jobs. The Danish data show that the form of flexibility that is most adequate in the learning economy – functional flexibility – is compatible with security among wage-earners. High mobility between employers has not resulted in insecurity among employees because the social security provision has been acceptable. The introduction of functional flexibility within firms tends to reduce the need for numerical flexibility and it creates more and more stable jobs even for unskilled workers.

Lesson no 3: On the importance of innovation in low-technology sectors

One of the interesting aspects of the Danish system is that its relative wealth has been built in spite of a specialization in low-technology sectors and the fact that most of its innovations are incremental and experience-based rather than radical and science-based. Supporting innovation in low-technology areas will remain an important priority for industrial policy. This contrasts with the 'new economy' discourse where there is a risk of forgetting about the renewal of competence in traditional sectors, including service sectors.

Lesson no 4: People and career patterns matter for the formation of networks

The Danish economy is characterized by intense interaction between firms, while the interaction between firms and universities is weakly developed. As demonstrated in this study this characteristic reflects the composition of the labour force in firms and the absence of academic personnel in many small and medium-sized firms. A general conclusion is that network formation and establishing new linkages may be stimulated more effectively by affecting career patterns. This calls for a reassessment of incentive systems in firms and at universities.

Lesson no 5: What matters most is learning to learn and learning organizations

The rapid rate of change undermines established competences and requires the continuing establishment of new ones. Firms that become learning organizations are more productive and more innovative. They create more jobs, and more stable jobs. Much of the resistance is found at the top rather than at the bottom of the organization. Promoting organizational change is becoming a crucial element of innovation policy. Education and training institutions need to be evaluated according to their capacity to make students learn to learn.

Lesson no 6: Social capital matters for growth and the need for a New New Deal

The only way to explain the strong economic performance of Denmark and other small economies with a weak specialization in high-technology products is to take into account the social capital that makes it easier for people to learn, collaborate and trade. The most important threat to this mode of production and

> innovation is the growing polarization and exclusion of those who do not fit into the learning economy. To give those a stronger learning capability and access to the networks where learning takes place is crucial for the sustainability of the learning economy.

THE CHALLENGE OF THE LEARNING ECONOMY AND THE NEED FOR A NEW TYPE OF POLICY COORDINATION AT THE EUROPEAN LEVEL

As pointed out in the introduction, there is a growing consensus, at least at the verbal level, in Europe on the need to focus on long-term competence building in firms and in society as a whole. At the same time, the prevailing institutional set-up and global competition tend to give predominance to short-term financial objectives in policy-making. At the institutional level this is reflected in the fact that Ministries of Finance have become the only agencies taking on a responsibility for coordinating the many specialized sector policies. Sector-specific ministries tend to identify with their own 'customers' and take little interest in the global objectives of society.

The concept of 'the learning economy' has its roots in an analysis of globalization, technical innovation and industrial dynamics (Lundvall and Johnson 1994; Lundvall and Borras 1999). But the concept also implies a new perspective on a broad set of policies, including social policy, labour market policy, education policy, industrial policy, energy policy, environmental policy and science and technology policy. Specifically, the concept calls for new European and national development strategies with coordination across these policy areas.

These sector-specific policies need to be brought together and attuned into a common strategy. In the learning economy it is highly problematic to leave policy coordination exclusively to Ministries of Finance and central banks – their vision of the world is necessarily biased toward the monetary dimension of the economy and thereby toward the short term.

Europe could decide to establish a 'European High-Level Council on Innovation and Competence-Building' with the President of the EU as its chairman and with at least as much political weight as the European Bank. Such a new institution could have as one of its strategic responsibilities the development of a common vision for how Europe should cope with the learning economy. The basis of such a vision must be a better understanding of the distinct European national systems of competence-building and innovation. Only in the framework of such an understanding can international benchmarking and policy-learning at the European level become meaningful. Similar and corresponding new institutions need to be built at the national and regional levels within member states.

Even the most recent framework programmes – the fifth and the sixth, now under preparation – remain focused on the creation and use of scientific knowledge. Even if it is structured with reference to social and ecological needs it is still the scientific community and research ministries in member states that dominate when it comes to the detailed design and implementation. Europe could decide to develop a 'Framework Programme on Innovation and Competence-Building' where science is treated as only one among several sources to competence-building. The European High-Level Council could be in charge of the design of the main lines of the programme. Again, similar efforts at the national and regional level within member states would make the initiative more forceful.

Bibliography

Abramovitz, M. and P. David (1996), 'Technological change and the rise of intangible investments: the US economy's growth-path in the twentieth century', in Foray, D. and B.-Å. Lundvall (eds), *Employment and Growth in the Knowledge-based Economy*, OECD Documents, Paris: OECD, 35–60.

Amable, B., R. Barré and R. Boyer (1997), *Les systémes d'innovation a l'ére de la globalization*, Paris: Economica.

Andersen, E.S., B. Dalum and G. Villumsen (1981), 'The importance of the home market for technological development and the export specialization of manufacturing industry', in Freeman, C. et al. (eds), *Technical Innovation and National Economic Performance*, Aalborg: Aalborg University Press, 49–102.

Andersen, E.S. and B.-Å. Lundvall (1988), 'Small national innovation systems facing technological revolutions: an analytical framework', in Freeman, C. and B.-Å. Lundvall (eds), *Small Countries Facing the Technological Revolution*, London: Pinter Publishers, 9–36.

Andersen, P.H. and P.R. Christensen (1998), *Den globale udfordring*, Copenhagen: Erhvervsfremmestyrelsen.

Andersen, T.M., B. Dalum, H. Linderoth, V. Smith and N. Westergård-Nielsen (1999), *Beskrivende økonomi*, Copenhagen: Djøf-Publishing.

Andersen, T.M., B. Dalum, H. Linderoth, V. Smith and N. Westergård-Nielsen (2001), *The Danish Economy: An International Perspective*, Copenhagen, Djøf-Publishing.

Archibugi, D. and J. Michie (1995), 'The globalization of technology: a new taxonomy', in *Cambridge Journal of Economics* **19**(1), 121–40.

Archibugi, D. and M. Pianta (1992), *The Technological Specialization of Advanced Countries*, Dordrecht: Kluwer Academic Publishers.

Archibugi, D. and Lundvall, B.-Å. (eds) (2001), *Europe in the Globalising Learning Economy*, Oxford: Oxford University Press.

Breschi, S. and F. Malerba (1997), 'Sectoral innovation systems', in Edquist, C. (ed.), *Systems of Innovation: Technologies, Institutions and Organizations*, London: Pinter Publishers, 130–56.

Carlsson, B. (1980), 'The content of productivity growth in the Swedish economy', Industriens Udredningsinstitut, *The Firms in the Market Economy*, Stockholm: IUI , 33–46.

Carlsson, B. and S. Jacobsson (1997), 'Diversity creation and technological systems: a technology policy perspective', in Edquist, C. (ed.), *Systems of Innovation: Technologies, Institutions and Organizations*, London: Pinter Publishers, 266–94.

CEC (Commission of the European Communities) (2000a), Council of the European Union, 9088/00, 14 June 2000.

CEC (Commission of the European Communities) (2000b), Communication from the Commission to the Council and the European Parliament, COM (2000) 567, final.

Christensen, J.F., P.T. Christensen, K. Foss and P. Lotz (1996), *Teknologisk service: Tendenser og udfordringer*, Copenhagen: Institutrådet and Danish Agency for Trade and Industry.

Christensen, J.L. (ed.) (1998), *Private investorers bidrag til innovation*, DISKO report no. 5, Copenhagen: Industry and Trade Development Council.

Christensen, J.L. and A. Kristensen (1994), *Innovation i danske industrivirksomheder*, Copenhagen: Danish Agency for Trade and Industry.

Christensen, J.L. and A. Kristensen (1995), *Innovation og erhvervsudvikling*, Copenhagen: Danish Agency for Trade and Industry.

Christensen, J.L. and A. Kristensen (1997), *Et historisk og internationalt perspektiv på innovation i dansk industri*, Copenhagen: Danish Agency for Trade and Industry.

Christensen, J.L., A.P. Rogaczewska and A.L. Vinding (1998), 'The NIS project: summary report of the focus group on innovative firm networks', Paris: OECD.

Christensen, J.L., B. Gregersen and A.P. Rogaczewska (1999), *Vidensinstutioner og innovation*, DISKO report no. 8., Copenhagen: Industry and Trade Development Council.

Cohen, W.M. and D.A. Levinthal (1990), 'Absorptive capacity: a new perspective on learning and innovation', *Administrative Science Quarterly*, **35**, 128–52.

Coleman, J. (1988), 'Social capital in the creation of human capital', *American Journal of Sociology*, **94** (Supplement), 95–120.

Coriat, B. (2001), 'Organizational innovation in European firms: a critical overview of the survey evidence', in Archibugi, D. and B.-Å. Lundvall (eds), *The Globalizing Learning Economy*, Guildford and King's Lynn: Oxford University Press, 195–218.

Dahlgaard, J. and Reichstein, T. (1999), 'Produktivitet og teknologisk forandring', Master thesis, Aalborg: Aalborg University.

Dalum, B., K. Laursen and G. Villumsen (1997), 'Is there such a thing as a "good" export specialisation pattern?: A European perspective', Mimeo, Aalborg: *Department of Business Studies*, Aalborg University.

Dalum, B., K. Laursen and B. Verspagen (1999), 'Does specialization matter for growth?', *Industrial and Corporate Change* **8**(2), 267–88.

Danish Competition Authority (1999), *Konkurrenceredegørelsen 1999*, Copenhagen: Konkurrencestyrelsen.

Dansk Management Forum (1996), *HRM – Human resource management i europæisk perspektiv*, Copenhagen: Copenhagen Business School.

Dosi, G. (1996), 'The contribution of economic theory to the understanding of a knowledge-based economy', in Foray, D. and B.-Å. Lundvall (eds), *Employment and Growth in the Knowledge-based Economy*, Paris: OECD, 81–94.

Dosi, G., C. Freeman, R.R. Nelson, G. Silverberg and L. Soete (eds) (1988), *Technology and Economic Theory*, London: Pinter Publishers.

Drejer, I. (1998), *Den vidensbaserede økonomi – en analyse af vidensintensitet og vidensstrømme i det danske innovationssystem*, DISKO report no. 4, Copenhagen: Industry and Trade Development Council.

Edquist, C. (ed.) (1997), *Systems of Innovation: Technologies, Institutions and Organizations*, London: Pinter Publishers.

Edquist, C. and B.-Å. Lundvall (1993), 'Comparing the Danish and Swedish systems of innovation', with C. Edquist, in Nelson, R.R. (ed.), *National Innovation Systems: A Comparative Analysis*, Oxford: Oxford University Press, 265–98.

Fagerberg, J. (1995), 'Is there a large-country advantage in high-tech?', *NUPI Working Paper No. 525*, January 1995, Oslo: NUPI.

Fagerberg, J. and B. Verspagen (1996), 'Heading for divergence? Regional growth in Europe reconsidered', *Journal of Common Market Studies* **34**, 431–48.

Fagerberg, J., B. Verspagen and M. Caniëls (1997), 'Technology, growth and unemployment across European regions', *Regional Studies* **31**(5), 457–66.

Foray, D. and B.-Å. Lundvall (1996), 'The knowledge-based economy: from the economics of knowledge to the learning economy', in Foray, D. and B.-Å. Lundvall (eds), *Employment and Growth in the Knowledge-based Economy*, Paris: OECD.

Freeman, C. (1987), *Technology Policy and Economic Performance: Lessons from Japan*, London: Pinter Publishers.

Freeman, C. (1995a), 'The national innovation systems in historical perspective', *Cambridge Journal of Economics* **19**(1), 5–24.

Freeman, C. (1997), *Innovation Systems: City-State, National, Continental and Sub-National*, Mimeo, Paper presented at the Montevideo conference, University of Sussex: SPRU.

Freeman, C. and B.-Å. Lundvall (eds) (1988), *Small Countries Facing the Technological Revolution*, London: Pinter Publishers.

Fukayama, F. (1995), *Trust: The Social Virtues and the Creation of Prosperity*, London: Hamish Hamilton.

Gellner, E. (1983), *Nations and Nationalism*, Oxford: Blackwell.

Gibbons, M., C. Limoges, H. Nowotny, S. Schwartzman, P. Scott and M. Troiw (1994), *The New Production of Knowledge*, London: Sage.

Gjerding, A.N. (1997), *Den fleksible virksomhed: Omstillingspres og fornyelse i dansk erhvervsliv*, DISKO report no. 1, Copenhagen: Industry and Trade Development Council.

Gjerding, A.N., B. Johnson, L. Kallehauge, B.-Å. Lundvall and P.T. Madsen (1990), *Den forsvundne produktivitet*, Copenhagen: Jurist og Økonomforbundets Forlag.

Government Institute for Economic Research (2000), *Social Capital; Global and Local Perspectives*, Helsinki: Government Institute for Economic Research.

Hatchuel, A. and B. Weil (1995), *Experts in Organisations*, Berlin: Walter de Gruyter.

Hansen, B. and S. Nielsen (1997), *Viden, teknologisk udvikling og vækst*, Masters Thesis, Aalborg: Aalborg University.

Hirschman, A.O. (1970), *Exit, Voice and Loyalty*, Cambridge, MA: Harvard University Press.

IFKA (1998), *Kompetenceløft i Danmark*, Copenhagen: Institut for Konjunktur Analyse.

Industry and Trade Development Council (1999), *Managementkonsulenter – Kortlægning af en branche i vækst*, Copenhagen: Industry and Trade Development Council.

Jeurissen, R.J.M. and H.J.L. van Luijk (1998), 'The ethical reputations of managers in nine EU-countries: a cross-referential survey', *Journal of Business Ethics*, **17**, 995–1005.

Jørgensen, K., F.S. Kristensen, R. Lund and S. Nymark (1998), *Organisatorisk fornyelse – erfaringer fra 24 danske virksomheder*, Copenhagen: Industry and Trade Development Council.

Katzenstein, P.J. (1985), *Small States in World Markets: Industrial Policy in Europe*, New York: Cornell University Press.

Kern, H. and M. Schumann (1984), *Das Ende der Arbeitsteilung – Rationalisierung in der Industriellen Produktion*, München: Bechs.

Kline, S.J. and N. Rosenberg (1986), 'An overview of innovation', in Landau, R. and N. Rosenberg (eds), *The Positive Sum Game*, Washington, DC: National Academy Press.

Kolb, D.A. (1984), *Experiential Learning*, London: Prentice Hall.

Kristensen, F.S. (1997), 'A study of four organizations in different competitive environments', *DRUID Working Paper* 97(13), Department of Business Studies, Aalborg: Aalborg University.

Kuznets, S. (1960), 'Economic Growth of Small Nations', in Robinson, E.A.G. (ed.), *Economic Consequences of the Size of Nations*, proceedings of a conference held by the International Economic Association, London: Macmillan, 14–32.

Lam, A. (1998), 'Tacit knowledge, organizational learning and innovation: a societal perspective', *DRUID Working Paper* 98(22), Department of Business Studies, Aalborg: Aalborg University.

Lauritzen, F., J. Nyholm, O. Jørgensen and U. von Sperling (1996), 'Technology, education and unemployment', in Foray, D. and B.Å. Lundvall (eds), *Employment and Growth in the Knowledge-Based Economy*, OECD Documents, Paris: OECD.

Laursen, K. (1998), 'A neo-Schumpeterian perspective on the determinants and effects of international trade specialisation', Unpublished PhD thesis, *IKE-Group/DRUID*, Aalborg University, Aalborg. A revised version of the thesis has been published with Edward Elgar, UK (2000).

Laursen, K. and N. Foss (2000), 'New HRM practices, complementarities, and the impact on innovation performance', *IVS Working Paper* no. 05, Copenhagen Business School.

List, F. (1841), *Das Nationale System der Politischen Ökonomie*, Basel: Kyklos (translated and published under the title *The National System of Political Economy* by Longmans, Green and Co., London 1841).

Lund, R. (1998), 'Organizational and innovative flexibility mechanisms and their impact upon organizational effectiveness', *DRUID Working Paper* 98(23), Department of Business Studies, Aalborg: Aalborg University.

Lund, R. and A.N. Gjerding (1996), 'The flexible company, innovation, work organisation and human resource management', *DRUID Working Paper* 96(17), Department of Business Studies, Aalborg: Aalborg University.

Lund Vinding, A. (2001), 'Absorptive capacity and innovative performance: a human capital approach', paper presented at the workshop: Innovation, technological change and growth in knowledge-based and service-intense economies, at the Royal Institute of Technology, Stockholm, 1–2 February.

Lundvall, B.-Å. (1974), 'Virker en høj arbejdsløshed dæmpende på inflationen?', *Nationaløkonomisk tidsskrift* 112(3).

Lundvall, B.-Å. (1985), *Product Innovation and User–Producer Interaction*, Aalborg: Aalborg University Press.

Lundvall, B.-Å. (ed.) (1992), *National Innovation Systems: Towards a Theory of Innovation and Interactive Learning*, London: Pinter Publishers.

Lundvall, B.-Å. (1996), 'The Social Dimension of the Learning Economy', *DRUID Working Paper*, 1, Aalborg University, Department of Business Studies.

Lundvall, B.-Å. (1998), 'Why study national systems and styles of innovation?', *Technology Analysis and Strategic Management*, 10(4), 407–22.

Lundvall, B.-Å. (1999), 'National business systems and national systems of innovation', in *International Studies of Management and Organization*, **29**(2), 60–77.

Lundvall, B.-Å. and B. Johnson (1994), 'The learning economy', *Journal of Industry Studies*, **1**(2), December 1994, 23–42.

Lundvall, B.-Å. and F.S. Kristensen (1997), 'Organizational change, innovation and human resource development as a response to increased competition', *DRUID Working Paper* 97–16, Department of Business Studies, Aalborg: Aalborg University.

Lundvall, B.-Å. and S. Borras (1999), *The Globalising Learning Economy: Implications for Innovation Policy*, Brussells: *DG* XII-TSER, The European Commission.

Lundvall, B.-Å. and P. Nielsen (1999), 'Competition and transformation in the learning economy – the Danish case', *Revue d'Economie Industrielle*, **88**, 67–90.

Lundvall, B.-Å. and P. Maskell (2000), 'Nation states and economic development – from national systems of production to national systems of knowledge creation and learning', in Clark, G.L., M.P. Feldmann and M.S. Gertler (eds), *Handbook of Economic Geography*, London: Oxford University Press, 353–72.

Lundvall, B.-Å. and M. Tomlinson (2001), 'Learning by comparing: reflection on the use and abuse of benchmarking', in Sweeney, G. (ed.), *Innovation, Economic Progress and Quality of Life*, Cheltenham: Edward Elgar, 120–36.

Lundvall, B.-Å. and D. Archibugi (2001), 'Introduction: Europe and the learning economy', in Archebugi, D. and B.-Å. Lundvall (eds), *The Globalizing Learning Economy*, Guildford and King's Lynn: Oxford University Press, 1–20.

Lundvall, B.-Å., B. Johnson, E.S. Andersen and B. Dalum (forthcoming), 'National systems of production, innovation and competence building', in Special Issue of *Research Policy* on Innovation Systems.

Madsen, P.T. (1999), *Den samarbejdende virksomhed*, DISKO report no. 6, Copenhagen: Industry and Trade Development Council.

Mandag Morgen (1996), *Analyse: Danmark kan ikke konkurrere på viden*, *Mandag Morgen*, **36**, 21 oktober 1996.

Mandag Morgen (1998), *Kompetencerådets rapport 1998*, Copenhagen: Mandag Morgen.

Maskell, P. (1998a), 'Low-tech competitive advantages and the role of proximity – the case of the European furniture industry in general and the Danish wooden furniture production in particular', *European Urban and Regional Studies*, **5**(2), 99–118.

Maskell, P. (1998b), 'Learning in the village economy of Denmark: the role of institutions and policy in sustaining competitiveness', in Braczyk, H.J., P. Cooke and M. Heidenreich (eds), *Regional Innovation Systems: The Role of Governance in a Globalized World*, London: UCL Press, 190–213.

Maurseth, P.B. and B. Verspagen (1999), 'Europe: one or more innovations systems?' in Fagerberg, J., P. Guerreri and B. Verspagen (eds), *The Economic Challenges for Europe: Adapting to Innovation-Based Growth*, Cheltenham, UK and Brookfield, US: Edward Elgar, 149–74.

Ministry of Business and Industry (1996), *Technological and Organisational Change*, The OECD Jobs Strategy, Country Report, Denmark, Copenhagen: Ministry of Business and Industry.

Ministry of Education (1997), *National kompetenceudvikling*, Copenhagen: Ministry of Education.

Ministry of Business and Industry (1996), *Technological and Organizational Change*, Copenhagen: Ministry of Trade and Industry.

Ministry of Trade and Industry (1998), *Erhvervsredegørelsen 1998*, Copenhagen: Ministry of Trade and Industry.

Nelson, R.R. (1988), 'Institutions supporting technical change in the United States', in Dosi, G., C. Freeman, R.R. Nelson, G. Silverberg and L. Soete (eds), *Technology and Economic Theory*, London: Pinter Publishers, 312–29.

Nelson, R.R. (1993), (ed.) *National Innovation Systems: A Comparative Analysis*, Oxford: Oxford University Press.

Nielsen, K. (1995), *Kvalifikationsudvikling*, Aalborg, DK: LEO-Gruppen.

Nielsen, P. (1999), *Personale og fornyelse*, DISKO report no. 7, Copenhagen: Industry and Trade Development Council.

Nyholm, J., L. Normann, C. Frelle-Petersen, M. Riis and P. Torstensen (2001), 'Innovation policy in the knowledge based economy: can theory guide policy-making?', in Archebugi, D. and B.-Å. Lundvall (eds), *The Globalizing Learning Economy*, Guildford and King's Lynn: Oxford University Press, 253–72.

Nonaka, I. and H. Takeuchi (1995), *The Knowledge Creating Company*, Oxford: Oxford University Press.

Nonaka, K. (1991), 'The knowledge-creating company', *Harvard Business Review* **69**(6), 96–104.

OECD (1992), *The Technology Economy Programme*, Paris: OECD.

OECD (1994a), *The Jobs Study*, Paris: OECD.

OECD (1994b), *The OECD Jobs Study, Evidence and Explanation, Part I*, Paris: OECD.

OECD (1996), *Technology and Industrial Performance*, Paris: OECD.

OECD (1997a), *Employment Outlook*, July 1997, Paris: OECD.

OECD (1997b), *Economic Surveys, Denmark 1997*, Paris: OECD.

OECD (1998a), *Science, Technology and Industry Outlook*, Paris: OECD.

OECD (1998b), *Technology, Productivity and Job Creation*, Paris: OECD.

OECD (1998c), *Student Migration to and between OECD Countries: Characteristics and Current Trends* (DEELSA/ELSA/WP2(98)7), Paris: OECD.

OECD (1999a), *Draft Chapter 4: Flexible Working Practices*, DEELSA/ELSA/WP5 (99)4, Paris: OECD.

OECD (1999b), *Boosting Innovation: The Cluster Approach*, OECD Proceedings, Paris: OECD.

OECD (2000a), *A New Economy: The Changing Role of Innovation and Information Technology in Growth*, Paris: OECD.

OECD (2000b), *Knowledge Management in the Learning Society*, Paris: OECD.

OECD (2001a), *The Well-being of Nations: The Role of Human and Social Capital*, Paris: OECD.

OECD (2001b), *The New Economy: Beyond the Hype, Final Report on the OECD Growth Project*, Paris: OECD.

Papaconstantinou, G., N. Sakurai and A. Wyckoff (1996), *Embodied Technology Diffusion: An Empirical Analysis for 10 OECD Countries*, Paris: OECD.

Pavitt, K. (1984), 'Sectoral patterns of technical change: towards a taxonomy', *Research Policy* **13**, 343–73.

Pedersen, P.J. (1977), 'Langtidssammenhæng mellem produktivitetsstigning og beskæftigelsesgrad', *Nationaløkonomisk Tidsskrift* **115**, 2, 175–92.

Pedler, M., J. Burgoyne and T. Boydells (1991), *Learning Company*, McGraw Hill.

Polanyi, M. (1958/1978), *Personal Knowledge*, London: Routledge and Kegan Paul.

Polanyi, M. (1966), *The Tacit Dimension*, London: Routledge and Kegan Paul.

Porter, M. (1990), *The Competitive Advantage of Nations*, London: MacMillan.

Putnam, R.D. (1993), *Making Democracy Work – Civic Traditions in Modern Italy*, Princeton, NJ: Princeton University Press.

Regeringen (1999), *Strukturovervågning*, Copenhagen: Regeringen, May 1999.

Romer, P.M. (1990), 'Endogenous technological change', *Journal of Political Economy*, **98**, 71–102.

Smith, N. (1997), 'Det effektive, rummelige og trygge danske arbejdsmarked', in *Arbejdsmarkedspolitisk Årbog 1998*, Copenhagen: Ministry of Labour, 102–20.

Solow, R.M. (1957), 'Technical change and the aggregate production function', *Review of Economics and Statistics*, **39**, 312–20.

Storper (1997), *The Regional World*, New York: Guilford Press.

Svennilson, I. (1960), 'The concept of the nation and its relevance to econo-mics', in Robinson, E.A.G. (ed.) (1960), *Economic Consequences of the Size of Nations*, Proceedings of a conference held by the International Economic Association, London: Macmillan, pp. 1–13.

Tomlinson, M. (2001), 'A new role for business services in economic growth', in Archebugi, D. and B.-Å. Lundvall (eds), *The Globalizing Learning Economy*, Guildford and King's Lynn: Oxford University Press, 97–110.

Voxted, S. (1998), *Efteruddannelsessystemets rolle og muligheder i det danske innovationssystem*, DISKO report no. 3, Copenhagen: Industry and Trade Development Council.

Voxted, S. (1999a), *Kan kurser ændre holdninger?*, Copenhagen: Industry and Trade Development Council.

Voxted, S. (1999b), 'Den nye industriarbejder', *Arbejdsliv*, 4.

Wagner, M. (1998), *Det polytekniske gennembrud* (The polytechnical break-through), Aarhus: Aarhus University Press.

Westling, H. (1996), *Co-operative Procurement: Market Acceptance for Innovative Energy-Efficient Technologies*, Stockholm: NUTEK 1996:3.

Westling, H. (1997), 'Buyer co-operation for more efficient solutions', presented at the *DA/DSM DistribuTECH Europe 97*, Amsterdam, 14–16 October 1997.

Whitley, R. (1994), 'Societies, firms and markets: the social structuring of business systems', in Whitley, R. (ed.), *European Business Systems*, London: Sage Publications.

Woolcock, M. (1998), 'Social capital and economic development: toward a theoretical synthesis and policy framework', *Theory and Society*, **2**(27), 151–207.

Ziman, J. (1979), *Reliable Knowledge*, Cambridge: Cambridge University Press.

Index